Karen Brow

Portugal

Charming Inns & Itineraries

Written by

CYNTHIA SAUVAGE, KAREN BROWN and CLARE BROWN

Illustrations by Barbara Tapp
Cover Painting by Jann Pollard

Karen Brown's Guides, San Mateo, California

[handwritten notes:]
EVORA
SALIMA
SAGRES
LISBON
NAZARE
Rent cell phone
when you rent car
AVEIRO (POTTERY)
2 hour river cruise
Estoril Cais car
Gulbenkian Museum
Funicular
Castle Sao Jorge
restaurant
Museu de Arte Antiga
Hieronymite Monastery

Karen Brown Titles

Austria: Charming Inns & Itineraries
California: Charming Inns & Itineraries
England: Charming Bed & Breakfasts
England, Wales & Scotland: Charming Hotels & Itineraries
France: Charming Bed & Breakfasts
France: Charming Inns & Itineraries
Germany: Charming Inns & Itineraries
Ireland: Charming Inns & Itineraries
Italy: Charming Bed & Breakfasts
Italy: Charming Inns & Itineraries
Mexico: Charming Inns & Itineraries
Mid-Atlantic: Charming Inns & Itineraries
New England: Charming Inns & Itineraries
Pacific Northwest: Charming Inns & Itineraries
Portugal: Charming Inns & Itineraries
Spain: Charming Inns & Itineraries
Switzerland: Charming Inns & Itineraries

Karen Brown Guides are available in bookstores; can be ordered online at
www.karenbrown.com, or by phone from Karen Brown Guides at (650) 342-9117.

Dedicated with all my love to
Kim and Christian
Little Christian
Adorable Camilla
and
Baby William

Front cover painting: Quinta das Lágrimas, Coimbra.

Editors: Karen Brown, June Eveleigh Brown, Clare Brown, Kim Brown Holmsen, Tony Brown, Lorena Aburto Ramirez, Iris Sandilands.

Illustrations: Barbara Tapp; Cover painting: Jann Pollard.

Webmistress: Lynn Upthagrove.

Technical support and graphics: Michael Fiegel.

Maps: Susanne Lau Alloway, Michael Fiegel.

Distributed by Fodor's Travel Publications, Inc., 280 Park Avenue, New York, NY 10017, USA.

Distributed in Canada by Random House Canada, 2775 Matheson Boulevard. East, Mississanga, Ontario, Canada L4W 4P7, phone: (905) 624 0672, fax: (905) 624 6217.

Distributed in the United Kingdom, Ireland, and Europe by Random House UK, 20 Vauxhall Bridge Road, London, SW1V 2SA, England, phone: 44 20 7840 4000, fax: 44 20 7840 8406.

Distributed in Australia by Random House Australia, 20 Alfred Street, Milsons Point, Sydney NSW 2061, Australia, phone: 61 2 9954 9966, fax: 61 2 9954 4562.

Distributed in New Zealand by Random House New Zealand, 18 Poland Road, Glenfield, Auckland, New Zealand, phone: 64 9 444 7197, fax: 64 9 444 7524.

Distributed in South Africa by Random House South Africa, Endulani, East Wing, 5A Jubilee Road, Parktown 2193, South Africa, phone: 27 11 484 3538, fax: 27 11 484 6180.

A catalog record for this book is available from the British Library.

ISSN 1533-5909

Contents

Introduction

Nazaré

Portugal, whose rich history is irrevocably tied to the sea, was once one of the world's greatest powers. Its finest hour was when the Portuguese discovered the coveted sea route to the Orient, which enabled them to monopolize the spice trade. At the same time as Columbus was discovering the New World, Bartolomeu Dias and Vasco da Gama were testing the frontiers in the opposite direction—Africa, India, and the East Indies. Mighty castles, spectacular fortresses, beautiful mansions, and elaborate cathedrals remain today as reminders of this period of great wealth and prominence. These stunning monuments—along with incredibly lovely places to stay, excellent weather, and genuine warmth of welcome—make Portugal an ideal travel destination.

About This Guide

Portugal: Charming Inns & Itineraries is written specifically for the traveler looking for a guide to more than the capital city and a handful of highlights—it is written for the visitor who wants to add a little out of the ordinary to his agenda. Our goal has been to discover and describe the most charming and historic places to stay in Portugal and to detail itineraries that will lead you to them by the most scenic and interesting routes. We do not claim to be objective reporters—that sort of information is available anywhere—but rather subjective, on-site raconteurs. We have definite biases toward places we have stayed at and enjoyed—from intimate bed and breakfasts in enchanting manor houses to spectacular castles snuggled in medieval villages. We believe that your accommodations weave the tapestry of your trip—they can make or break a visit to any country, and can add immeasurably to your memories. Happily, prices in Portugal are still reasonable enough to allow you the pleasure of indulging yourself. If you follow our itineraries (every one of which we have personally traveled) and trust in our recommendations for places to stay, you will be assured of staying in the most interesting lodgings Portugal has to offer while visiting the country's most intriguing destinations.

This guide is divided into three sections. The first section is the introduction, which is packed with general information on Portugal. The second section features itineraries that guide you throughout Portugal and direct you to the most interesting sightseeing. The third section features places to stay with descriptions of recommended accommodations in every price range.

About Portugal

The following information is given in alphabetical order.

AIRFARE

Karen Brown's Guides have long recommended Auto Europe for their excellent car rental services and we are now very pleased to introduce their air travel division, Destination Europe, to our readers. An airline broker working with major American and European carriers, Destination Europe offers deeply discounted coach- and business-class fares to over 200 European gateway cities. It also gives Karen Brown travelers an additional 5% discount off its already highly competitive prices. You can make reservations online via our website, *www.karenbrown.com*, (click "Discount Airfares" on our home page) or at (800) 223-5555. When phoning be sure to use the Karen Brown ID number 99006187 to secure your discount on the lowest prices they currently offer.

BANKS

Banks in Portugal are open from 8:30 am to 3 pm, Monday through Friday. All exchange foreign currency: look for a *cambio* (exchange) sign outside the bank. You can exchange money at the *cambio* counters in the airports and you can also find small *cambio* offices along city streets. Usually your hotel will exchange your money, though generally at a less favorable rate. We have often found the best rate of exchange is given at ATMs, so if you do not already have one, it might be wise to get an access code for your bank card or credit card so you can get cash overseas.

CAR RENTAL

Readers frequently ask our advice on car rental companies. We always use Auto Europe, a car rental broker that works with the major car rental companies to find the lowest possible price. They also offer motor homes and chauffeur services. Auto Europe's toll-free phone service from every European country connects you to their U.S.-based, 24-

hour reservation center. Auto Europe offers our readers a 5% discount, and occasionally free upgrades. Be sure to use the Karen Brown ID number 99006187 to receive your discount and any special offers. You can make your own reservations online via our website, *www.karenbrown.com* (select Auto Europe from the home page), or by telephone (800-223-5555).

CELLPHONES

Cellphones are wonderful to have as many properties do not have direct-dial phones in the guestrooms and if you used the hosts' personal phone for phone calls or computer hookup, it would be an inconvenience both to you and to them, as well as hard to determine charges. Also, cellphones are wonderfully convenient when you are on the road and want to call for directions, advise of a changed arrival time, or simply make sure that someone is home.

Cellphones can be rented through your car rental company, at the airport or train stations, or you can purchase an international phone once you are overseas. If you are considering taking your cellphone from home, check with your carrier to make sure that your phone has international capability. Sometimes it is necessary to make arrangements before you depart to activate a special service. We would also recommend getting international phone access numbers and inquiring about international access charges or rates so there are no billing surprises.

CLIMATE

Portugal enjoys Europe's best climate since the moderating influence of the Atlantic keeps all seasons relatively mild in most parts of the country. There is a natural progression of temperature variation from north to south. It is seldom hot in the north and almost never cold in the Algarve. The Alentejo (the central plain) is very hot in summer, at which time an air-conditioned car and an air-conditioned room are very important. The highest and lowest temperatures show greater divergence as you move away from the coast and in the higher mountain ranges, such as the Serra da Estrela, there is enough snow for skiing in winter. In most of the country winter usually means simply an increase in rainfall. The ideal times to visit, in our estimation, are the spring and fall when the weather is usually excellent and there are fewer tourists. Try to avoid summer if possible—especially the Algarve, which is swarming with tourists in July and August. Another advantage to traveling off-season is that rates are usually less expensive.

CLOTHING

As holds true throughout Europe, standard attire is generally less casual than in the United States. Although women wear slacks just about anywhere they would at home, dresses are generally worn in the evening, and short shorts are rarely seen outside the coastal resorts. While ties and jackets are actually required in only the most elegant establishments, you will find that they are worn regularly.

CURRENCY–EURO

All pricing, including room rates, is quoted in euros, using the "€" symbol. The euro is now the official currency of most European Union countries, including Portugal, having completely replaced national currencies as of February 2002. Visit our website (*www.karenbrown.com*) for an easy-to-use online currency converter.

When traveling, an increasingly popular and convenient way to obtain foreign currency is simply to use your bankcard at an ATM machine. You pay a fixed fee for this but, depending on the amount you withdraw, it is usually less than the percentage-based fee charged to exchange currency or travelers' checks. Be sure to check with your bank or credit card company about fees and necessary pin numbers prior to departure.

DRIVING

DRIVER'S LICENSE: Portugal requires only that you have a valid driver's license from your home country.

GASOLINE: Gasoline is expensive and should be factored into your budget if you plan to drive extensively. Gasoline is available in almost every town, and service stations are open from around 7 am to 10 pm, while a few are open 24 hours a day. Using a little common sense, you should have no trouble finding gasoline. Most of the gas stations take credit cards, but be sure to look for their sign before you pump.

ROADS: Enormous changes are taking place in the highway system and each time we visit we find the roads much improved. A fantastic amount of construction was completed prior to Expo 98. One of the major projects was a spectacular new bridge, Ponte Vasco da Gama, which was built close to the Expo center, at the eastern edge of Lisbon. At the present time, the roads in Portugal run the gamut from outstanding national highways to barely-two-lane country roads. By far the best are the four-lane highways, designated by "A" (for example, the highway from Lisbon to Porto is A1). After traveling over 6,000 kilometers exploring every nook and cranny of Portugal, we concluded that you should take "A" roads whenever possible to go from one sightseeing spot to another. If an "A" road is not available, take the next best highway, one that starts with the letters "IP" (for example, IP5)—these are always quite good and sometimes exceptionally fine highways, usually with two lanes that frequently become three lanes for passing purposes. "N" roads should be avoided whenever possible because they are usually two-lane roads congested with truck traffic. Country lanes and backroads vary in quality, but are far less congested than "N" roads.

ROAD SIGNS: "A" roads are well marked, but many others are very poorly designated. You can guess by looking at the map what road you are *probably* on, but it is often difficult to reconfirm the number by seeing a sign. The road number is almost never signposted, but is sometimes found on a concrete marker indicating each kilometer along the road. However, these markers are often missing, upended, or simply unreadable at normal speeds. Destinations along the route are better marked—usually the next town of any size is indicated along with either the name of the next large town or the last town on the road. All this makes for an adventure of following a map through unfamiliar territory.

ROADS—TOLLS: Tolls are charged on some of the major freeways/motorways. As you approach the freeway, you pull out a ticket from an automated machine at the toll station. Keep this ticket handy because when you exit the freeway, you need to hand it to the agent and pay according to distance traveled. Cash only is accepted for payment. The tolls are not extravagant—and certainly worth the convenience. Tolls are also charged to cross two bridges: the Ponte 25 de Abril, in and out of the heart of the Lisbon, and the Ponte Vasco da Gama, in and out of Lisbon, just to the east of the city.

SEAT BELTS: Use of seat belts is mandatory in Portugal, so get into the habit of buckling up when you get into the car.

TRAFFIC: It is difficult to drive in the large cities. The volume of traffic, lack of street signs, parking problems, one-way streets, and streets that never run parallel make driving a trial for all but the bravest of souls. Our advice is to buy a detailed map and pinpoint the location of your hotel before you arrive in a city. Make your way to where you are staying and leave the car in the hotel parking lot (or one recommended by the hotel), then take cabs or walk around the large cities. Taxis are plentiful and reasonable. In downtown Lisbon you can use the subway system (the Metro, marked with signs bearing a large "M"). In smaller towns always try to park on or near a main square for easy recall, and then venture by foot into streets that were never designed with cars in mind. Traffic regulations are similar to most other countries.

Driving is on the right-hand side of the road, passing on the left. There are many roundabouts where vehicles already on the circle always have the right of way. The speed limits are generally as follows: 60 kph in built-up areas, 90 kph on normal roads, 120 kph on express highways. There are frequently police officers with scanners on the side of the road, so drive carefully.

Beyond the cities, the *Guarda Nacional Republicana*, a national police force, is in charge of traffic. They conduct spot checks constantly around the country, pulling over cars (using criteria known only to them) and checking for valid documents—be sure to carry your car papers at all times.

ECONOMY

Portugal has long been known as a travel bargain, although now that it has joined the European Union (EU), prices are slowly creeping upwards. Nevertheless, the cost of traveling in Portugal is much less than in most other countries in Europe. The socialist revolution in 1974 caused tourism to grind to a virtual halt for about four years, but since then, a more moderate government has sought to revitalize the industry and, as a result, the quality of accommodations throughout the country has greatly improved.

ELECTRICAL SUPPLY

If you are taking any electrical appliances made for use in the United States, you will need a transformer plus a two-pin adapter. A voltage of 220 AC current at 50 cycles per second is almost countrywide, though in remote areas you may encounter 120V. The voltage is often displayed on the socket. Even though we recommend that you purchase appliances with dual-voltage options whenever possible, it will still be necessary to have the appropriate socket adapter. Also, be especially careful with expensive equipment such as computers—verify the adapter/converter capabilities and requirements.

ENGLISH SPOKEN

England and Portugal have been constant allies throughout history, and partly because of this heritage of friendship, Portugal is a favorite destination for the British who love Portugal and, in turn, are warmly welcomed. As a result, English is widely spoken in tourist areas. You won't need to use your phrase book in the large hotels in major cities. Likewise, in the pousadas there is always someone who speaks enough English to ease your way through from check-in to checkout. If you stay in private homes or hotels off the beaten path, there is a chance you might have a language problem, although most of the owners speak at least a little English. If not, just pull out your trusty phrase book and point—the Portuguese are friendly and you'll eventually make yourself understood (and probably learn some Portuguese while you're at it). If you make advance reservations, be sure to take your letters of confirmation with you—it will save a lot of pointing.

FESTIVALS AND FOLKLORE

The major national holidays are April 25 (1974 Revolution), May 1 (Day of the Worker), June 10 (death of the great poet, Camoes), October 5 (Establishment of the Republic), and December 1 (Independence from Spain, 1640). Of course, Christmas, New Year's Day, and Easter are also major holidays.

In addition, every Portuguese town has its patron saint, and every saint its day of honor, so there are as many festivals as there are Portuguese towns. If you know where you want to go ahead of time, contact the Portuguese National Tourist Office (see p. 23) for a list of festival dates so that you might arrange your visit to coincide with one or several of these colorful local events. (Be forewarned, however, that hotel space can be a problem during festival time.)

Each week in most towns there is a major market day (*feira* or fair) that is held in one of the main squares—we have mentioned a number of these in the itinerary section. You should try to visit these to see a wider selection of folk art and handicrafts (and at better prices) than you will find in the shops.

All over Portugal, from April to October, major festivals often include the local variant of bullfighting. Unlike the Spanish version, in Portugal the bull is not killed, and part of the show features an amazing performance by the bullfighter on horseback. If you've been put off by the better-known Spanish spectacle, the Portuguese interpretation might be an acceptable alternative.

The archetypal musical form in Portugal is the *fado*, a mournful lament on the fateful adversity of life, usually sung by a female accompanied by one or more 12-string guitarists. The Coimbra-style *fado* is characterized by a happier, sometimes satirical tone. Performances, often included on city tours, are most common in Lisbon cafés and clubs and, to a lesser extent, in other cities.

FOOD AND DRINK

The government rates restaurants from one to four crossed forks and spoons (four is best). However, its rating system is based on such matters as the number of choices on the menu, the wine cellar, and whether the menu is translated, rather than the quality of the food, so ratings can be misleading. It is fun to sample some of the regional fare in the modest restaurants where the locals go—usually the price is extremely reasonable and the food excellent. Servings tend to be quite generous.

Not surprisingly, given its proximity to (and its economic dependence upon) the sea, the Portuguese menu features an incredibly wide variety of seafood. Many of these are totally unknown to Americans (even where the menu is translated, it doesn't necessarily help). Items such as *enguias* (baby eels) and numerous shellfish are best viewed as an adventure—you will find many of them excellent and should definitely experiment. By far the most common single item on the menu is *bacalhau* (cod). This is often dried, salted, soaked to restore the softness, then cooked mixed with other items such as eggs and potatoes—there are said to be 350 ways to fix cod, and I certainly believe it.

Pork, lamb, and veal are the most prevalent meats served in restaurants. You'll find that vegetables accompany the main course with more frequency than in other European countries.

Wine is ubiquitous. In the large, fancy restaurants a good selection of imported wines is usually available in addition to the extensive native listing. In smaller ones the options are mostly Portuguese, which is often a rich selection indeed, and fun to sample. We found ourselves returning repeatedly to the very smooth reds from the Colares region, but almost every area has some good local wine that is quite economical. You'll seldom be disappointed with the *vinho da regiao* (regional wine). Unlike most countries where wine comes in three varieties—*tinto* (red), *blanco* (white), and *rosado* (rose)—in Portugal there is also *vinho verde* (green), a light wine with a slight sparkle. This is a young wine produced in the north and actually comes in both red and white versions (not really green), although the white is much more common. Portugal's most famous drink is, of course, *porto*, the well-known fortified wine from the Upper Douro River region. It comes in seemingly endless varieties from vintage (single good year) to blended (several years mixed), and from deep red and sweet (usually for dessert) to white and dry (for an aperitif).

Cerveja (beer) is another favorite liquid refreshment and is always good, sometimes excellent, especially on hot days in a shady outdoor café. *Sagres* is the most common local variety, but imported beers are also widely available (at a higher price, of course).

Another customary beverage ordered in Portuguese restaurants is, believe it or not, water: the bottled kind. Though there is nothing wrong with *agua da torneira* (tap water), *agua mineral* (mineral water) is popular in either *litro* or *meio litro* (liter or half-liter) sizes. It may also be ordered *com* (with) or *sem* (without) gas (carbonation). You'll notice that the Portuguese often dilute their wine with it.

Once you leave the large cities and tourist-frequented restaurants, you'll find that menus are often poorly (and sometimes amusingly) translated or not translated at all. The following list includes some of the terms of traditional specialties to be found at each mealtime.

PEQUENO ALMOCO (breakfast): Breakfast is often "Continental," which means you are served *pao* (bread) and/or *pao doce* (sweet rolls) along with *café* (coffee), *chá* (tea), *leite* (milk) or *chocolate* (hot chocolate). However, the pousadas always offer a large breakfast (usually served buffet style), which includes tea, coffee, hot chocolate, fruit juices, various breads, cereals, fresh fruits, cold meats, cheeses, and sometimes scrambled eggs and sausage. The larger city hotels usually offer a Continental breakfast with other items at an extra charge such as *ovos* (eggs), which may be ordered *mexidos* (scrambled), *mal pasados* or *quentes* (soft-boiled), *escalfados* (poached), *fritos* (fried), or *cozidos* (hard-boiled). Bed and breakfast accommodations vary greatly in what they offer. Some serve a large breakfast, but most serve a Continental one. Breakfast is always included in the room rate unless we state otherwise in the description.

ALMOCO (lunch): This is usually taken between 12:30 and 1:30 pm and normally consists of several courses: *acepipes* (appetizers), *sopas* (soup, usually of the thick variety), *carne* (meat dishes), *peixe e mariscos* (fish and shellfish), *sobremesa* (desserts), and, of course, *vinho*. No one orders all these courses—two or three is most common. Restaurants will usually offer an à-la-carte *ementa* (menu) and a smaller menu (daily special-price meal). The latter will have fewer choices and frequently two prices—one includes soup, a main course, and dessert; the other adds another main course. This menu is almost always a bargain if you like its selections. If you prefer a lighter lunch, just stop at a small bakery shop (*pastelaria*) or bar. Even though you might not see it on the menu, at either place you can almost always order either a ham or cheese sandwich (*sande*) along with a cold drink, coffee, or tea.

CHÁ (tea): This follows the British tradition of tea accompanied by various pastries and is to be found in numerous *casas de chá* (teahouses), especially in the larger cities. The Portuguese were the first to import tea from the Orient in any appreciable amount. The word *chá* comes from the Chinese word for it, while "tea," the word used in most western languages, comes from the Chinese word for leaf.

JANTAR (dinner): This meal is taken around 8 pm and usually consists of the same combinations mentioned above under *almoco* (lunch).

MENU—VOCABULARY: Some of the words you are likely to puzzle over on your menu are the following: *acorda*—a thick soup with various bases (one of which is almost always garlic); *aldeirada*—a hearty fish chowder; *azeite*—olive oil, about the only kind of oil used to cook with in Portugal, and used in many, many dishes; *caldo verde*—a potato and cabbage or kale soup; *cataplana*—this actually refers to the utensil, a flat frying pan with a curved bottom and a hinged lid, which is frequently used over an open fire to cook mixtures of seafood (clams, shrimp, etc.) and other meats and sausage.

MENU—CONDIMENTS: *Alho* (garlic), *coentros* (coriander), *piri-piri* (a spicy chili sauce).

MENU—MEAT (*CARNE*): *Anho* (lamb), *bife* (beefsteak), *cabrito* (kid), *leitao* (suckling pig), *porco* (pork), *vitela* (veal). *Costeleta* is a chop and *lombo* is a filet. Several of these items are also commonly used in *guisado* (stew). They may be *assado* (roasted), *grelhado* (grilled), *nas brasas* (charcoal grilled), or *salteado* (sauteed). If you want poultry instead of meat, look for *frango* (chicken) on the menu.

MENU—FISH AND SHELLFISH (*PEIXE E MARISCOS*): *Ameijoas* (clams), *bacalhau* (cod), *camaroes* (shrimp), *chocos* (cuttlefish), *espadarte* (swordfish), *lagosta* (crayfish), *lavagante* (lobster), *linguado* (sole), *lula* (squid), *peixe espada* (scabbard fish), *pescada* (hake), *pregado* (turbot), *salmao* (salmon), *truta* (trout), *tum* (tuna).

MENU—VEGETABLES (*LEGUMES E HORTALICAS*): *Alcachofra* (artichoke), *arroz* (rice), *batata* (potato), *cebolha* (onion), *cenoura* (carrot), *cogumelos* (mushrooms), *espargos* (asparagus), *espinafre* (spinach), *grelos* (turnip greens).

MENU—TOSSED SALAD (*SALADA MISTA*): *Alface salada* (lettuce salad) usually includes any or all of the following: olive, tomato, onion, and raw vegetables. But remember that there is only one salad dressing: *vinagre* (vinegar) and *azeite* (olive oil).

MENU—FRUITS: *Ameixas* (plums), *figos* (figs), *macas* (apples), *morangos* (strawberries), *peras* (pears).

MENU—DESSERT: There is usually a wide variety of sweets available for dessert, including pies, cakes, baked custards, and fruits. One of the most popular desserts, found throughout Portugal, is a rich confection based on sweetened egg yolks, which has as many names as versions.

In the few instances where a property we recommend in this book actually has a restaurant and serves meals to non-guests, we have indicated this with the symbol ¶ in the list of icons at the bottom of the description.

GEOGRAPHY

Mainland Portugal is roughly a rectangle approximately 570 kilometers long by 160 kilometers wide. It is bordered on the north and east by Spain (with about 1,300 kilometers of common border) and on the south and west by the Atlantic Ocean. The northern half of the country is studded with low mountain ranges, with only the Serra da Estrela approaching imposing dimensions (its highest peak, Torre, rises to 1,980 meters). Plains characterize the southern half of the country, with less frequent mountain outcroppings. The Serra de Monchique divides the southern tip from the rest of the country and shelters the famous Algarve from the cooler north. Portugal's population is about 10 million, with a density of population similar to Ohio or Pennsylvania.

GOVERNMENT

Portugal has a parliamentary democracy similar to France, based on the constitution of 1976. The President is elected for five years with a maximum of two terms; the Prime Minister is elected for a four-year term. The Revolution of 1974, and the resulting constitution, instituted an essentially socialist government, bringing about a great deal of nationalization. Subsequent modifications have tended to reverse that trend to some extent.

HISTORY

EARLY PERIOD: Traces of cave-dwelling prehistoric man—Neolithic, Megalithic, and Magdalenian—have been discovered all over the Iberian Peninsula. Most recently, in 1992, Nelson Rebanda discovered prehistoric rock drawings in the granite hills rising from the Côa Valley, south of the River Douro near the Spanish border. The main park office is located in the small town of Vila Nova de Foz Côa. At this time there are two sites open to the public, but you need to make a reservation (usually from one to four weeks in advance) through the Parque Arqueológico Vale do Côa—tel: 279.76.43.17, fax: 279.76.52.57. The excursion, which costs about Esc 500 per person, involves a jeep ride out to the site and then a guided walking tour of about an hour. For those who are interested in archaeology, this excursion is a rare treat.

ROMAN PERIOD: Hispania was the most heavily colonized of all Rome's dominions, and their 600-year presence is the wellspring for modern Portuguese culture—its language, legal system, and religion. The Portuguese pride themselves on the fact that the Lusitanians, under their leader Viriato, resisted Roman domination longer than any other people (he was finally assassinated by the Romans in 139 BC and is now considered a national hero). When the Germanic tribes overran the Roman Empire from the north, Portugal suffered the same fate.

VISIGOTH PERIOD: By the 5th century AD the Visigoths had subdued the Iberian Peninsula almost completely (the Basque area of Spain was an exception) and had adopted Roman Catholicism as their own. As kingdoms were combined and divided over the next centuries, their feudalistic system presaged the traditional Portuguese regions. Their political structure, involving a monarch who served at the pleasure of the feudal lords, was subject to considerable instability as the kaleidoscope of dynastic unions changed constantly. This characteristic strife provided the opportunity, in 711, for the Moors (Islamic Africans) to invade and sweep across the Peninsula from south to north in the space of two decades.

MOORISH PERIOD: The Moors were a tolerant people and allowed a diversity of religions to coexist. At that point in history they represented the highest level of civilization in the West and exerted influence on the development of Portuguese culture, especially in the southern part of the country. By the 10th century the Emirate of Cordoba, which included present-day Portugal, was perhaps the most advanced area in Europe. Nevertheless, the Christians regrouped in the inaccessible mountains of Asturias to launch a crusade to reconquer their territory from the Moslems.

RECONQUEST PERIOD: Legend has it that a Christian leader Pelayo set up the Kingdom of Asturias after the defeat of the Moors at Covadonga in 718. The Christians established their capital at Leon in 914. Under their control were Asturias, Galicia, and part of Burgos. They discovered the remains of Saint James the Apostle in Galicia, and he became the patron saint of the Reconquest.

By 1095 the northern part of Portugal was held by the Christians, and King Alfonso VI of Castile and Leon created the separate county of Portucalia (named for Portus Cale, the modern city of Porto), granting it to Count Henry of Burgundy. In 1139 Henry's son, Alfonso Henriques, assumed the title of Alfonso I and proclaimed independence from Castile and Leon. Struggles with the Moors consumed the next 100 years, with the Algarve finally falling to the Christians in 1250. The stage was thus set for the definitive establishment of the modern Portuguese nation.

MODERN PERIOD: The first monarch to move substantially in that direction was the esteemed King Dom Diniz (1279–1325), credited with developing the agricultural economy of the country and securing its territory from the aggressive, emerging nation next door. (Not yet known as Spain, the kingdoms of Castile and Leon controlled almost the entire border with Portugal and were almost equivalent to it in size.) When not distracted with stimulating farming and establishing and fortifying towns (which may still be found atop hills along the Spanish border), Dom Diniz was fascinated by

Sagres

Introduction–About Portugal

Portugal's only other neighbor, the Atlantic Ocean. He strengthened the country's merchant marine fleet and sought out the most capable European navigators to teach in Portugal. It's believed that early Atlantic expeditions resulted in the discovery of the Azores during this period. Thus, King Diniz initiated what was to culminate in Portugal's finest hour in the 15th and 16th centuries.

In 1385 King João I finally defeated the Castilians in a decisive battle at Aljubarrota, consolidating the country's independence for the next two centuries and allowing full attention to be given to conquering the sea. His youngest son, Prince Henry, established a school of navigation at Sagres on the southwestern tip of Portugal in 1418 and expansion activity began in earnest.

Prince Henry became known to history as Henry the Navigator, and though he never went on the voyages himself, he was obsessively dedicated to organizing them. Portuguese sailors and navigators began a series of voyages down the coast of Africa, each expedition pushing the frontier farther south. Economic motivation was strong, since dwindling European gold supplies were being poured into the thriving spice trade through middlemen of the Middle East and Venice. Portugal was hemmed in by Spain, so Africa, and later the Orient, provided the only direction for expansion.

In 1482 an expedition reached the mouth of the River Congo, and six years later Bartolomeu Dias sailed far enough around the Cape of Good Hope to realize that he was probably in the Indian Ocean. The king at the time was João II, arguably Portugal's greatest monarch and styled "The Perfect Prince," although it was he who turned away Columbus before the Spanish Queen Isabella took up his offer. João II was a vigorous supporter of these enterprises, but apparently believed his own navigators when they opined that Columbus's proposed route to the Orient was impractical. In 1494 (after Columbus's discovery of the New World) João II negotiated the Treaty of Tordesillas, which divided the world between Spain and Portugal for exploration and colonization. Portugal got everything east of the line approximately following the 50° W line of longitude and Spain everything to the west.

Under King Manuel I, who succeeded João II in 1495, Vasco da Gama finally reached India in 1498. Manuel I built the incredible Hieronymite monastery in Belém, near Lisbon, to commemorate the event. The Portuguese then attained Newfoundland, Greenland, Labrador and, in 1500, Brazil. By 1513 they had sailed to China and Timor in the Orient, then proceeded to Japan a few years later. Portugal's empire, unlike Spain's, was based primarily on maritime trade, and the eastern "colonies" were simply trading enclaves. While they sparked a lot of activity, they were apparently not that profitable, with what profit there was going primarily to the crown rather than creating an entrepreneurial class.

By 1580, when King Sebastião attempted a crusading expedition to Morocco and disappeared, the Portuguese were in no shape to resist the pretensions of Sebastião's uncle, Phillip II of Spain, to the throne. Thus began the long-dreaded "Spanish Captivity" of 60 years. During this period Portugal began to lose its empire one piece at a time, mostly to the Dutch. At the same time, Lisbon became the third-largest city in Europe, surpassed only by Paris and Naples in population. When a subsequent Spanish Phillip increased Portugal's taxes to help finance Spain's Thirty Years War with France, it proved to be the last straw. In 1640 the Spanish were overthrown and the Duke of Bragança assumed the throne as João IV. The remainder of the century was mostly dedicated to restoring Portugal's devastated economy.

Toward the end of the 17th century gold was discovered in Brazil, and a new era of prosperity followed for the Portuguese monarchs. The flow of the precious metal (soon to be accompanied by diamonds) increased throughout the first half of the 18th century, but since it was used to finance imports, the nation's internal economy derived little benefit. It was during this period that the art of working gold reached its zenith, as can be seen in various museums and cathedral treasuries throughout the country. The revenue from Brazil also allowed João V (1706–1750) to construct the giant palace monastery at Mafra. By the time he died in 1750 Portugal had regained some of its former importance in Europe.

His son and successor was Jose I, one of those obscure monarchs, like Louis XIII in France, eclipsed by the power and achievements of their ministers. In Louis' case it was Cardinal Richelieu and in Jose's it was the Marques de Pombal, Sebastião Jose de Carvalho e Melo. Pombal was, in the style of the mid-18th century, a product of the Enlightenment and a believer in the notion that the best ruler was the enlightened despot. The King was a product of the lavish court and a believer in things more pleasurable than the dreary job of governing. They were made for each other. Then, on November 1, 1755, a tremendous earthquake destroyed most of Lisbon and caused severe damage to other cities in the region. In the ensuing chaos Pombal seems to have kept his head and consolidated his power, which he wielded for the next 22 years. Most of his administration seems to have been marked by failure, although he was often in the European limelight. He was anticlerical to the extreme of expelling the Jesuits entirely. He attempted to establish state monopolies in various economic sectors, but there is little evidence that they made much economic sense. He did reorganize much of the administration of Brazil (his legacy there is as an important, progressive figure). When Jose died in 1777, his successor Maria I relieved Pombal of his duties and he retired to his estates in the town that bears his name.

In 1807 Napoleon's forces entered Portugal and marched toward Lisbon. The Prince Regent João (later King João VI) accepted British advice and hastily moved the court to Brazil, where it remained for 14 years to govern the still-vast Portuguese Empire. The Portuguese who remained behind wasted no time in striking back at the French. An agreement was negotiated with England (no friend of Napoleon), and a combined force of British and Portuguese armies headed by the Duke of Wellington soon drove the French back across the Spanish border.

The 19th century in Portugal was witness mostly to struggles between the constitutionalists' desire to end absolutism and their royalist opponents. João VI had made Brazil a kingdom in its own right and left his son, Pedro IV, to rule. Two years later Pedro proclaimed independence for that immense and wealthy colony (naming himself Emperor), and Portugal was powerless to hold on to it. On João's death in 1826,

Pedro was theoretically both Emperor of Brazil and King of Portugal. Since that was not possible, he attempted to install his daughter Maria on the Portuguese throne. There followed an eight-year battle between the forces of Pedro's brother Miguel and those loyal to Pedro's daughter Maria. Pedro himself was forced to abdicate his Brazilian throne in favor of his son, so returned to Europe to support the claims of his daughter. He managed to defeat his brother and banish him into exile. Maria II was then crowned queen at the age of 15. Her faction was in favor of a constitution and it was duly pronounced the same year as her coronation.

Having been through 25 years of strife, Portugal now found itself saddled with a huge debt, without its main source of income (Brazil) and with two contentious factions promoting different constitutions. On a liberal move, all religious orders were abolished and their property confiscated. (This is why, as you will see in the hotel descriptions, many former monasteries are now government property and some are pousadas.) The rest of the century saw numerous small-scale revolts and a struggle to match the pace of economic development being experienced in the rest of the continent, while also defending the remaining overseas possessions from encroachment by other European powers. Failure to do all this was a major determinant in the revolt of October 5, 1910, which overthrew the monarch (Manuel II) and established the Republic—the third in Europe (after Switzerland and France).

The next 15 years brought over 40 changes of government by various means, mostly coups. Portugal entered World War I on the Allied side and fought in Africa and Europe. In 1928 Antonio Oliveira Salazar, the Finance Minister, was given the task of rebuilding the national economy. Due to his success, he was named Prime Minister in 1932 and arranged the promulgation of a new constitution which created the "New State," a kind of corporative republic. Salazar liked his job and remained as Prime Minister for the next 36 years. The regime was primarily authoritarian, with control maintained by repression and sometimes brutality. Though not generally considered as bad as Generalissimo Franco's contemporaneous regime in neighboring Spain, it was essentially a dictatorship. Portugal remained neutral during World War II, but was commonly perceived as sympathetic to its old British allies. Lisbon became a rendezvous spot for spies from both sides, as spy-novel fans will undoubtedly recall.

After World War II it was Salazar's primitive economic theories that prevented development in national industry, even though conditions conducive to an industrial boom existed, since Portugal had made a tidy profit selling tungsten from its colonies to both sides during the war.

By the 1960s Portugal's control over its so-called "overseas provinces" began to weaken. India reclaimed Goa and national liberation movements developed in Angola and Mozambique. During the entire decade Portugal was being drained of both money and young men as the wars continued. The inability or unwillingness of the Salazar regime to move toward decolonization fueled the fires of resentment among even those elements of society—the peasants, the armed forces—who might have been his staunchest supporters. As more and more families lost sons in faraway lands, and pressure mounted on the armed forces to save the colonies, the regime lost support. The officers' corps was increasingly being recruited from the lower middle class as the elite refused to serve for the first time. In 1968 ill health and his personal unpopularity forced Salazar to step down. A few liberalizing gestures proved insufficient to quell unrest and, finally, on April 25, 1974, a radical military group carried out an almost bloodless coup. Within a few months the colonies were liberated.

The original architects of the revolution were mostly communist-oriented elements of the armed forces that had joined in an organization called the Armed Forces Movement (MFA). The MFA set up a junta to run the government until elections could be held. The more moderate socialist party was in disarray and unable to mount opposition to the extremists. Within less than a year some 60% of the economy had been nationalized and several million acres of farmland had been collectivized. Even small businesses were summarily seized in dramatic fashion.

Elections for a constitutional convention were finally set for April 25, 1975. The MFA had not constituted itself as a political party and presented no candidates. The socialist party's strong showing indicated a clear preference for an evolutionary rather than revolutionary approach. The MFA junta continued to move to the left, in contrast to the will of the people. Opposition to the leaders of MFA grew, both within and outside the military. By the close of 1975 Portugal seemed again on the brink of a civil war, but fortunately, the MFA saw the writing on the wall and capitulated.

The revolution ended and a period of leftist socialism under a very radical, though democratic, constitution was ushered in. The economy was in chaos resulting from the rash behavior of the MFA. Subsequent governments have addressed this problem and have backed off from many of the radical policies of the revolution in favor of a more moderate approach. On January 1, 1986, Portugal achieved full status in the European Union.

ICONS

Icons allow us to provide additional information about our recommended properties. When using our website to supplement the guides, positioning the cursor over an icon will in many cases give you further details. For easy reference an icon key can be found on the last page of the book.

We have introduced these icons in the guidebooks and there are more on our website, *www.karenbrown.com.* ❋ Air conditioning in rooms, ☕ Breakfast included in room rate, ♻ Children welcome, ♨ Cooking classes offered, ▦ Credit cards accepted, ☎ Direct-dial telephone in room, ⌂ Dogs by special request, ▥ Elevator, 🏋 Exercise room, ☗ Mini-refrigerator in room, ⊘ Non-smoking rooms, P Parking available, ‖ Restaurant, ≈ Swimming pool, 🎾 Tennis, ▨ Television, ⚭ Wedding facilities, ♿ Wheelchair friendly, ⊥ Beach nearby, ♟ Golf course nearby, ⋔ Hiking trails nearby, 🐎 Horseback riding nearby, ⛷ Skiing nearby, ⚓ Water sports nearby, ♟ Wineries nearby.

INFORMATION

A rich source of free information about Portugal is the Portuguese National Tourist Office. It has branches around the world that can provide you with general information about the country or, at your request, specific information about towns, regions, and festivals. Some of the offices are shown below:

ICEP Portugal
Avenida Duque d'Avila, 185
1050-082 Lisbon, Portugal
Tel: 217.90.95.00, Fax: 213.55.68.96

ICEP Portugal
590 Fifth Avenue, 4th Floor
New York, New York, 10036, USA
Tel: (212) 354-4403, (800) PORTUGAL, fax: (212) 764-6137

ICEP Portugal
88 Kearny Street, Suite 1770
San Francisco CA 94108
Tel: (415) 391 7080, fax: (415) 391 7147

ICEP Portugal
60 Bloor Street West, Suite 1005
Toronto, Ontario M4W3B8, Canada
Tel: (416) 921-7376, fax: (416) 921-1353

Websites: *www.portugalinsite.pt, www.portugal.org, www.orderportugal.com*

E-mail: tourism@portugal.org

If you send a request for information addressed to the *Posto de Turismo* (Tourism Office) of almost any town in Portugal, you will be inundated with colorful and informative brochures. The tourist offices throughout the country are usually prominently located in the center of town and offer an incomparable on-site resource, furnishing town maps and details on local and regional highlights. During tourist season, they are frequently open seven days a week and their hours are usually longer than most other establishments. The *Turismo* sign identifies them.

MUSEUMS

Museums are usually open Tuesday through Sunday, 10 am to 12:30 pm and 2 pm to 5 pm. Some palaces also close on Wednesday.

PORTUGUESE LANGUAGE

Here are a few Portuguese words.

IN THE CITY: *Avenida:* avenue, usually a larger street; *bairro:* district, section, or neighborhood of a city; *calcada:* another name for a street, often a very small one; *centro:* downtown (when looking for the heart of the city where the sights are usually located, follow signs to the *centro*—the signs usually show a bull's eye); *doca:* dock; *largo:* square, usually a wide spot at an intersection; *praça:* square, ranging from tiny to grand, the central ones often surrounded by the town's main official buildings; *rua:* street.

OUTSIDE THE CITY: *Adega:* winery; *auto-estrada:* four-lane expressway; *estrada:* highway; *praia:* beach; *quinta:* country estate, usually private; *rio:* river—the name will follow, as in *Rio Tejo*, River Tagus.

SIGHTS: *Artesanato:* store which sells handicrafts—you'll find at least one in towns of any size; *azulejos:* ceramic tiles, a ubiquitous decorative element in Portugal. The craft of making these tiles was extremely advanced during the Moorish occupation of the Peninsula and in Portugal endured long afterward; *cabo:* cape—there are many of these along the Atlantic coast which provide wonderful views over the ocean; *miradouro:* viewpoint with special views.

BUILDINGS: *Castelo:* castle, often with extensive fortifications sheltering a town and a church within; *museu:* museum; *paço:* palace (but not a royal palace) or else a place the king has visited; *palacio:* former royal palace; *ponte:* bridge; *solar:* manor house; *torre*—tower; *torre de menagem:* castle keep, the strongest, innermost, and, usually, the tallest tower.

RELIGIOUS PLACES: *Capela:* chapel; *convento:* convent; *igreja matriz:* parish church; *mosteiro:* monastery; *se:* cathedral.

NAMES AND TITLES: *Dom:* title of honor reserved in Portugal (unlike in Spain) for royalty and high ecclesiastical officials; *Dona:* feminine title of honor—seldom used; *Nossa Senhora:* Our Lady (the Virgin Mary), used in the names of most churches, as in *Nossa Senhora da Assuncao*, (Our Lady of the Assumption); *Rainha:* queen; *Rei:* king—seldom used, *Dom* usually used instead; *Santa:* female saint; *São* or *Santo:* male saint.

AND DON'T FORGET YOUR MANNERS: *Adeus:* goodbye; *bom dia:* good morning; *boa noite:* good evening; *boa tarde:* good afternoon; *desculpe:* excuse me; *obrigado:* thank you (male speaker); *obrigada:* thank you (female speaker); *por favor:* please.

SHOPPING

CERAMICS: The most popular souvenir to take home is ceramics. Throughout Portugal, you will see colorful pottery for sale and each region has its own patterns and colors. The colors are usually cheerful and the patterns frequently folkloric. The porcelain works at Vista Alegre (near Aveiro) are world famous.

EMBROIDERY: Beautiful embroidered shawls, bedspreads, and tablecloths are popular items. The island of Madeira is especially famous for its embroidery work.

FILIGREE WORK: Since the time of King João V who reigned in the 1700s, intricate gold and silver filigree jewelry has been very popular in Portugal. It is still being made, the center of the craft being Gondomar, near Porto.

LACE: Portugal's handmade lace is beautiful. Most of the craft is located along the coast near fishing villages.

PORT WINE: Port wine is served throughout Portugal—you will taste some delicious varieties that you never knew existed. Bring a bottle home to renew memories of your holiday.

RUGS: Throughout Portugal you will see beautiful hand-woven woolen carpets accenting floors of hotels and homes, the best known types coming from Arraiolos, the center of this cottage industry. For their quality and charm, they are well priced.

WROUGHT-IRON ITEMS: Portugal produces many handsome items made of wrought iron. In addition to new pieces, you can also find some lovely old fixtures in antique shops.

TELEPHONES

It is more expensive to call home from Portugal than vice versa. The best way to phone overseas is to charge your call to a calling card. Large hotels and pousadas usually have direct-dial phones in the rooms, but you can use a public telephone. Many of the telephone booths are set up to accept special phone cards that can be purchased at post offices. You buy these cards in a predetermined amount, and your credit is used up according to the length of your conversation.

TIME

You will find the typical Portuguese schedule easy to adjust to. Breakfast is at the same time as at home. Restaurants start serving the midday meal around 1 pm and dinner is typically served from 8 pm on.

TIPPING

As everywhere, tipping is not clear-cut. Many restaurants include *servicio* in the bill but a tip of about 5% is usually given anyway when the service is good. If service is not included, the tip is usually about 10%. Tip taxi drivers about 10% of the meter's fare. Also it is customary to tip the porter who carries your suitcases and the concierge if you request special service.

TRAINS

There is a rail network throughout Portugal. The fastest, most luxurious service is on the Alfa Line, which runs between Lisbon and Porto with a stop in Coimbra. Second-best is the Rápido Inter-Cidades Line, which (as the name implies) connects most of the major cities. In addition there are local trains, but these are usually very slow. Rail Europe offers a special 15-day pass that is extremely flexible. You can choose to travel any 4 days during the 15-day period and the days do not need to be consecutive. The Eurail Pass is also valid within Portugal, although there is a small supplemental charge for certain trains. It is possible to research schedules and availability online. Also, important to note, many special fares and passes are only available if purchased in the United States. For information, the best possible fares, and to book tickets online, visit our website, *www.karenbrown.com*.

TRIP CANCELLATION INSURANCE

Because unexpected medical or personal emergencies—or other situations beyond our control—sometimes result in the need to alter or cancel travel plans, we strongly recommend travel insurance. Prepaid travel expenses such as airline tickets, car rentals, and train fares are not always refundable and most hotels and bed and breakfasts will expect payment of some, if not all of your booking, even in an emergency. While the owners might be sympathetic, many of the properties in our guides have relatively few rooms, so it is difficult for them to absorb the cost of a cancellation. We recommend insurance to cover these types of additional expenses arising from cancellation due to unforeseen circumstances. A link on our website (*www.karenbrown.com*) will connect you to Access America, which offers a variety of insurance policies that can be purchased online.

About Regions of Portugal

Portugal is officially divided into eighteen political districts. But for the traveler, the tourist department breaks down the country into eight "user-friendly" geographic regions, each of which has a unique personality and offers its own special charm. Two of these regions are islands: Madeira and the Azores; the other six are on the mainland. Our itineraries weave throughout these mainland regions, visiting their sites of rare beauty and exploring their rich history. Following is a capsule summary highlighting regional information to help you plan your holiday. After each of these brief overviews, we list the towns where we recommend places to stay and the featured hotels and/or bed and breakfasts in each town. Also given is the map number of the town so that you can quickly pinpoint where it is located. For detailed information on individual properties, look in the description section at the back of the book where they are featured alphabetically by the town name.

Some of the recommended places to stay are located in fabulous towns, some are in buildings with historic or old-world charm, some have incredible views or spectacular settings, some offer their own special ambiance. To assist you, we have coded the hotels and bed and breakfasts as follows:

x   *Characterful Town*   Place to stay in, or just outside, a town with special character.

H   *Historic Building*   Place to stay in a building with historic or old-world charm.

❀   *Outstanding Setting*   Place to stay with outstanding views or dramatic location.

♥   *Special Ambiance*   Place to stay with some kind of special ambiance, such as lovely gardens, antique décor, and beautiful furnishings.

Regions of Portugal

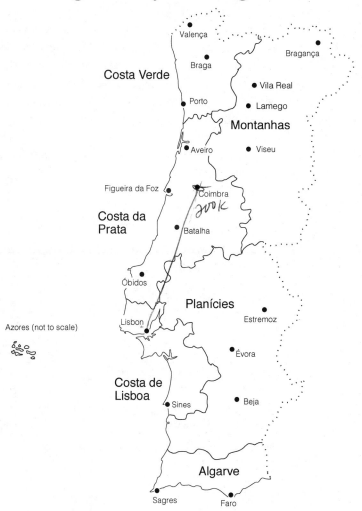

ALGARVE: The Algarve is the strip of land that embraces the entire width of the southern tip of Portugal where you find an excellent climate and strong Moorish influence. This magical area is dotted with bright white houses reflecting the brilliant sun, further enhanced by whimsical chimneys and colorful bougainvillea. The gentle air is fragrant with the scent of orange and almond blossoms. This is also the playground of Portugal and golf courses abound. The coast is divided into two parts. The section east of Faro that stretches to the Spanish border is called *sotavento*. The beaches here are dotted with sand dunes and the coastline is not as rugged as the portion to the west of Faro, which is called *barlavento*. Here you find the Algarve's most outstanding feature—spectacular long stretches of sand accented by giant outcroppings of majestic rocks, glowing in glorious hues of gold, ochre, and red. The area is extremely popular, especially in summer when the beaches are packed. Try to visit in the spring or fall when the weather is lovely and there are fewer tourists. SIGHTSEEING: Faro, Lagos, Monchique, Portimão, Sagres, Silves, Tavira. HANDICRAFTS: Wicker, straw hats, copper objects, ceramics.

Codes: **X** *Characterful Town,* **H** *Historic Building,* ✿ *Outstanding Setting,* ♥ *Special Ambiance*

Town	Place to Stay	Code	Map
Estói (Faro)	Monte do Casal	H ♥	4d
Odiáxere (Lagos)	Quinta das Barradas	H ♥	4c
Porto de Mós (Lagos)	Romantik Hotel Vivenda Miranda	✿ ♥	4c
Praia da Rocha (Portimão)	Albergaria Vila Lido	H ♥	4c
Praia do Vau (Portimão)	Casa Três Palmeiras	✿ ♥	4c
Praia de Galé	Vila Joya	✿ ♥	4c
Sagres	Casa de Chá da Fortaleza do Beliche	H ✿ ♥	4c
Sagres	Pousada de Sagres–Infante	✿ ♥	4c
São Brás de Alportel	Pousada de São Brás de Alportel– São Brás	♥	4c
Tavira	Quinta do Caracol	*x* H ✿ ♥	4c

AZORES: The Azores consist of a group of nine volcanic islands located in the middle of the Atlantic Ocean, about on a parallel with Lisbon. There are frequent two-hour flights from Lisbon to three Azorean airports: Ponta Delgada (on São Miguel), Lajes (on Terceira), and Horta (on Faial). Discovered in 1427, the islands became a strategic base between Portugal and the New World. Not only were many naval battles fought here, but also the islands became a favorite target for pirates. Word quickly spread of the mild climate and fertile land of the Azores and from the 15th to the 18th centuries settlers came to the islands to make a living from agriculture, cattle, and fishing. The early settlers were very religious and soon built churches in their new homeland, with many of these baroque beauties remaining today. (Columbus came to pray in a small chapel in the Azores when making his way across the Atlantic.) Fortresses, too, hark back to this era when the Azores was a port of call for ships laden with treasures from both the Orient and the New World. It is obvious that, even though far from the homeland, the archipelago is an integral part of Portugal. The architecture is similar and many of the streets are lined with small, whitewashed houses that have windows, doors, and gables trimmed in bright hues of blue or yellow, so like what you see on the mainland. However, the most endearing feature of these remote islands is the landscape. Emerald-green fields (frequently bordered by vibrant-blue hydrangeas) terrace down to a deep-blue sea, and turquoise-colored lakes of great beauty are tucked in volcanic craters. Most of the hotels are built in a contemporary style.

SIGHTSEEING: Local festivals abound on all the islands in the Azores with colorful costumes adding greatly to the gaiety. Also charming small baroque churches, phenomenal volcanoes, gorgeous crater lakes, deserted beaches, splendid landscapes.

HANDICRAFTS: Blue-decorated ceramics, delicate embroidery, decorative wicker, artwork created from whalebone, ship models.

NOTE: We currently do not have a hotel recommendation for the Azores.

COSTA DA PRATA: The Costa da Prata (Silver Coast) includes a long strip of land that stretches along the coast, beginning north of Lisbon and ending just before Porto. This is a lovely, forested region with fishing villages, medieval towns, monasteries, convents, churches, castles, and archaeological sites, including the 12th-century Abbey of Santa Maria in Alcobaça, where the tragic love story of King Pedro I and his beloved Inês de Castro outshines even that of Romeo and Juliet. The region has lots of colorful military history and it was here that Napoleon was defeated in battle. SIGHTSEEING: Alcobaça, Aveiro, Batalha, Buçaco, Coimbra, Conímbriga, Fátima, Óbidos, Tomar. HANDICRAFTS: Porcelain, ceramics, crystal.

Codes: *x* *Characterful Town,* **H** *Historic Building,* 🛐 *Outstanding Setting,* ♥ *Special Ambiance*

Town	Place to Stay	Code	Map
Atouguia da Baleia	Casa do Castelo	♥	3a
Batalha	Pousada da Batalha–Mestre Afonso Domingues	*x* 🛐	2c
Batalha	Quinta do Fidalgo	*x* H ♥	2c
Buçaco	Bussaco Palace	H 🛐 ♥	2a
Castelo de Bode	Pousada de Castelo de Bode–São Pedro		2c
Coimbra	Quinta das Lágrimas	*x* H 🛐 ♥	2a
Condeixa-a-Nova	Pousada de Condeixa-a-Nova–Santa Cristina	♥	2c
Mealhada–Luso	Vila Duparchy	H ♥	2a
Murtosa (Torreira)	Pousada do Murtosa/Torreira–Ria	🛐	2a
Óbidos	Casa d'Óbidos	*x* 🛐 ♥	3a
Óbidos	Estalagem do Convento	*x* H ♥	3a
Óbidos	Pousada de Óbidos–Castelo	*x* H ♥	3a
Ourém	Pousada de Ourém–Conde de Ourém	*x* H 🛐	2c
Ourém	Quinta da Alcaidaria–Mór	H ♥	2c
Taipa (Aveiro)	Casa do Sol Nascente	♥	2a
Valado dos Frades (Nazaré)	Quinta do Campo	H ♥	2c

Introduction–About Regions of Portugal

COSTA DE LISBOA: Costa de Lisboa is a superb region near Lisbon that includes chic Cascais, and charming Sintra. SIGHTSEEING: Cascais, Estoril, Lisbon, Mafra, Palmela, Queluz, Setúbal, Sintra. HANDICRAFTS: Wicker, embroideries, lace, ceramics, copper.

Codes: **x** *Characterful Town,* **H** *Historic Building,* 🏵 *Outstanding Setting,* ♥ *Special Ambiance*

Town	Place to Stay	Code	Map
Alcácer do Sal	Pousada de Alcácer do Sal–D. Afonso II	H	3c
Cascais	Casa da Pérgola	x H ♥	3c
Cascais	Hotel Albatroz	x H 🏵 ♥	3c
Cascais	Senhora da Guia	x ♥	3c
Guincho (Cascais)	Fortaleza do Guincho	H 🏵	3c
Lisbon	As Janelas Verdes	x H ♥	3c
Lisbon	Hotel Britania	x	3c
Lisbon	Hotel Lisboa Plaza	x ♥	3c
Lisbon	Hotel Metropole	x	3c
Lisbon	Solar do Castelo	x H 🏵 ♥	3c
Lisbon	York House	x H ♥	3c
Monserrate (Sintra)	Quinta da Capela	x H 🏵 ♥	3c
Palmela	Pousada de Palmela–Castelo de Palmela	H 🏵 ♥	3c
Queluz	Pousada de Queluz–Dona Maria I	x H ♥	3c
Rio Frio (Palmela)	Pallácio de Rio Frio	H♥	3c
Santiago do Cacém	Pousada de Santiago do Cacém–Quinta da Ortiga	H♥	4a
Setúbal	Pousada de Setúbal–São Filipe	H 🏵 ♥	3c
Sintra	Casa Miradouro	x H ♥	3c
Sintra	Hotel Palácio de Seteais	x H 🏵 ♥	3c
Sintra	Lawrence's Hotel	x H ♥	3c
Sintra	Quinta das Sequoias	x H 🏵 ♥	3c
Vila Nogueira de Azeitão	Quinta das Torres	H♥	3c

COSTA VERDE: Costa Verde (Green Coast) is a region tucked in the northwest corner of Portugal, stretching north from Porto to the border with Spain. Although small in size, this verdant area of fertile valleys and wooded hills is rich in history and charm. This region is home to Portugal's famous port wine and *vinho verde*, produced from grapes that lace the banks of the Douro River. Also here are towns dating back to the Roman times, such as picturesque Barcelos and Ponte de Lima, which is surrounded by estates of great wealth—many of which have been converted into lovely bed and breakfasts that are featured in this guide. Here too is Portugal's second largest city, Porto, situated at the mouth of the Douro. SIGHTSEEING: Barcelos, Braga, Guimarães, Peneda-Gerês National Park, Ponte de Lima, Porto, Viana do Castelo. HANDICRAFTS: Embroideries, tapestry, filigree, jewelry, ceramics, wrought iron, wicker.

Codes: **x** *Characterful Town,* **H** *Historic Building,* 🪴 *Outstanding Setting,* ♥ *Special Ambiance*

Town	Place to Stay	Code	Map
Amares	Pousada de Amares–Santa Maria do Bouro	H 🪴 ♥	1a
Anha (Viana do Castelo)	Quinta do Paço d'Anha	H ♥	1a
Barcelos	Quinta do Convento da Franqueira	x H 🪴 ♥	1a
Braga–Monte do Bom Jesus	Hotel do Elevador	🪴 ♥	1a
Braga–Monte do Bom Jesus	Hotel do Parque	🪴	1a
Canedo (Celorico de Basto)	Casa de Canedo	H 🪴 ♥	1c
Gerês–Caniçada	Pousada do Gerês–São Bento	🪴 ♥	1a
Guimarães	Pousada de Guimarães–Nossa Senhora da Oliveira	x H ♥	1a
Guimarães	Pousada de Guimarães–Santa Marinha	x H 🪴 ♥	1a
Molares (Celorico de Basto)	Casa do Campo	H 🪴 ♥	1c
Nespereira (Guimarães)	Casa de Sezim	H ♥	1a
Ponte de Lima–Arcos	Casa da Lage	x H ♥	1a
Ponte de Lima–Arcozelo	Casa do Arrabalde	x H ♥	1a
Ponte de Lima–Arcozelo	Casa do Outeiro	x H ♥	1a
Ponte de Lima–Arcozelo	Quinta de Sabadão	x H ♥	1a
Ponte de Lima–Beiral do Lima	Casa da Várzea	x H	1a
Ponte de Lima–Calheiros	Paço de Calheiros	H 🪴 ♥	1a

Introduction–About Regions of Portugal

Town	Place to Stay	Code	Map
Ponte de Lima–Estorãos	Moinho de Estorãos	**H** ♣ ♥	1a
Ponte de Lima–Facha	Casa das Torres	**H**♥	1a
Ponte de Lima–Gemieira	Casa do Barreiro	*x* **H** ♥	1a
Ponte de Lima–Moreira do Lima	Casa de Covas	**H**♥	1a
Ponte de Lima–Queijada	Quinta do Baganheiro	**H** ♣ ♥	1a
Ponte de Lima–Ribeira	Casa de Crasto	*x* **H**	1a
Porto	Hotel Infante de Sagres	*x* ♥	1c
Quintiães (Barcelos)	Casa dos Assentos	*x* **H** ♣ ♥	1a
Taboadelo (Guimarães)	Paço de São Cipriano	**H**♥	1c
Valença do Minho	Pousada de Valença do Minho–São Teotónio	*x* ♣	1a
Viana do Castelo	Casa do Ameal	♥	1a
Viana do Castelo	Pousada de Viana do Castelo–Monte de Santa Luzia	♣ ♥	1a
Vila Nova de Cerveira	Pousada de Vila Nova de Cerveira–D. Diniz	*x* **H** ♥	1a

MONTANHAS: Montanhas (The Mountains) is a large, remote region in the northeast corner of Portugal with snow-capped mountains, dense forests, and valleys strewn with mighty rocks. Here you find fascinating scenery, historic old villages, and prehistoric archaeological sites, including the newly discovered prehistoric drawings etched into the rocks in a remote valley near Vila Nova de Foz Côa. Because it is isolated, many old traditions, customs, and festivals remain. There is a strong Celtic influence in the songs and dances. If you just deviate slightly from the main roads, you discover tiny hamlets untouched by time. The most beautiful section of the Douro River, whose banks are covered with vineyards, stretches across the center of the region. SIGHTSEEING: Bragança, Lamego, Vila Nova de Foz Côa, Vila Real. HANDICRAFTS: Embroidery, ceramics, black pottery, lace, copper, wrought iron.

Codes: *x* *Characterful Town,* **H** *Historic Building,* ⚜ *Outstanding Setting,* ♥ *Special Ambiance*

Town	Place to Stay	Code	Map
Alijó	Pousada de Alijó–Barão de Forrester	♥	1d
Almeida	Pousada de Almeida–Senhora das Neves	x ⚜	2b
Belmonte	Pousada de Belmonte–Convento de Belmonte	H ⚜	2b
Bragança	Pousada de Bragança–São Bartolomeu	⚜	1b
Britiande (Lamego)	Casa de S. Antonio de Britiande	x H ♥	1c
Canas de Senhorim	Solar Abreu Madeira	x H ♥	2b
Caramulo	Pousada do Caramulo–São Jerónimo		2a
Casal de Loivos (Pinhão)	Casa de Casal de Loivos	H ⚜ ♥	1d
Chaves	Forte de Sao Francisco Hotel	x H	1b
Chaves	Quinta da Mata	x H ⚜ ♥	1b
Lamego	Quinta da Timpeira	x H ♥	1c
Mangualde	Estalagem Casa d'Azurara	H ♥	2b
Manteigas	Pousada de Manteigas–São Lourenço	⚜ ♥	2b
Marão	Pousada do Marão–São Gonçalo		1c
Miranda do Douro	Pousada de Miranda do Douro–Santa Catarina		1d
Monsanto	Pousada de Monsanto		2d
Oliveira (Mesão Frio)	Casa das Torres de Oliveira	H ⚜ ♥	1c
Pinhão	Vintage House	x H ⚜	1d
Rede (Mesão Frio)	Pousada de Mesão Frio–Solar da Rede	H ⚜ ♥	1c
Vidago	Vidago Palace Hotel	x H ⚜ ♥	1b
Vila Real	Casa Agrícola da Levada	x H♥	1c
Vilarinho de S. Romão (Pinhão)	Casa de Vilarinho de S. Romão	♥	1d

PLANÍCIES: Planícies (The Plains) is Portugal's largest region, a hunk of land covering one third of the country that stretches from the middle of Portugal south to the Algarve. This is one of our favorite parts of Portugal because its beauty is still so pure, with vast open spaces, marvelous walled hilltop towns, centuries-old olive trees dotting gentle hills, and shepherds tending their sheep with their faithful dogs nearby. SIGHTSEEING: Arriaolos, Elvas, Estremoz, Évora, Marvão, Monsaraz, Vila Viçosa. HANDICRAFTS: Rugs, tapestries, embroideries, wrought iron, leather goods, pottery.

Codes: x *Characterful Town,* **H** *Historic Building,* ❧ *Outstanding Setting,* ♥ *Special Ambiance*

Town	Place to Stay	Code	Map
Aldeia da Serra (Redondo)	Hotel Convento de São Paulo	**H** ❧ ♥	3d
Alvito	Pousada do Alvito–Castelo de Alvito	**H** ♥	3d
Arraiolos	Pousada de Arraiolos–Nossa Senhora da Assunção	*x* **H** ❧ ♥	3d
Beja	Pousada de Beja–São Francisco	**H** ♥	4b
Crato	Pousada do Crato–Flor da Rosa	**H** ❧ ♥	3b
Elvas	Pousada de Elvas–Santa Luzia		3d
Estremoz	Monte dos Pensamentos	*x* **H**	3d
Estremoz	Pousada de Estremoz–Rainha Santa Isabel	*x* **H** ❧ ♥	3d
Évora	Pousada de Évora–Lóios	*x* **H** ♥	3d
Évora	Solar Monfalim	*x* **H**	3d
Marvão	Albergaria El Rei Dom Manuel	*x*	3b
Marvão	Pousada do Marvão–Santa Maria	*x* **H** ❧ ♥	3b
Monsaraz	Estalagem de Monsaraz	*x* ♥	3d
Monsaraz	Hotel Rural Horta da Moura	*x* ♥	3d
Santa Clara-a-Velha	Pousada de Santa Clara-a-Velha	❧ ♥	4c
Serpa	Pousada de Serpa–São Gens	❧	4b
Sousel	Pousada de Sousel–São Miguel	❧ ♥	3b
Torrão	Pousada do Torrão–Vale do Gaio	❧ ♥	3d
Vila Nova de Milfontes	Castelo de Milfontes	*x* **H** ❧ ♥	4a
Vila Viçosa	Casa de Peixinhos	*x* **H** ♥	3d
Vila Viçosa	Pousada de Vila Viçosa–D. João IV	*x* **H** ♥	3d

About Itineraries

The itinerary section of this guide features itineraries covering most of Portugal. They may be taken in whole or in part, or tied together for a longer journey. As an example, the *Exploring the Alentejo* itinerary, which ends in Estremoz, can connect to the *Medieval Monuments* itinerary, which when taken in reverse, begins in Estremoz. The two can be joined to make a perfect loop from Lisbon. Also the *Port to Port* itinerary, which begins in Lisbon and ends in Porto, dovetails nicely with the *Back to the Beginning* itinerary, which begins in Porto and ends in Bouro. Each of the itineraries highlights a different part of the country, and they are of different lengths, enabling you to find one or more to suit your individual taste and schedule.

Each itinerary is preceded by a map showing the route and the towns where we suggest sightseeing and recommend hotels. All the maps in this guide are intended to provide a general impression of a region and itinerary route, and an approximate location of the towns. These maps are drawn by an artist and are not intended to replace commercial maps. For identifying, navigating, and exploring country roads and for finding these secluded countryside properties, it is important to purchase detailed maps. We recommend buying maps before your trip, both to aid in the planning of your journey and to avoid having to spend time vacation time searching for the appropriate maps. (We use the one-page map of Portugal, Michelin Map 940, to outline our journey.) Since we often had difficulty finding all the maps we wanted from one source, we stock a full inventory of all the Michelin maps referenced in our guides. You can easily order maps online through our website, *www.karenbrown.com,* and we will ship them out immediately.

At the beginning of each itinerary we suggest our recommended pacing to help you decide the amount of time to allocate to each area. Each itinerary map shows all the towns and villages in which we have a recommended place to stay. Our suggestion is to choose a place to stay that appeals to you and use it as your hub, going out to explore each day in a new direction. We *highly* recommend staying several nights in one spot whenever possible.

About Places to Stay

BED AND BREAKFASTS

More and more Portuguese are opening their homes to guests. The Department of Tourism publishes an official guide called *Turismo Do Espaço Rural* listing bed and breakfasts in the countryside throughout Portugal that maintain set standards of quality and offer genuine hospitality. There are three classifications of houses: *Agroturismo,* farm estates where the guests can participate in the work; *Turismo Rural,* rustic houses in or near a town; and *Turismo de Habitação,* manor houses with quality furnishings, frequently antiques. Accommodations vary from basic to luxurious. We have featured many of the finest manor houses in this guide. Breakfast is always included in the room rate, and sometimes dinner is available. Within this group of bed and breakfasts some of the owners have banded together to form an affiliation called *Solares de Portugal.*

CREDIT CARDS

All pousadas accept major credit cards but in the smaller hotels and inns, credit cards are rarely accepted, cash being the preferred method of payment. Whether or not an establishment accepts credit cards is indicated in the list of icons at the bottom of each description by the symbol ▭. We have also indicated the specific cards accepted by using the following codes: AX–American Express, MC–MasterCard, VS–Visa, or simply, all major. *Note:* Even if an inn does not accept credit card payment, it will perhaps request your account number as a guarantee of arrival.

For obtaining cash, an increasingly popular and convenient way to obtain euros is simply to use your bankcard at an ATM machine. You pay a fixed fee for this but, depending on the amount you withdraw, it is usually less than the percentage-based fee charged to exchange currency or travelers' checks. Be sure to check with your bank or credit card company about fees and necessary pin numbers prior to departure.

ELECTRICAL APPLIANCES

You need a transformer plus an adapter if you plan to take an American-made electrical appliance. Even if the appliance is dual voltage, as many of them are these days, you'll still need a two-prong adapter plug. The voltage is usually 220, but occasionally a 110 outlet (meant for an electric razor) is provided in the hotel bathroom.

ESTALAGEMS

Estalagems are privately owned inns that are supposed to maintain similar standards to the pousadas. We discovered some charming examples, but our experience indicates that there is more variation in the quality of the estalagems than in the pousadas.

HOTELS

You could travel throughout Portugal staying only in government-owned pousadas and be assured of exceptional accommodations. However, we also recommend and describe many outstanding, privately owned hotels that offer great charm.

MAPS

Each itinerary is preceded by a map showing the route and each hotel listing is referenced on its top line to a map at the back of the book. To make it easier for you, hotel location maps are divided into a grid of four parts—a, b, c, and d—as indicated on each map's key. All maps are an artist's renderings and are not intended to replace detailed commercial maps.

We recommend you purchase the Michelin Map 940, which features just Portugal (not the Michelin that has Spain and Portugal together). This map has an extensive index, and you should be able to find almost all of the places we mention.

If you are also going to Spain, an excellent choice is the *Michelin Tourist and Motoring Atlas of Spain and Portugal,* a book of maps with a scale of 1:400,000 (1 cm = 4 km). While the atlas proves invaluable for detailed routes, we find it too detailed for getting an overview of our trip and rely upon the one-page map of Portugal, Michelin Map 940, to outline our journey.

Since we often had difficulty finding all the maps we wanted from one source, we stock a full inventory of all the Michelin maps referenced in our guides. You can easily order maps online through our website, *www.karenbrown.com,* and we will ship them out immediately.

MINIMUM STAYS

Many of the places in our guides have a minimum number of nights for which a reservation will be accepted. You might find that in high season, even though this minimum stay is not mentioned in the property's description, there often is a minimum stay of anywhere from two to seven nights.

POUSADAS

The Portuguese government operates through Enatur, S.A., a system of hotels called pousadas—literally "stopping places" or, more commonly, "inns." This company was created in 1976 to handle the entire management of the country's pousadas and over the years more and more hotels have been added to the affiliation. The goal of these pousadas is to introduce the traveler to the people, culture, traditions, art, and food of the various regions of Portugal. Visit their website: *www.pousadas.pt.*

Our book includes all but two recently opened pousadas. We have visited each and every one of them that we recommend. Some are absolutely outstanding, while others are a bit bland. Nevertheless, they are all in strategic locations and offer without exception rooms that meet standards of cleanliness and comfort—even if lacking charm. Because there is not a large choice of places to stay in Portugal, and because the pousadas are both easy to find and conveniently situated, we feature almost all of them for your consideration.

COST: Room rates throughout the pousada affiliation have recently increased. However, for the quality of accommodation, they still offer good value. Some of the pousadas are delightfully simple, others fabulously deluxe, and their rates are based accordingly. Prices are seasonal, the low season being November though March, and the high April through October. In our descriptions we quote the rate for high season, including taxes and breakfast. Sometimes special rates are available for seniors.

DINING: All of the pousadas have good to excellent dining rooms featuring regional culinary specialties. These dining rooms are open to the public and make a reliable place to stop for lunch if you have a leisurely day. The dining rooms are always attractive, open every day, and frequently have a stunning view.

HISTORICAL BUILDINGS: In addition to seeing many of the recently renovated pousadas, we also visited several that had just opened in historic buildings. We just cannot rave enough about the incredible job the government is doing in rescuing irreplaceable historical monuments whose beauty would soon have been lost forever. The cost of these renovations has been extraordinary. When you are a guest, you cannot help feeling a bit pleased that by staying in a pousada, you are a part of this remarkable project of preserving the past.

HOW TO FIND: An advantage to choosing a pousada is that there are always signs guiding you to it from the edge of town. This may seem trivial to you now, but just wait—after the frustration of getting lost trying to find some of our other recommendations, you might decide to stay only at pousadas in the future! Having asked many owners of other hotels why they weren't better marked, the answer was always the same—the bureaucracy wouldn't allow them to put up signs. Being government-owned, the pousadas happily don't have this problem.

TYPES: Most of the pousadas are positively enchanting—installed in historic buildings such as castles, monasteries, convents, or medieval manor houses. Others, not quite as glamorous, have been constructed within the last 50 years—usually in the style of the region where they are located. A few of the pousadas we visited (mostly those built since the 1940s) seemed a little tired. However, there is an ongoing program of refurbishment, and their turn will soon come for a face-lift. We revisited several places that had just reopened after extensive renovation and were astounded by the tremendous improvement—the new facilities were without exception outstanding. So whether the pousada is an absolute jewel that you will always remember or a more basic hotel, we have included them all because you can depend on a high level of service, a good restaurant, and an immaculate room.

RATES

The rates shown in this guide are those given to us by each of the properties for 2003 for two people sharing one room in high season, including tax. Breakfast is almost always included in the room rate, which is confirmed in the list of icons at the bottom of each description by the symbol ☕. Please **always check prices** when making reservations. Prices can vary according to season, local special events, and additional features such as sitting rooms, balconies, and views. Remember that we show the rate for the high season (which is usually April through October), so if you travel off peak, you can frequently save money.

RESERVATIONS

Whether or not to reserve ahead is not a question with a simple answer—it depends upon the flexibility of your timetable and your temperament. It also depends to a large extent on the season in which you are traveling. For example, during the peak season, accommodation at the Pousada do Castelo in Óbidos normally requires reservations many months in advance. Other popular hotels with limited rooms are similarly booked. Prudent tourists make arrangements months in advance to secure desirable accommodations during local festivals. On the other hand, throughout much of the year space can be obtained in most places with one day's notice or less. If you have your heart set on a particular place, there are several ways of making reservations.

When making your reservations, be sure to identify yourself as a "Karen Brown traveler." The innkeepers appreciate your visit, value their inclusion in our guide, and frequently tell us they take special care of our readers. We hear over and over again from hotel owners that the people who use our guides are wonderful guests, and some of the properties extend special offers to Karen Brown members. Visit our website, *www.karenbrown.com*, for membership information.

TELEPHONE, FAX, LETTER, OR E-MAIL: If you want to make the booking yourself, you can phone, fax, write, or e-mail for a reservation. Note: for e-mail addresses, all properties featured on the Karen Brown Website have their e-mail address published on their web page (this information is constantly kept updated and correct). You can link directly to a property from its page on our website using its e-mail hyperlink. Remember that Portugal is five hours ahead of New York, so plan your call accordingly to avoid waking someone up in the middle of the night. If you call or fax, the system is to dial the international access code (011), then the country code for Portugal (351), and then the telephone number listed in the hotel's description. Don't worry that phone numbers have different numbers of digits—that's the way it works in Portugal. We have a sample reservation letter in English and Portuguese on page 46, which you can photocopy and use to make reservations. Always spell out the month as Europeans reverse the American month/day numbering system.

POUSADA RESERVATIONS–MARKETING AHEAD: Reservations for all of the pousadas (and many of the other hotels featured in this guide) can be made with Marketing Ahead in New York. You can call, fax, e-mail, or use the hot link from our website to make reservations. Identify yourself as a Karen Brown reader using the code number KBG2003MA to get 5% discount (individuals only please—this offer is not available through your travel agent). Reservations are confirmed within 48 hours and require a $50 deposit (per hotel). Reservations must be prepaid 30 days prior to departure from the USA and cover the room, tax, and breakfast. Vouchers showing proof of payment will be mailed to you. The price in dollars is guaranteed upon prepayment (prices displayed locally in euros may fluctuate with the exchange rate). For further information contact Marketing Ahead, 433 Fifth Avenue, 6th Floor, New York, NY 10016, tel: (212) 686-9213, toll-free: (800) 223-1356, fax: (212) 686-0271, e-mail: *mahrep@aol.com* or simply click across from our website, *www.karenbrown.com*.

POUSADA RESERVATIONS–POUSADAS DE PORTUGAL: If you see in the hotel's description that it is a pousada, you can call or fax it directly. However, if you are reserving multiple pousadas, you might want to consider booking through the central reservations office: Pousadas de Portugal (Reservations), Avenida Santa Joana Princesa 10A, Lisbon 1700, Portugal, tel: 218.44.20.01, fax: 218.44.20.85. Note: Be sure to inquire about their mid-week specials and senior citizen discounts.

UNITED STATES REPRESENTATIVE: KB Travel Service is a company whose professional travel consultants specialize in Karen-Brown-recommended hotels and personal trip planning and consultation. If you are interested in assistance with your trip, we recommend that you contact them directly to check on the services offered and the fees. KB Travel Service, 16 E. Third Ave., San Mateo, Ca. 94401, tel: 1-800-782-2128, email: info@kbtravelservice.com, website: www.kbtravelservice.com.

WEBSITE

Please supplement this book by looking at the information provided on our Karen Brown website (*www.karenbrown.com*), which serves as an added dimension to our guides. Many properties are featured on our website (participation is the choice of an individual property) with a link to their own websites and e-mail for even more detailed information, directions and reservations. Also featured on our site are comments, feedback, and discoveries from you, our readers; information on our latest finds; post-press updates; contest drawings for free books; special offers; unique features such as recipes and favorite destinations; and special savings offered by certain properties.

WHEELCHAIR ACCESSIBILITY

If an inn has *at least* one guestroom that is accessible by wheelchair, it is noted with the symbol ♿. This is not the same as saying it meets full disability standards. In reality, it can be anything from a basic ground-floor room to a fully equipped facility. Please discuss your requirements when you call your chosen place to stay to determine if they have accommodation that suits your needs and preference.

SAMPLE RESERVATION REQUEST LETTER

HOTEL NAME AND ADDRESS

Exmos. Senhores:

Escrevemos para fazer uma reserva para _____ noite(s)
We are writing to make a reservation for (number of) night(s)

Desde o dia _____ de _____ até o dia _____ de _____
From   (date) of (month)   to   (date) of (month).

(Months: Janeiro, Fevereiro, Março, Abril, Maio, Junho, Julho, Agosto, Setembro, Outubro, Novembro, Dezembro)

_____ quarto(s) individual(ais)   com cama extra—with an extra bed
    single room(s)   com vista do mar—with a view of the sea
                                     com terraço—with a terrace
_____ quarto(s) duplos   com banho—with bath
    double room(s)   num andar alto—on an upper floor
                                     num andar baixo—on a lower floor
_____ suite(s)   a frente—in the front
    suite(s)   antrás—in the back

Somos _____ pessoas.
We have (number of) persons in our party.

Tenha a bondade de avisar sóbre se e disponível o quarto, o preço dêle, e se é preciso uma garantia. Esperando a sua resposta, subscrevemo-nos atenciosamente,

Please advise availability, the rate, and the deposit necessary. Awaiting your reply, we remain, sincerely,

YOUR NAME, ADDRESS, & PHONE/FAX/E-MAIL—clearly printed or typed

Lisbon Highlights

Brangaça
Porto
Ciombra
Lisbon
Évora
Lagos

★ Suggested hotels
● Orientation/Sightseeing
- - - Itinerary route

Praias
N247 Sintra
Colares N249
Monserrate
Cabo
da Roca
ATLANTIC
OCEAN
Queluz
IC19
Guincho
Praia do Guincho N247 Cascais Lisbon
A5
Estoril N6
Belém

Lisbon Highlights

Palácio da Pena, Sintra

Any trip to Portugal should include some time in the capital and largest city, Lisbon. Sitting on seven low hills near the mouth of the River Tagus (Tejo), it qualifies as one of the world's most beautifully situated cities. Just above Lisbon the Tagus spreads out into a 7-kilometer-wide estuary, which carries it the final 16 kilometers of its 1,000-kilometer course to the Atlantic. The sunset glow on the estuary has given it the name of *Mar de Palha*, or Sea of Straw. This is the centerpiece of Lisbon's charm and one of its most attractive features. It also provides an excellent sheltered harbor, which has been the city's most significant economic attribute and the reason for its long-term importance.

Recommended Pacing: If you select a couple of museums that appeal to you and skirt the exterior of the others, you can accomplish the recommended sightseeing in a day, which means that you will need a minimum of two nights' accommodation in Lisbon. Add an extra night if you are making the daytrip to Estoril, Cascais, and Sintra.

Lisbon was probably first settled by the Phoenicians around 1200 BC and, after falling to the Greeks and Carthaginians in succession, was taken by the Romans in 205 BC. From 714 to 1147 AD it was in Moorish hands; then around 1260 it became the seat of the Portuguese monarchs and has been the capital ever since.

The city really reached its maturity in the 16th century when so many exploratory sea voyages were launched from here. The flourishing trade with the Orient, which resulted from the discovery of the route around Africa, made Lisbon the European center of such commerce and brought a high level of prosperity to the city.

In 1755 an exceptionally violent earthquake hit Portugal and much of Lisbon was reduced to rubble, especially the lower town. The subsequent tidal wave was an awesome catastrophe, sweeping away thousands of people. Uncontrollable fires augmented the citywide destruction. The quake was a major event in Europe and dampened the carefree optimism prevailing at the time. The **Marques de Pombal**, who was Foreign Minister serving under the inexperienced King Jose I, used the tragedy as his springboard to nearly dictatorial power. He immediately began the reconstruction of the city, following the fashionable design of the time: wide, tree-lined boulevards and streets laid out in a square pattern. The reconstruction was mostly limited to the flatter, lower town: The hillsides still retain the winding lanes of the original city. Most of what you see today in Lisbon reflects the fine style of the 18th century as set forth by Pombal.

Driving in Lisbon, as in any large European city, can be trying, to say the least. We strongly suggest using taxis where walking is not feasible. If your plans include renting a car, our advice is to take delivery after staying in Lisbon—it is expensive to park here, and it is always easier to follow directions to one of the major highways out of the city (which are well marked) than it is to try to find your way to your city hotel.

A good way to begin your visit to the capital is to take one of the numerous city tours, which will acquaint you with Lisbon's layout and give you an idea of which sights you wish to return to at your leisure. The center of business activity is the district known as the **Baixa**, or lower town. This is the area between the Praça do Comércio on the riverbank, through Dom Pedro IV Square (called the Rossio), and along the expansive Avenida da Liberdade to the Praça do Marques de Pombal. The **Praça do Comércio** is a gigantic 9-acre square surrounded by mostly government buildings, with an equestrian statue of King Jose I in the middle. The square was spruced up in preparation for the Expo that took place in the spring of 1998. You may hear or see the name **Terreiro do Paço** in reference to it: that means "Palace Square" and refers to a palace destroyed by the earthquake. Just off the southeast corner of the square is the ferry dock where you can take a boat to the city of **Barreiro** on the left bank of the Tagus. From another dock just east of there you can take a tranquil two-hour cruise on the river and glean a unique perspective of the city.

The area north of the square (reached through a baroque triumphal arch) consists of Lisbon's major shopping streets, which feed into the Praça like spokes of a wheel. Pombal's intent was to organize the district by product category; hence names such as *Rua do Ouro* for the goldsmiths and *Rua da Prata* for the silversmiths. The distinction is no longer maintained, however, and all kinds of vendors are found on all the streets.

At the north end of this bustling area is the **Rossio**, or **Dom Pedro IV Square**, where its namesake stands atop a 22-meter column between baroque fountains. This square was refurbished for the 1998 Expo. At the end of the square is the national theater with a statue of Gil Vicente, considered to be the father of Portuguese theater. He occupies a literary position in Portuguese similar to that of Shakespeare in English, though he lived more than a century earlier. Just behind the national theater, many colorful restaurants line the streets with tables set outside for dining when the weather is warm.

Beyond the theater is the **Restauradores Square,** honoring the uprising in 1640, which put an end to the Spanish occupation of Portugal. This lively square forms one end of the magnificent **Avenida da Liberdade**, lined with trees, tall, modern office buildings, and hotels. At the other end of the avenue is a monument to Pombal and, behind it, the elegant **Edward VII Park** created in honor of the 1902 visit of that English king. Here you find formal gardens and splendid views from the upper end of the park.

A couple of blocks north of the Edward VII Park sits the Gulbenkian Foundation, established by an Armenian oilman who lived much of his life in Portugal and bequeathed his fortune to establish the foundation. The organization supports cultural activities and the building houses two museums. The **Calouste Gulbenkian Museum** contains the eclectic personal collection of the benefactor: Ancient Egypt, Greece, and Rome are represented along with a large collection of Oriental art.

To the west of the Baixa is the section known as the **Bairro Alto**, or upper town. An easy way to get there is to take the funicular from the Avenida da Liberdade (you'll see the station at the north end of the Praça dos Restauradores).

Bairro Alto, Lisbon

The funicular runs up the street called Calcada da Gloria, at the top of which sits the **Belvedere of São Pedro de Alcantara** overlooking panoramas of the city to the north. Down the Rua da Misericordia to the south is the 16th-century **São Roque Church**, which has a handsome interior. Attached to the church is a worthwhile museum of religious art. A little farther in the same direction lies the **Square of Luis de Camoes** (he wrote *The Lusiads*, Portugal's greatest epic poem). To the left runs the **Rua Garrett**, also known as the Chiado—an elegant, animated street lined with shops and cafés. If you follow it to its end and turn left on Rua do Carmo, in addition to more boutiques, you'll come across ruins of a Carmelite church (to the left). To the right is an Eiffel-designed elevator, which takes you down to the Rua do Ouro in the Baixa.

The area to the east of the Baixa is the medieval city crowned by the São Jorge Castle. The section nearest the river is known as the **Alfama** and is characterized by ancient stepped streets winding through picturesque old houses with wrought-iron balconies and washing hanging to dry from flower-bedecked windows. At the edge near the Praça do Comércio is **Lisbon Cathedral**, a late-12th-century edifice largely restored after the earthquake. It contains several small chapels and an impressive **Treasury** (*Tesouro*). A bit farther up on the Rua Limoeiro is the Santa Luzia belvedere with superb views over the rooftops of the ancient Alfama and the rest of the city beyond.

At the apex of the hill is the **Castle of São Jorge**, built on the site of the earliest town settlement. Originally converted from a Moorish castle, it has been remodeled many times over the centuries. There are terrific vistas from the terrace and castle battlements over the city's hills and the Tagus. Plan your excursion so that you can dine at the charming restaurant, Casa de Leão, built within the old castle. This delightful restaurant, operated by the pousada chain, is quite popular, so it's best to make a reservation. The restaurant terrace is a romantic spot to watch the sunset.

A few hundred meters east of the castle is **São Vicente de Fora Church**, which has some beautiful azulejos in the adjoining cloisters. In the former refectory of the attached monastery is the **Royal Pantheon of the House of Bragança**, containing the family tombs from that famous royal line since the 17th century. If you are here on Tuesday or Saturday, seek out the colorful flea markets in progress in nearby Campo de Santa Clara and Campo Santana.

Along the river to the west of the Praço do Comércio on the Rua das Janelas Verdes is the excellent **Museu de Arte Antiga** (Ancient Art). Besides a first-rate collection of Portuguese art, there are good works by Spanish, Flemish, and German artists. The gold- and silversmith work is also superior, as is the exhibit of antique furniture. This museum is definitely worth a visit.

Several kilometers to the west of the city (too far to walk) is the Belém district, reached by car, taxi, or train. You will pass under the approach to Europe's longest suspension bridge, the **25 de Abril** (commemorating the Revolution of 1974), its kilometer-long span towering 60 meters above the Tagus and strongly reminiscent of the Golden Gate bridge in San Francisco.

A second, equally dramatic bridge into Lisbon, the Ponte Vasco da Gama, was completed in time for the 1998 Expo. Across the street to the north of the **Praça do Albuquerque** is the rose-colored **Belém Palace**, where the President of Portugal resides.

In the former riding school of the palace is the fascinating, not-to-be-missed **Coach Museum** with a stunning collection of royal carriages from the 16th to 19th centuries.

Just beyond the palace is the famous **Hieronymite Monastery**, considered a masterpiece of Manueline architecture with its impressive **Saint Mary's Church** and an awe–inspiring cloister with elegant, sculpted arcades. King Manuel I commissioned this marvel as a gesture of gratitude for Vasco da Gama's discovery of the route to India, which resulted in the glorious era of Portuguese wealth and prominence. In the former dormitory flanking the church is the **National Archaeology Museum** with an impressive collection of prehistoric Iberian material. Farther west is the **Naval Museum**, which will appeal to those who enjoy historical displays of model ships.

Royal Coach, Coach Museum, Lisbon

Across the grassy Imperial Square in front of the monastery are two reminders of the past: the five-story **Belém Tower** and the **Monument to the Discoveries**. The tower was constructed as a fortress in the early 16th century in the middle of the Tagus, which obviously has changed course a bit, since the tower now sits on the right bank. The Monument to the Discoveries was erected in 1960, on the 500th anniversary of the death of **Prince Henry the Navigator**, who opened the doors to the 16th-century period of discovery. Between the two is a museum of folk art and crafts from around Portugal.

EXCURSIONS FROM LISBON: There are several ways to explore the "Portuguese Riviera," which is the name given to the area to the west of the city, between Lisbon and the Atlantic. Numerous bus tours are available, although their one-day duration can't really do justice to this beautiful area. Another way, of course, is by car from Lisbon. Finally, there is excellent train service from Lisbon to Cascais-Estoril and from Lisbon to Sintra. In fact, if you are not particularly enamored of the hustle and bustle of Lisbon, you might seriously consider choosing one of the lovely hotels in or near Cascais, Monserrate, or Sintra instead of staying in the city. From there you can make excursions to Lisbon by train—the trains make the 35-minute trip from the coast to the capital every half-hour between 5:30 am and 10 pm and every hour from 10 pm to 2 am. The Sintra route takes you right to the Rossio in the center of town, and the Cascais train arrives at the Estacão do Cais Sodre, a few blocks west of the Praça do Comércio. A return to the relative calm of a hotel at the seaside or up in the hills is not a bad way to end a day of city sightseeing. Be sure to confirm the train schedules at the hotel desk since they may change.

If you opt to stay in Lisbon, below is a description of the route to the Portuguese Riviera by car:

ESTORIL, CASCAIS, AND SINTRA: Leave Lisbon going north on the Avenida da Liberdade. When you reach the roundabout at Marquis de Pombal, take the A5 (blue signs) marked to Cascais and Estoril. The toll road ends at Cascais.

The old-world resort of **Estoril** has been a favorite stomping ground of the European jet set for a century. The once-magnificent beaches have deteriorated somewhat, but the lovely private villas will still impress you. This coastal area enjoys an especially mild climate all year round. All sorts of activities, outdoor and indoor, from golf to gambling, abound in this somewhat exclusive resort town.

Although technically separate, Estoril now forms a contiguous developed unit with **Cascais**, former summer home of the Portuguese royal family (19th century) and now that of the President. Originally a tiny fishing village, today it is a pleasant and colorful resort town resplendent with boutiques, narrow winding streets, seafood restaurants, and flowery parks. In the center of town brightly painted boats are still hauled up on the shore at night and the fishermen sit talking in the evening as they mend their nets.

Just out of Cascais on the coast road (N247-8) is a giant sea-formed abyss called **Boca do Inferno** (Hell's Jaws). Here breakers smash into the rocky caverns, creating intriguing patterns among the oddly shaped rocks of the promontory. As you continue along this road, you'll be treated to spectacular ocean views. You come upon a good viewpoint at **Cabo Raso**, then skirt the long **Praia do Guincho** with its forested borders.

Palácio de Seteais, Sintra

Warning: There is said to be a strong undertow here. Set on a promontory overlooking the crashing surf is the imposing **Fortaleza do Guincho**, which once protected this dramatic stretch of coastline and now offers luxurious accommodation. Another 6 kilometers bring you to a junction for Malveira where you turn left and enter the lower edge of the beautiful wooded **Serra da Sintra**. Watch for a left turn onto N247-4 which leads out to **Cabo da Roca**, the westernmost point of the European continent—an isolated, elevated promontory from which to survey the vastness of the Atlantic.

Return to N247 and turn left. You are still skirting the western edge of the Serra and will shortly come upon the little town of **Colares**, justly famous for its superior wines. Following N375 southwest will take you through the lush green hills of the Sintra region. After a few kilometers on the tranquil country road, a large stone arch at the entrance to the **Palácio de Seteais** (seven sighs) will catch your eye. The palace is now a luxury hotel and has an excellent restaurant, which you should visit if you happen to be driving by at mealtime. Otherwise, consider settling on the wisteria-covered terrace for a light snack—anything to enjoy the gorgeous views and tranquil setting of this magnificent property! Soon afterward you reach **Sintra** (often spelled Cintra in English).

Just as you enter town, you'll see a sign to the right, leading up a narrow, zigzag lane to the remains of the 7th-century **Castelo dos Mouros** whose ramparts provide enchanting views of the serra. A kilometer up the road is the fantastic 19th-century **Palácio da Pena**, a colorful, flight-of-fancy construction, which includes elements of every architectural period imaginable. There are guided tours of the interior, featuring art objects and furnishings supposedly left exactly as they were when the monarchy was overthrown in 1910. The terraces, guard paths, and ornate onion dome afford marvelous views to Lisbon and the Tagus to the east and the Atlantic to the west. This is a castle you mustn't miss—it's fabulous.

In Sintra is another **National Palace** near the middle of town on the Praça da Republica. This one was originally built in the 14th century as a royal residence and subsequently much remodeled. Guided tours will take you through its wonderfully furnished rooms and halls.

Sintra is an especially romantic little town, nestled in the heavily wooded hills that rise from the coast. This was once an area of great wealth and many of the fabulous old *quintas* (farm estates) tucked in the countryside outside of town have been turned into small, deluxe hotels, which are described in the hotel section of this book: **Quinta das Sequoias** and **Quinta da Capela** are both gorgeous and lovely places to stay. In the center of town you find many boutiques, a variety of good restaurants, and wonderful accommodation. We recommend a delightful bed and breakfast, **Casa Miradouro**, on the bottom of edge of town and a beautiful, historic hotel, **Lawrence's**, located just up from the main square. In addition to its other attributes, Sintra is surprisingly cool in the summertime. Lord Byron resided here for a while in the early 19th century, and it is easy to see why he chose this beautiful location.

To return to Lisbon, leave Sintra on N249 and after about 15 kilometers, watch for the turnoff to **Queluz**, where you'll discover the rococo **Palácio Nacional de Queluz**, a beautiful former summer palace of the Bragança royal house that has been converted into a pousada. Its 18th-century style includes Versailles-like formal gardens and a particularly harmonious blend of decorative elements inside. For its restaurant, the pousada uses the fabulous Cozinha Velha, located just across the street. This is a charming, extremely cozy dining room built within the old kitchen of the royal palace.

After seeing Queluz, get on the IC19 for the 12-kilometer drive back to Lisbon.

Belém Tower, Lisbon

The Alluring Algarve

★ Suggested hotels
● Orientation/Sightseeing
▲ Archaeological sites

Brangaça
Porto
Ciombra
Lisbon
Évora
Lagos

to Lisbon
to Lisbon

N120

Vila Nova de Milfontes ★

Odemira ●

N120

★ Santa Clara -a-Velha

IP-2

IP-1

Mertola ●

N122

Monchique ●

Silves ●

Alte ●

Querença ●

Santa Bárbara de Nexe ●

São Brás de Alportel ★

Odiáxere ★

Portimão ●

N125

Loulé ●

IP-1

Cabo de São Vincente ●

Porto de Mós ★

Lagos ★

Praia do Vau ★

Praia da Rocha ★

Praia de Galé ★

Albufeira ●

Vilamoura ●

Val do Lobo

Almansil ●

▲ Estói ★

Faro ●

Olhão ●

Tavira ★

Cacela Velha ●

Sagres ★

Spain

The Alluring Algarve

Praia da Rocha

This itinerary introduces you to one of Portugal's most alluring tourist areas: its southern strip called the Algarve. The name comes from the word *Al-Gharb*, the Arabic word for west, so-called because it was the most westerly European stronghold of the Islamic civilization that occupied most of the Iberian Peninsula during the Middle Ages. Due to its somewhat isolated geographical situation—separated from the rest of the country by a chain of mountains—it was both the first area taken by the Moors in the 8th century and the last to be regained by the Christians, thus spending the longest time under Arab domination. As might be expected, it retains the greatest cultural influence of that civilization.

Recommended Pacing: The Algarve stretches between Spain and the Atlantic Ocean, a total span of 160 kilometers. Because the distance is so short, we recommend that you do not move around from night to night—instead, choose one place to settle in the Algarve and use it as a hub to explore the whole region. A four-night stay will give you a day to explore alluring villages, a day for a trip to Sagres, and a day to relax on the beach.

The map has stars indicating towns where we recommend accommodations. Frequently the hotel is *not* actually in the town where the star is shown, but instead nearby on the coast or in a tiny hamlet in the countryside. Luckily, there is a rich selection of places to stay, so you are sure to find one well suited to your personality and pocketbook. From your base you can venture out each day on a new adventure. We suggest places to include on your excursions. However, as you explore the coast, you are sure to discover your own favorite villages and secluded beaches.

Although the Algarve lies along Portugal's southern coast, it is easily accessible. One option is to fly to Faro, an airport with flights arriving from all over Europe—and, of course, from Lisbon. A suggestion is to either begin or end your holiday in the Algarve, either picking up your car rental when you arrive or dropping it off as you leave.

Another option is to drive from Lisbon to the Algarve (or vice versa). You can take either the coastal road, N120 (which parallels the coast but is rarely close enough to see the water) or else the inland route on the IP1. If you choose the coastal road, a convenient point to break your journey is **Santiago do Cacém**, where there is the **Pousada de Santiago do Cacém–Quinta da Ortiga** (see listings). Although it is a bit farther, we recommend the inland route on the IP1 because the roads are better and because there is not a lot to see along the coast. Either way, you can easily make the journey in a day since the Algarve is only about 300 kilometers from Lisbon.

Another way to travel to the Algarve is by bus. The bus system within Portugal is excellent. One of the main, countrywide bus companies is EVA, which has some of the fastest service to the Algarve. For example, from Lisbon it is about four and a half hours to Albufeira and five hours to Faro.

The Algarve's favorable geographic setting provides it with some of the best weather in Europe. Snuggled in a protected pocket that is bound to the north by mountains, to the west by the craggy cliffs of Cape Saint Vincent, and to the east by bucolic deltas of the Spanish border, the coast is blessed with a mild climate all year round. Because the weather is so favorable, a string of resort areas has sprouted up along the Atlantic beaches, which the Portuguese call the Costa do Sol (Sun Coast).

If possible, time your vacation in the spring or fall since the area is swarming with tourists in the summer. Because of so many travelers, the main road that parallels the coast is lined with souvenir shops, amusement parks, bright plastic water slides, and fast-food restaurants. Much of this is geared to appeal to families traveling with children. However, do not be discouraged—off the main road, if you know where to look, you will find everything from quaint fishing villages to swanky resorts and casinos, along with ample opportunities for all kinds of outdoor activities from sports to sunbathing. As might be expected, the Algarve's forte is its cornucopia of fresh seafood dishes. The ubiquitous *caldeirada de peixe* (bouillabaisse) comes in as many forms as there are chefs. Various mixtures of fish and shellfish are prepared *a cataplana* (a lidded, round-bottomed skillet) over an open flame. Versions of this concoction also include cured ham and/or pork along with the typical clams and other fish.

Sightseeing Suggestions

ALBUFEIRA

Albufeira is a bustling seaside fishing village-turned-resort. The architecture of its boxy, flat-roofed, whitewashed houses stepping up the cliffs from the beach harks back to its Moorish heritage. Its Moorish background also lingers in the name "Albufeira," which means "castle on the sea" in Arabic. The town boasts a large, busy beach, which is reached by a tunnel from the main square. The predominantly white buildings are colorfully decorated with bright awnings. Shops and restaurants abound here, as do street vendors with multi-hued umbrellas covering their wares. Brightly colored boats are still drawn up onto the sand at night. The town has the potential to be outstanding, but its quaintness has been sullied a bit by the fact that it is such a magnet for swarms of tourists. Nevertheless, it's an inviting place to stroll around the steep, narrow streets and inspect the shops and attractive cafés. Try to visit early in the morning before the mobs of tourists arrive. If you want to stay in a deluxe hotel near Albufeira, the **Vila Joya**, west of town at Praia de Galé, has an outstanding position on the bluffs above the sea.

ALMANSIL

Almansil is not worth a special visit on its own merits, but if you enjoy beautiful churches, you will find one of the loveliest in Portugal just outside the town. This 18th-century gem is the **Igreja Matriz de São Lourenço**, which was built in tribute to São Lourenço who answered the town's prayers for water. Its altar is an intricately painted, gilded masterpiece, but most impressive are the stunning azulejo panels depicting scenes from the saint's life.

ALTE

Alte is an out-of-the-way, picturesque, whitewashed village tucked up in the hills about 20 kilometers northeast of Albufeira. Off the tourist path, small rural villages such as Alte offer a glimpse of the "real" Algarve as it used be—a far cry from the glitter and fast pace of the coast.

CACELA VELHA

Cacela Velha is one of the quaintest of the small villages between Tavira and the Spanish border and makes a fun stop if you are exploring the coast. Fishing used to be the main industry here and there are still fishing boats drawn up on the beach. The fishermen live in the whitewashed houses with bright-blue trim on the bluff above the sea. For added character, the town also has the picturesque remains of an old fortress.

FARO

Faro, the capital of the Algarve, was an important Moorish seaport. In 1249 **Afonso III** recaptured it from the Moors and promptly set about rebuilding the city walls. However, the walls could not protect the town from the British, who in 1596 sacked and burned it to the ground. One of the leaders of the expedition, the **Earl of Essex**, stayed in the Bishop's Palace and helped himself to 200 of its priceless, leather-bound, gilt-tooled books. He took these back to England and gave them to his good friend, Sir Thomas Bodley, at Oxford, who was delighted to receive them for his now world-renowned Bodleian Library. After the British destroyed Faro, it was rebuilt, but the 1755 earthquake leveled it again.

Today Faro is a sprawling industrial center, so head straight to the historic old town and the port with its tree-lined avenues. Make your way to the **Cathedral**, which is beautifully decorated with 17th-century azulejos. Located behind the cathedral, the **Archaeological Museum** is housed in a lovely 16th-century cloister of the **Convento de Nossa Senhora da Assunção**. Here you find both Moorish and Roman artifacts (all uncovered in nearby sites), plus lovely azulejos and a nice collection of paintings. Also alongside the cathedral is the **Chapel of the Bones**, an enticingly macabre building entirely faced with the bones of exhumed monks! A short walk from the cathedral is a little gem you must not miss, the **Teatro Lethes**. Originally a small chapel, it was converted into an enchanting tiny opera house by an Italian family who made their fortune in Portugal after being shipwrecked en route to London. At the north end of the harbor is a **Maritime Museum** with models of boats and ships. The area to the east of the harbor is the traditional downtown area with shops and pedestrian streets. The **beach** at Faro—actually an offshore strip of sand—is about 9 kilometers away and can be reached by car or ferry (from June to September) from the Porta Nova pier at the harbor.

If you want to stay in the Faro area, we suggest several outstanding places: the friendly, homelike **Monte do Casal** near Estói; and the newly renovated **Pousada de São Brás de Alportel** in the hills north of Faro in São Brás de Alportel.

LAGOS

Lagos, which shelters the widest bay in the Algarve, was once the primary departure point for the crusaders. There were also trade ships sailing out of Lagos, including many en route to Africa. In 1441 Prince Henry's explorer, Nuno Tristão, brought back slaves from the Sahara and the first **slave market** to appear in Europe was set up in Lagos under the arches of the Customs House. Most of the early voyages of exploration departed from here, and **Prince Henry the Navigator** (whose statue adorns the Praça da Republica) called it home for a while.

The tree-lined Avenida dos Descobrimentos (Discoveries) separates Lagos from the sea. For strolling, the most interesting section is the area between the Avenida dos Descobrimentos and the Praça de Gil, which is decorated with a statue of **Dom Sebastião**, King of Portugal from 1557 to 1578. Dom Sebastião died in Morocco in 1578 during the **Battle of Alcácer Quibir**. During this ill-advised expedition, 8,000 of his soldiers were slain and 15,000 more captured and sold into slavery. The handsome king, who was only 24, became a legend. Since nobody actually witnessed his death, a cult called "Sebastianism" evolved, which proclaimed that the popular monarch was not killed and would someday return to rule Portugal. The belief gave rise to numerous imposters pretending to be Sebastião and offering themselves as king. Sebastião's demise paved the way for Spain's Phillip II to take over the throne, forcing Portugal to become part of the hated Spanish Empire.

At the edge of Lagos, jutting out over the entrance to the harbor, is the 17th-century **Forte Ponta da Bandeira**, a sturdy, square, stone fortress with jaunty little watchtowers perched on each corner. A drawbridge from the Avenida dos Descobrimentos leads into the inner courtyard. Inside are displays of the Great Discoveries and also a small 17th-century chapel.

Within town stop to visit the 18th-century **Santo Igreja de António** with its remarkable blue and white azulejos. In the church there is also a statue of Lago's patron saint, **Santo António**, which—according to tradition—was always carried into battle for good luck. Adjoining the church is a small archaeological museum.

Lagos is also famous for a naval battle fought just off shore in 1693 when the celebrated French admiral, Tourville, sank 80 Dutch and English ships in an awesome engagement.

Just before town is a sign for the beautiful cove at **Praia de Dona Ana**, a beach uniquely situated beneath giant red cliffs eroded into impressive shapes by ceaseless waves. A bit farther west is another lovely beach at **Porto de Mós** where we feature the delightful **Romantik Hotel Vivenda Miranda**. In the countryside outside Lagos, near Odiáxere, is the charming **Quinta das Barradas**.

LOULÉ

About 10 kilometers northwest of Faro lies the picturesque mountain village of **Loulé**, known for its local handicrafts and its collection of intricately carved chimneys so characteristic of the Algarve.

MILREU

The Roman ruins of **Milreu** are located near Estói. The small site, dating back to the 1st century, is thought to be the Roman predecessor of Faro. Two marble columns mark the spot where a temple once stood, and nearby are the foundations of houses and baths, some still with mosaics. There is not a wealth of things to see because most of the artifacts found here have been removed—many are now housed in the **Archaeological Museum** in Faro.

MONCHIQUE

Monchique is a spa town nestled in the wooded hills above the coast with wonderful views to the sea. The town is popular for those who want to escape the heat and fast pace of the coast. Also, Monchique is known for its local handicrafts, the most notable being wicker baskets, leather goods, copper and brass items, woolen sweaters, and heavy woven-wool spreads, which make handsome bedcovers or rugs. On a clear day, the view of the distant coast is lovely.

OLHÃO

Olhão is a sardine- and tuna-fishing port about 8 kilometers east of Faro, with beaches much less crowded than those at Faro. You can take a ferry from Olhão out to either **Armona** or **Culatra**, islands just off the coast where you can enjoy peaceful beaches. Olhão gained great fame when in 1808 some brave local fishermen sailed all the way to Rio de Janeiro in their small boat to tell King Dom João VI the joyful news that Napoleon's troops had been defeated and forced out of Portugal.

PORTIMÃO

Portimão, one of the largest towns along the Algarve, is a bustling, commercial fishing port situated at the mouth of the River Arade. As you approach the town, it seems to hold little promise, but ignore the hodgepodge of its surroundings and head straight for the heart of the old town. Here you will find some charm still remains that hints of the town's 18th-century grandeur. One of the highlights is the delightful Nossa Senhora da Conceição church, which, although rebuilt after the earthquake of 1755, actually dates back to the 14th century. Peek inside to see its lovely azulejos.

Nossa Senhora da Conceição, Portimão

Although Portimão is worth a brief stop, its nearby beaches make this destination truly special. The most celebrated of these, made famous by a group of English writers in the early 1900s, is **Praia da Rocha**, one of the coast's original beach resorts, as evidenced by the old mansions and villas along the shore. It has an exceptionally high number of sunny days and is pleasant even in winter. The vast Praia da Rocha is one of the most dramatic beaches we have ever visited. Buff-colored soft sand, towering ochre and red cliffs, and rock formations in the beach and offshore make Praia da Rocha truly unforgettable. A small fort overlooks the bay and right across the street from it, we recommend a delightful, fresh, and pretty small hotel, the **Albergaria Vila Lido**. On the western part of the beach there is a tunnel through the red cliffs to an eastern section with a few hotels and restaurants. The eastern part of the beach has an abundance of beautiful shells, particularly scallops, replenished with each tide. Be sure to stroll along the beach at dusk—the sunsets are unforgettable. As the sun slips toward the horizon, the sand and the rock formations turn stunning shades of mellow gold and red. When the tide is low, you can walk for a great distance, ducking through natural tunnels and exploring whimsical caves.

Praia da Rocha blends into an equally gorgeous beach, **Praia do Vau** where the **Casa Três Palmeiras** (see listing) is perched on the cliffs with a view that is unsurpassed anywhere on the Algarve—even at the most deluxe hotels.

QUERENÇA

If you want to explore off the beaten path, you will enjoy **Querença**, a pretty village snuggled in the hills about 10 kilometers north of Loulé.

SAGRES

Sagres has the distinction of sitting on the most southwesterly point in Europe and is one of the most historically important places in Portugal. Located on this windswept, barren tip of the continent was an incredibly advanced school of seafaring—the scene of exciting advances in navigation that changed the world forever. The Sagres **School of Navigation** was founded by **Prince Henry the Navigator**, a man of incredible genius and foresight who surrounded himself with the most gifted men of the times — astronomers, geographers, cartographers, ship designers, and seamen. The advances in technology made here during the 15th century made possible the great voyages of discovery to the Cape of Good Hope by Bartolomeo Dias in 1488 and, ultimately, to India by Vasco da Gama in 1498. The Portuguese thus accomplished what Columbus failed to do and opened a sea route from Europe to the spice-rich Orient. It was also here that the caravel (a fast, wide-hulled boat with a large number of masts) was designed and built in secret. With its increased speed, stability, and ability to carry a large crew, the caravel set the style for ships for the next century.

Unfortunately, the famous English pirate, Sir Francis Drake, destroyed most of the school's original buildings in 1597. Close to where the school once stood, there is an excellent hotel, the **Pousada de Sagres–Infante**, which is set on a headland above the sea. On a promontory to the west of the pousada is the fort where Prince Henry's school is said to have been located. On the ground in the courtyard is an immense stone *rosa dos ventos*, or compass rose, supposedly used for instruction during Prince Henry's time.

Along with fishing and diving, a popular pastime in this area is renting bicycles to tour the area out to the cape. The secluded beaches in this area, punctuated with the craggy rock outcroppings so strongly associated with the Algarve, make attractive destinations, especially at sunset. The beaches here are far less congested than farther east.

A few kilometers west of Sagres is the little 17th-century fort of **Beliche**, which has been converted into a delightful tearoom and restaurant with four bedrooms operated by the pousada chain. It is called the **Casa de Chá da Fortaleza do Beliche**.

Just beyond Sagres is **Cape Saint Vincent**. This rocky promontory has been the scene of numerous sea battles throughout the history of Portugal, guarding as it does the entrance to the narrow channel into the Mediterranean. Giant fingers of rock jut out into the ocean where they are battered by crashing waves. The view is breathtaking and, considering the

Cape Saint Vincent

wild setting, it's easy to see how earlier Europeans might have equated this desolate spot with the end of the earth. You can climb the lighthouse installed in an old convent for an even more panoramic view of the Atlantic. The cape's name stems from the legend that the remains of Saint Vincent, Portugal's patron saint, washed ashore here before later reappearing in Lisbon.

SILVES

Silves—dramatically positioned high over the river with brooding, 12th-century battlements—was once the capital of the Moorish Al-Gharb, rivaling Granada in splendor and culture. Now it's a small town with some handsome burghers' houses in the shadow of its **castle**. This red sandstone castle was built during the Moorish occupation, but after they were ousted, it was used as a Christian fortress.

TAVIRA

Tavira is one of the most appealing towns in the Algarve. In its heyday Tavira was an important tuna center. Fishing is still important, but now the town is no longer directly on the sea since the earthquake of 1755 silted up the estuary. The town hugs the banks of the Sequa and Gilão rivers, which merge in Tavira and form an estuary that spreads out to the sea. Quaint houses line the river, which also has a picturesque Roman bridge spanning it. Although there are some sleazy-looking housing developments on the outskirts, the historic center of town still exudes an appealing charm. There are 21 old churches, colorful houses, narrow winding streets, and remains of the old town walls. Just a short walk from the center of town we highly recommend a simple, exceedingly charming, intimate bed and breakfast, the **Quinta do Caracol**.

VILAMOURA

If you are addicted to golf, the place to be is **Vilamoura**, which is surrounded by golf courses. The whole area has boomed, with new high-rise hotels springing up in every available niche of space. In this modern development are nightclubs, elegant shops, restaurants, and even a casino. Vilamoura is about 6 kilometers inland from the sea—the closest beach is at **Quarteira**, a once-quaint town that is now a jungle of high-rises. However, it still has a marvelous long stretch of sandy beach sheltered by red cliffs. Just to the east of Quarteira is **Val do Lobo**, another commercial coastal development that exudes more quality and refinement, with many deluxe, whitewashed, low-rise hotels and condominium complexes—usually with a Moorish flavor.

Exploring the Alentejo

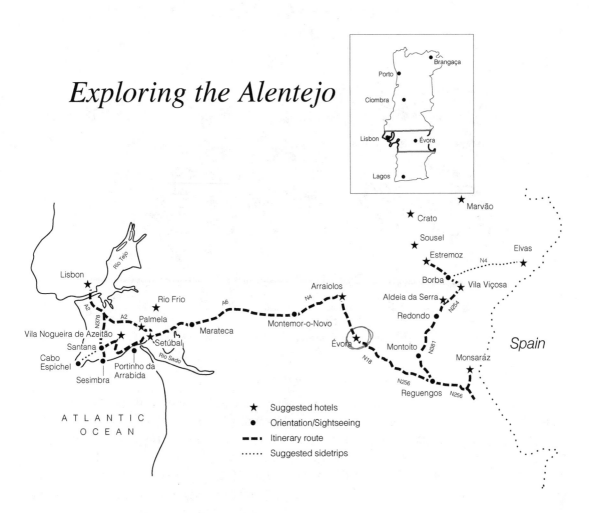

Exploring the Alentejo

Convent of Arrabida

After a drive along the Costa de Lisboa and some spectacular views of the Atlantic, this itinerary takes you into the heart of the Alentejo, with its fortified towns and romantic, walled medieval villages clinging to the top of strategic hilltops. Because this itinerary follows in reverse the natural route that the Spaniards would have chosen in their days of conquest, you'll be seeing some of the most heavily fortified villages and castles in the country. Throughout much of the Portugal's early history, Spain was a constant threat, making defense spending a high priority for many early monarchs.

Recommended Pacing: We love the Alentejo with its landscape of endless cultivated fields dotted with isolated whitewashed farmhouses. Centuries-old olive trees accent gently rolling hills and shepherds sit in pastures guarding large flocks of sheep—never lonely because their faithful dogs are always close at hand. Along the route you visit some of Portugal's most fascinating fortified towns, and while there, stay in outstanding hotels and pousadas housed in marvelous historic buildings—sightseeing attractions in their own right. You can drive to Évora in a day but if you have the luxury of time, spend a night in the countryside at Setúbal or Palmela before spending a night in Évora. Finish the itinerary with a night in Estremoz. If you want to make a loop back to Lisbon, this itinerary ties in perfectly with following one, *Medieval Monuments*. Just follow its routing in reverse.

Leave **Lisbon** following the A2 (blue toll road) south toward Setúbal, crossing the impressive **25 de Abril suspension bridge** soaring 60 meters above the River Tagus and reminiscent of San Francisco's Golden Gate bridge. The views from the bridge looking back toward Lisbon are fabulous, but since there is no place to stop, the driver won't have much chance to see them. However, an equally impressive view is yours for the picture-taking from the statue of **Cristo-Rei** in **Almada** (watch for the exit just after leaving the bridge). The bishops of Portugal built the statue in 1959 in thanks for Portugal's non-involvement in World War II. The statue itself is not particularly interesting, but the city vista is unforgettable.

After crossing the bridge, take the second exit in the direction of Sesimbra. Follow N378 to the little town of Santana in the Arrabida Nature Park, then bear right on N379, through green fields dotted with white houses and windmills, to **Cabo Espichel**. Here you find the pilgrimage church, **Nossa Senhora do Cabo**, dedicated to Our Lady of the Cape. The chapel is bound by two long, low arcaded wings that stretch out on either side. In the 16th and 17th centuries, these extensions provided a hospice for the pilgrims who came here to worship. Today, the structures have fallen prey to neglect; yet they stand hauntingly wistful, stretching out on the windswept promontory. Walk to the bluff's edge where you have magnificent views of the clear, deep-blue ocean and the rugged, craggy coast.

Head back toward Santana and take a right before town to drive by the well-restored **Castle of Sesimbra**. Occupying a defensive position held by numerous masters, it is a massive square structure with turrets and towers recalling earlier battles. There are expansive views from its ramparts of town, the sea, and the surrounding countryside. There is also a restored 18th-century church within the castle.

Continue on to **Sesimbra**. This colorful little fishing village with its pretty harbor nestled beneath rugged cliffs makes an appealing spot for a little wandering.

Return to Santana and turn right on N379, then right again after 10 kilometers on N379-1, passing through the lovely pine forests of the **Serra da Arrabida**. As you approach the coast, you have a choice of roads—take the one on the right that traces the coast. You will pass a sign indicating a road leading to the dramatic 16th-century **Convent of Arrabida**, a walled group of buildings, like a tiny ghost town, cupped in the hillside overlooking the sea. Continue toward the coast. If it's time for lunch, watch for the sign to the quaint fishing-village-cum-resort of **Portinho da Arrabida**—the one-way road that dips steeply down to the harbor is a bit scary, but the village is a fun place to stop and stretch your legs.

The road continues on to **Setúbal,** a bustling city, and the third largest seaport after Lisbon and Porto. Setúbal is the gateway to the cork-producing region (cork is one of Portugal's biggest exports). The only part of Setúbal that offers a bit of charm is the old town around **Bocage Square**. (Bocage, one of Portugal's most famous poets, was born in Setúbal in the 18th century.) Stroll along the picturesque winding streets and alleyways, some of which have been converted to pedestrian-only use. A couple of blocks northeast of the square is the **Municipal Museum**, housed in a 17th-century convent. The 15th-century **Igreja de Jesus** adjoining it is thought to be the earliest example of that highly Portuguese-style, late-Gothic architecture called Manueline, named for King Manuel I.

Exploring the Alentejo

Across the estuary from Setúbal is the burgeoning resort area of **Troia**, which can be reached by ferry, with or without your car (though there is little reason to take a car). Check with the tourist office on Bocage Square for current schedules and departure points. The peninsula boasts what is reputedly the longest fine, white-sand beach in the country—nearly 32 kilometers long. If you take the trip, visit the ruins of **Cetobriga**, a Roman city that was destroyed by an earthquake at the beginning of the 5th century.

In the Palmela-Setúbal area we recommend three places to stay, each delightful in its own way. The first choice for a place to stay is right in Setúbal. Look up from the Bocage Square and you will see on the hill watching over the city, the 16th-century **Pousada de Setúbal–São Filipe**. The castle was commissioned by Philip II of Spain (later Philip of Portugal) who employed the Italian military architect Filipo Terzi to design a castle impregnable against attack by the British. (King Philip II was a bit sensitive about the English navy who had defeated his Spanish Armada.) Even if you do not spend the night, climb the stairs inside the castle walls to the pousada and enjoy refreshments on the magnificent outdoor terrace with its stunning views of the sea, the port, and the countryside of the **Serra da Cerrábida**, a mountain range protecting the mouth of the River Sado. If you spend the night, ask if you can see the underground maze of tunnels. One of these passageways cuts through the hill all the way down to the harbor where escape boats were secreted. This was an emergency escape route in case the castle was invaded.

Another choice for accommodation is nearby in Palmela. This is also a pousada tucked into an ancient fortress, perched 250 meters above the town. The **Pousada de Palmela– Castelo de Palmela**—one of Portugal's finest—occupies a 15th-century convent constructed within the confines of the castle. The stronghold was used by the Romans and the Moors and was destroyed and rebuilt numerous times throughout its history. The fortress was taken from the Moors in the 12th century and was the headquarters of the Portuguese Knights of Saint James in the 13th century. It was abandoned after the earthquake of 1755 and restored in 1979 with the opening of the pousada. Don't miss the views from the ramparts, especially from the 14th-century keep (next to the ruins of the

Palmela Castle

Church of Santa Maria, victim of the 1755 quake). Walking the castle grounds is like a return to the legendary time of chivalry. Just below the castle is **Palmela**, a picturesque white town crossed by narrow streets winding to quaint little squares. Both the **Church of São Pedro** and the **Church of the Misericordia** are worth a visit for their azulejo interior decoration. The 15th-century **Church of Santiago**, next to the pousada, is another fine example of azulejo adornment, and its upper choir is thought to be the first in Portugal.

Our third suggestion for a hotel in this area is the **Quinta das Torres**, a farm estate in the rich wine-growing area of **Vila Nogueira de Azeitão**. This is the home of Portugal's internationally famous Lancers wine, produced under the Jose Maria da Fonseca label. The winery also produces an excellent dry white (Branco Seco B.S.E.) and a fine, full red (Dao Terras Altas). On weekdays from 9 am to 11:30 am and 2 pm to 5 pm, the winery welcomes visitors for tours and wine tasting—an experience that shouldn't be missed. The visit includes a small museum housing an interesting collection of wineglasses and 17th- and 18th-century azulejos. If you happen to be in town on the first Sunday of the month, be sure to seek out the colorful local market in Azeitão.

Leaving the Palmela-Setúbal area, get on the A6 and head east. After about 17 kilometers, the A6 ends and you continue on toward to the Moorish-appearing white town of **Montemor-o-Novo**, birthplace of São João de Deus, founder of the Brothers Hospitallers, whose statue is in the church square. The medieval fortified castle above town, occupying the former site of a Roman fortress, provides good views of the olive-tree-dotted countryside.

Continue along the N4 to **Arraiolos**, a picturesque town climbing to a 14th-century castle overlooking the Alentejo Plain. A beautiful blue and white church shares the hilltop. Not for the last time, you'll notice that the otherwise whitewashed houses are colorfully painted halfway up. The town is noted for its woven woolen carpets (*tapetes*), continuing a craft practiced here since the 16th century. The designs have an almost Oriental quality and are done in a variety of vivid colors. Another famous local product is sausage. Nestled in a pocket of the valley just outside Arraiolos (on the road to Pavia) is an exquisite, 16th-century convent, which has been converted into the charming **Pousada de Arraiolos–Nossa Senhora da Assunção**. If you want to stay overnight and take your time picking out a perfect carpet in Arraiolos, this pousada is an excellent choice.

From Arraiolos take the N370 south to the walled city of Évora—Portugal's pride. We recommend two places to stay here. One is the **Pousada de Évora–Lóios,** located in a former monastery, elegantly restored to retain the serenity required by its previous occupants. The pousada is easy to find as it is just across from the columns of the Roman Temple of Diana. The other choice is the **Solar Monfalim**, a small, family-run hotel, also in the center of town.

Whitewashed, stone-framed **Évora** is called the "Museum City" due to its quantity of historically interesting architecture. It is thought that the Romans had a settlement here in the 1st century AD that was greatly expanded by the Moors from the 8th to the 12th centuries, when Gerald the Fearless captured it for the Christians. During the next three centuries Évora was the preferred residence of the monarchs of Portugal. A Jesuit university was founded here in the mid-16th century, at the height of Évora's glory as the intellectual center of the country. When Phillip II succeeded to the Portuguese throne in 1580, he quickly annexed Évora to Spain and a long period of decline followed, although the first episode in the war of liberation against Spain occurred here in the 1630s. Today

Roman Temple, Évora

the town is a lively market center for the produce from the surrounding Alentejo Plains and a justifiably famous tourist attraction. Many of the major sights are around the pousada and Portugal's best-preserved Roman structure, **Templo Romano**, is found right outside its door. Across the square is the **Art Museum** with one of the country's top collections, and the impressive 13th-century **Évora Cathedral** (called *Se* in Portuguese), one of whose 16th-century towers has an intriguing tiled spire. Both merit a visit. Next to the pousada's entrance is the **Church of Saint John the Evangelist**, privately owned by the Cadaval family, but sometimes open to the public (ask at the pousada desk). This has some pretty azulejos. Past the church is the **Palace of the Dukes of Cadaval**, whose north tower formed a section of the old Roman wall.

Above all, take time to stroll around the ancient streets and see the marvelous medieval and Renaissance buildings. At various points you can also get views of the city walls, which are of Roman, Visigothic, and medieval origin.

Another must is a visit to the **Praça do Giraldo**, a bustling square and center of the town's activity, with medieval arches and a marble Renaissance fountain—the last sight seen by the many Inquisition victims who went to the stake here. This is the main shopping district, where you might want to examine the woolen goods for which the area is so well known.

Take N18 southeast from Évora and bear left after 16 kilometers on N256. Another 20 kilometers of fairly flat highway through rich plains studded with white farmhouses and dusty-green olive groves brings you to the little agricultural town of **Reguengos de Monsaraz**. The roadside scenery in this major wool-producing region is pastoral and picturesque. You are likely to see flocks of sheep under the watchful eye of shepherds, traditionally clad in brown sheepskin coats whose long tails ward off damp and cold during the hours spent sitting on the ground.

Beyond Reguengos de Monsaraz, stay on the N256 for another 14 kilometers to a turnoff to the left to Monsaraz. Watch for the vantage point along the way where you can see the hilltop towns of **Mourao** and its sister, **Monsaraz**, to the north. It's obvious that defense against Spanish invasion was uppermost in the mind of King Dom Diniz when he ordered these two fortified towns constructed in the 14th century. Monsaraz is steeped in authentic medieval atmosphere, but so small that it will take you only a little time to explore its tiny streets and admire its simple whitewashed and blue-trimmed houses. We recommend the **Estalagem de Monsaraz** and the **Hotel Rural Horta da Moura** as places to stay here.

Like Évora, Monsaraz was reclaimed from the Moors by **Gerald the Fearless** in the 12th century and formed an important part of the defensive scheme of subsequent Portuguese monarchs. The narrow town streets are made for wandering, and the Rua Direita, lined with ancient white houses sporting coats of arms, will transport you back in time. From the town's 13th-century castle ramparts, it's apparent why this spot was chosen for defense—the spectacular views stretch forever across the Alentejo Plain into Spain.

When you are ready to move on, return to N256 and Reguengos and turn north. From Vila Viçosa take N255 for 6 kilometers to **Borba**, another attractive white village. Both Borba and Vila Viçosa owe their prosperity to the marble of the nearby Montes Claros. Marble quarries and mounds of giant marble boulders flank the road between the two towns. As you enter town, watch for the imposing 18th-century fountain sculpted from the pale-pink, locally manufactured marble.

From Borba turn west on N4 and head directly to Estremoz; however, if you are game for more sightseeing, turn right on N4 to Elvas.

Elvas, only 11 kilometers from the Spanish border, was once the major defensive stronghold in the country. The 16th-century **Amoreira Aqueduct**, built on Roman foundations, is the most dramatic monument in town and, remarkably, is still used to carry water to the city. Equally impressive are the town walls whose elaborate construction, with two walls built in the 13th century and one in the 17th, attest to the continuing importance of the city. Two forts flank the city on the north and the south. The **Forte de Nossa Senhora da Graça** on the north offers splendid views of the countryside and the **Forte de Santa Luzia**, on the same side of the town as the pousada of the same name, is alleged to be the best-preserved 17th-century fort in Portugal.

The walled, medieval old city can be entered through the Porta de Olivença. A street of the same name leads directly to the center of town and the Praça de Republica. Just northeast of here are the **Church of Nossa Senhora da Consolaçao** and the **Church of Nossa Senhora da Assunçao**, both boasting lovely azulejo interiors.

Elvas is a bigger city and less pure in ambiance than some of the picture-perfect, fortified hilltowns you have been visiting. However, the narrow cobblestoned streets of the old city are lined with enchanting old residences and picturesque cafés and shops (you might want to pick up a box of Elvas's famous plums).

After stopping in Elvas, return to the N4 and head west to **Estremoz**. This fortified hill town is another of Portugal's jewels. The magic begins at the entrance to the walled town where, as in days of yore, you must pass over a moat to enter. The town is a maze of twisting small streets and on one of these, well marked by signs from the entrance, you will find one of our recommended places to stay, the **Pousada de Estremoz–Rainha Santa Isabel**. The simpler, less expensive **Monte dos Pensamentos** is located on the main highway just a short distance outside town.

Pousada de Estremoz–Rainha Santa Isabel, Estremoz

Roman Viaduct, Elvas

Medieval Monuments

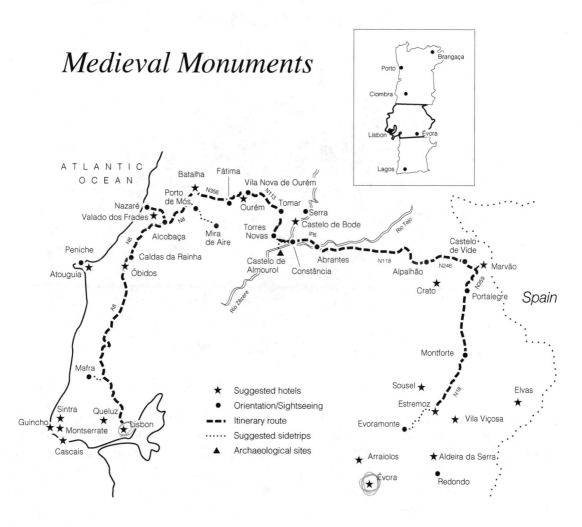

Medieval Monuments

Monastery of Santa Maria da Victoria, Batalha

This itinerary routes you to a number of the most notable medieval monuments in Portugal. It begins with a tour of the ancient region known as Estremadura, which comes from the Latin for "beyond the River Douro," now encompassing only the strip between the Tagus and the sea north of Lisbon. This was one of the earliest areas wrested from the Moors in the 12th century and boasts some of the best-preserved historic sights in Portugal.

Next the itinerary turns inland, crossing the fertile country known as Ribatejo, meaning "the banks of the River Tagus," where farming and cattle raising are the primary industries, and ends in the Upper Alentejo. Alentejo means "beyond the Tagus," which makes sense when you realize these regions were named by the Christians as they made their way down from the north. This area was of particular importance in the 13th and 14th centuries because, once recaptured, it formed the border between the Portuguese kingdom and the Moors to the south and between Portugal and the most accessible route from Spain to the east.

Recommended Pacing: If you are not a leisurely sightseer and leave Lisbon early, you can follow this itinerary and be in Batalha with its magnificent monastery by nightfall. A one-night stay should give you all the time you need unless you decide to take a sidetrip through Porto de Mós to visit the caves near Mira de Aire. Marvão is such an attractive town that it merits an overnight stay. Finish the itinerary with a night in Estremoz. If you want to make a loop back to Lisbon, this itinerary ties in perfectly with the preceding one, *Exploring the Alentejo*. Just follow its routing in reverse.

Before or after a visit to **Lisbon**, you'll want to make your way into the interior, where the rhythm and structure of everyday life in the mainly agricultural villages will impart a strong sense of how life has always been lived in Portugal's countryside. This itinerary includes some of the highlights of Portugal's historic past.

Leave Lisbon on the A8 (blue toll road) heading northwest. After about 20 kilometers take the turnoff to Malveira. From there, follow signs for another 11 kilometers to **Mafra**, a small village that is home to the **Convento de Mafra**, one of Portugal's most impressive national monuments, a 40,000-square-meter monastery. Built in the 18th century by King João V, it is reminiscent of the 16th-century Escorial in Spain, having been intentionally designed to surpass it in grandeur. It took some 50,000 workers 13 years to complete (1717–1730). The basilica occupies the center of the 240-meter façade and is impressive in its proportions. The vestibule contains a number of huge marble statues of saints. The palace and the monastery can be visited (except Tuesdays) by guided tours, which take you through the 90 rooms and apartments. Especially noteworthy is the baroque library housing 36,000 volumes, as well as religious manuscripts on parchment. Behind the building is the **Tapada Nacional**, a national park encircled by a 19-kilometer-long wall, which was originally the royal hunting grounds.

Church, Óbidos

The entire complex is a monument to the power of the Portuguese throne in its heyday, when Brazilian gold flowed into the national coffers.

After you have toured the palace, return to the A8 and head north to **Óbidos**, one of Portugal's most picturesque white towns, encircled by walls stretching across a grassy-green hillside. King Diniz's queen, known as Santa Isabel, admired the town so much that he gave it to her, and for the next five centuries the town was considered a possession of the ruling queen. Óbidos is a national monument and has been carefully preserved. The town is so small that it takes no time at all to walk from one end to the other, and although it is quite touristy, it is definitely as pretty as a picture and well worth a visit. In Óbidos you can stay either within the walls at the **Pousada de Óbidos–Castelo**; just outside the walls at the delightful **Estalagem do Convento**; or just below the village at a charming inn, the **Casa d'Óbidos**.

Medieval Monuments

Óbidos's most obvious attraction is its **castle** looming above town and the extensive, well-preserved, 12th-century fortifications that surround the old section. The castle was originally built by Dom Diniz in the 13th century, then mostly destroyed by the 1755 earthquake, and later restored. There are superb views of the countryside from the castle ramparts.

The ancient, narrow streets are very beguiling—filled with handicraft shops (lace, leather, baskets, and ceramics)—and the flower-bedecked buildings are charming to see and to explore. The Rua Direita is the main street, which leads from the handsome main gate to the castle, passing the market square and the most interesting church, Saint Mary's. Next door is the **museum**, with a collection of religious art and a room with antique arms and a model of the Lines of Torres Vedras. The town is made for leisurely wandering and taking pictures of enchanting nooks and crannies off cobblestoned streets overshadowed by dazzling-white houses with iron balconies and colorfully painted doors.

Leave Óbidos heading north on N8 to **Caldas da Rainha** (the Spa of the Queen), founded in the 15th century by Queen Leonor, wife of João II. The Dom Carlos I Park is on the right as you enter town. In the middle of the park is the Museu de Jose Malhoa with a collection of modern Portuguese paintings and ceramics. At the north end of the park is a statue of the queen and, if you turn right here, you'll soon come across the Manueline church, Nossa Senhora do Populo, its interior colorfully adorned with azulejos. Next to it is the bathhouse founded by the queen in 1504, which is still in use. If you happen to be here on Monday, it's worth walking north a couple of blocks to see the lively market in the main square.

Continue on N8 to **Alcobaça**, which derives its name from its situation at the confluence of the Alcoa and Baca rivers. It is also the home of the **Real Abadia de Santa Maria de Alcobaça**, one of Portugal's most outstanding monuments, which dominates the center of town. Founded in 1178 by Portugal's first king, Dom Afonso Henriques, the Cistercian monastery is a marvel of medieval architecture. The church is impressive for its extreme length compared to its narrow width. In the transept of the church are the intricately carved limestone tombs of Inês de Castro and King Pedro I, whose tragic love story has set the theme for numerous literary works.

Inês, a lady-in-waiting to Prince Pedro's wife, proved irresistibly attractive to the young prince and when his wife died, he installed Inês as his mistress, since her humble origins precluded marriage to the future king. Although their love was idyllic, many of the nobles feared that the illegitimate offspring of this union would aspire to the throne, so they convinced the king, Afonso IV, to condone her murder. When Afonso died and Pedro became king, he set out to avenge her death by hunting down and punishing the noble murderers one by one. Legend has it (probably fictitiously) that Pedro exhumed the skeleton of his dead paramour, had her crowned queen in regal dress, and forced the nobility to file by and kiss her hand. At any rate, he did spend much time and energy during his short reign (1357–1367) exalting her memory and, as you can see, provided quite handsomely for their eternal resting-places. They are allegedly positioned so that when their souls were resurrected, their first sight would be of each other.

On the opposite side of the pretty cloister from the church are the abbey buildings, including the impressive kitchen through which flows a branch of the River Alcoa, which provided the monks with fish. Next to it is the spacious refectory, sometimes used today as a community theater. Town activity centers around the large main square, its numerous shops proffering a wide variety of the distinctive blue-and-white ceramics typical of the area.

From Alcobaça, take the N8-5 directly west to **Nazaré**. This is the coast's best-known tourist attraction, especially in the summer when native costumes add to the local color. At the extreme north end of the Nazaré beach looms the promontory called **Sitio**. You can ride the funicular up from the lower (Praia) area, or you can take N242 toward Marinha Grande and turn left when you get to the top of the hill. The Sitio is worth a visit if only for the panoramic views from the belvedere. While you're there, stop in to see the colorful azulejos in the church nearby.

The main hub of activity is the Praia area down below. Souvenir and handicraft shops line the north end of the beachfront, which they share with a myriad of small restaurants featuring an endless variety of seafood. Street vendors offering everything from model boats to sardines drying on wire racks complete the picture of a bustling resort town. Away from the beach you'll encounter a labyrinth of narrow winding streets crowded with mostly residential buildings.

At the end of the day you can see the town's age-old livelihood carried out as dark-clad fishermen in long caps haul in their day's catch. Before Nazaré had a real harbor, the fishermen pulled their colorfully painted boats from the water onto the beach (traditionally by oxen, now more often by tractors) for safekeeping overnight. Now the boats dock in the new marina. If you want to spend the night in the area, the friendly **Quinta do Campo** offers accommodations in a farm estate about midway between Nazaré and Alcobaça.

Return to Alcobaça and head north on the N8. If time permits, consider a 5-kilometer detour to the ancient town of **Porto de Mós** (turn right at Cruz da Legua). It has a fabulous small fortified **castle** sitting on an isolated hill overlooking the River Lena, its handsome lines lending it a distinctly French appearance. It was originally built as a fortress in the 9th century, but was remodeled in the 15th for use as a palace. The National Agency for Historical Monuments has recently restored it. Unique green tiles on the towers shimmer in the sun, creating a striking vision.

Return to the N8 and continue on to Batalha. Here you will discover one of Portugal's gems, the stunning **Monastery of Batalha**, a combination of Gothic and Manueline styles. Tall stained-glass windows are the first and only things you notice upon entering until your eyes adjust to the interior dimness. To the immediate right is the stark, white Founder's Chapel sheltering the tomb of João I and his English wife, Philippa of Lancaster. Other notables rest in carved niches around the walls, including João's son, Henry the Navigator, founder of the school of navigation at Sagres that made possible the great voyages of discovery in the 15th and 16th centuries (although Henry himself never went).

On the left, across the nave, is the entrance to the Royal Cloister whose delightful garden patio is overlooked through graceful, carved Gothic arcades—almost no two alike. To the right as you enter is the Chapter House, which contains the Tomb of the Unknown Soldier from World War I, where two modern-day soldiers keep vigil. Actually there are two unknown soldiers, too, one who died in Europe and one who died in Africa, along with an eternal flame fueled by pure Portuguese olive oil. The former refectory on the opposite side of the cloister houses a Museum of the Unknown Soldier featuring the tributes paid by foreign dignitaries upon visiting the tomb.

Beyond, and in sharp contrast to, the Royal Cloister is the plainly severe Cloister of Dom Afonso V, added later. From here you exit and walk to the right around the outside to reach the dramatic unfinished chapels (Capelas Imperfeitas), built in rich Manueline style to be King Duarte's chapel. Both his tomb and his wife's are there, but the massive, ornately carved buttresses climb to the open sky, patiently awaiting the weight of a roof, which was never completed.

As in Alcobaça, shops and cafés are found in the immediate vicinity of the monastery and, beyond that, the town features some pretty 17th- and 18th-century houses and a nice parish church. There is a choice of two places to stay. Ideally situated, the **Pousada da Batalha–Mestre Afonso Domingues** sits in the shadow of the monastery. The inn is named for the principal architect of the Monastery de Maria da Vitoria, dedicated to Our Lady of Victory, and built by João I to commemorate and give thanks for the victory of the Portuguese at Aljubarrota. Just a few minutes' drive from the monastery is lovely bed and breakfast, the **Quinta do Fidalgo**.

An interesting side trip from Batalha is to head south through **Porto de Mós**, with its splendid castle, and then southeast on N243 toward **Mira de Aire**, an important textile area. Here there are four caves you can visit: the **Grutas de Alvados**, with a series of interesting chambers; the nearby **Grutas de Santo Antonio**, some 6,000 square meters in area (both of these are reached before Mira de Aire); the **Grutas Mira de Aire**, supposedly the deepest in Europe; and, north of Mira de Aire near **São Mamede**, the **Grutas de Moeda**, smaller and at a depth of 45 meters. If you are only casually interested in caves, the second and third are the most interesting.

Leave Batalha heading east on N356 toward Fatima. Just beyond **Reguengos do Fetal** are good views back over the ground you just covered, its green hills dotted with windmills. Another 10 kilometers brings you to Cova de Iria and **Fatima** which, like Lourdes in France, is a pilgrimage center of international renown (follow the signs reading "**Santuario**"). Legend has it that the Virgin appeared to three shepherd children—Lucia, Francisco, and Jacinta—on May 13, 1917, and on the 13th of each month thereafter until October, bearing a message of peace. The spot began to draw religious pilgrims almost immediately, although the immense neoclassical basilica, enveloped by a 40-acre park, was not constructed until the 1950s. Popes Paul VI and John Paul II have both visited here. A small chapel marks the spot where the apparition occurred and, at almost any hour, you will witness the faithful on their knees, traversing the broad esplanade which fronts it. On the 13th of each month from May to October, in accordance with the legend, attendance multiplies and includes a torchlight procession at night.

Continue north for 11 kilometers, join the N113, and turn left to the town of **Vila Nova de Ourém**. On the outskirts of town, we recommend a wonderful bed and breakfast, the **Quinta da Alcaidaria–Mór**, where you will be welcomed by the gracious Vasconcelos Alvaiàzere family (see listing under Ourém). From Vila Nova de Ourém, you're bound to notice the picturesque fortified town crowning a hill overlooking town—this is the ancient town of **Ourém**, today virtually abandoned, which is reached up a steep, winding road. The Count of Ourém turned the original castle into a palace in the 15th century and this is now open to the public as a pousada, the **Conde de Ourém**. Leave your car just inside the walled entrance (or drive to the center if you are staying at the pousada) and walk around the charming, lonely village and up to the castle. The visit imparts an almost

Convento de Cristo, Tomar

eerie feel for life in the distant past. The vistas from the belvedere over the green countryside are striking.

Descend to Vila Nova and continue east on N113 another 20 kilometers to **Tomar**, one of the oldest cities in Portugal. The site was originally awarded to the Knights Templar when Afonso Henriques, Portugal's first king, persuaded them to help fight the Moors in the 12th century. When the Pope subsequently disbanded them, King Diniz created the Order of the Knights of Christ to replace them, and the new order appropriated the castle as their headquarters. The wealth of this new order, always close to the royal family, was later to facilitate the great age of discovery. Henry the Navigator was its Grand Master during much of the 15th century, and the order sponsored numerous exploratory voyages along the coast of Africa, its holdings there and in the East Indies making it the richest knightly order in Christendom. Times changed, however, and in the early 16th century the order became monastic.

The old **Templar Castle** walls surround the **Convento de Cristo** convent inside. Be sure to allow enough time to investigate fully the elaborate complex and its multiple cloisters. The Templar church, called the rotunda, has 16 sides, in imitation of the Church of the Holy Sepulchre in Jerusalem. Two stellar examples of Manueline-style architecture are found here in the entrance and window of the church, both painstakingly and ornately carved. Manueline decorative motifs, as you'll note here, emphasized marine elements such as masts, ropes, and anchor chains, as well as natural ones such as trees.

The town of Tomar occupies an appealing spot on the bank of the River Nabao. There is an unusually pretty riverside park with a lovely waterfall along the edge of the placid river as it flows through the center of town. Besides its enchanting setting, as you might suspect, other notable sights in town consist mainly of churches and chapels.

From Tomar head south on N110 to Castelo de Almourol and then go east on the IP6 to **Abrantes**, an old-world town dominated by castle ruins. At Abrantes, cross the Rio Tejo and follow N118 east to Alpalhão, where you commence the climb toward Castelo de Vide on N246.

Castelo de Vide offers a charming reminder of the distant past. Tiny cobblestoned lanes, often stepped, run between barely separated buildings constructed in a time when nothing larger than a horse had to pass between them. At the foot of the castle is the *Judaria*, or Jewish Quarter, which will reward a short stroll with glimpses of the past through the doors and windows. Walk up to the São Roque Fort for some excellent views of the town and surrounding countryside.

Leave town on N246-1 in the direction of Marvão. You traverse a tree-lined country road flanked by pasture land and olive groves as you ascend the Serra. Watch for signs to the unpretentious but welcoming **Pousada do Marvão–Santa Maria**, which you reach along a winding road with extensive panoramas. The hilltop town of **Marvão** rises more than 760 meters above sea level and is visible up to the right upon your approach. As romantic as its setting appears today, from its massive and apparently impregnable fortifications it's plain to see why, historically, unwelcome aggressors would consider this strategic position next to impossible to overcome.

This picturesque little mountain town is completely ringed by the imposing ramparts of its 13th-century **castle**, another of King Diniz's defensive installations against the ever suspect Spaniards (it was previously also a Roman stronghold called Herminio Minor). The narrow streets betray the town's age and, along with a profusion of wrought-iron windows and flowery balconies on whitewashed houses, paint an authentic and charming picture of life here as it has been for centuries. Meander through the quaint village up to the castle ramparts, which you can stroll around for glorious views over red rooftops to the Serra stretching for many kilometers beyond. Another worthwhile visit is to the pretty little church of **Nossa Senhora da Estrâla**.

Leaving Marvão, descend the hill to the main road and continue straight ahead on N359 through rocky terrain only occasionally interrupted by signs of habitation to **Portalegre**, a commercial city dominated by its cathedral. For a dramatic and elevated view of the town as well as the surrounding mountain scenery, take N246-2 to the left on the southern edge of town and, after about 8 kilometers, take a small road to the right. After a couple of kilometers bear left to the highest peak in the area, São Mamede (1,066 meters). You'll get captivating glimpses of Portalegre, with its cathedral spires jutting against the sky, as you make your way down.

From Portalegre head south on N18 through cultivated green countryside sprinkled with cattle, olive trees, and cork oaks to **Estremoz**. The major attractions of Estremoz are its picturesque setting and Moorish character. The medieval atmosphere has been largely retained in the narrow lanes and historic buildings, both employing the local white marble in their construction. This is most apparent in the area in the upper town. You will especially want to explore the neighborhood around the Largo do Castelo Square and see the **Chapel of the Saint Queen** with its lovely azulejo interior. Queen Isabel, wife of Dom Diniz, died here in 1336 after an arduous journey, and the painted tiles depict the various miracles attributed to her life's work spent in the service of the poor. She was beloved of the Portuguese people and was canonized in the 16th century.

Estremoz is host to the **Pousada de Estremoz–Rainha Santa Isabel**, beautifully located in the center of town. The 13th-century, 30-meter keep that flanks the pousada is called the "Tower of Three Crowns" because its construction spanned the reigns of three monarchs. There are fabulous views from its battlements. Nearby is the **Church of Saint Mary**, which dates from the 16th century.

Besides the Pousada de Estremoz–Rainha Santa Isabel, there is another choice for accommodation in Estremoz. If you are looking for a less expensive place to spend the night, consider the **Monte dos Pensamentos**. This simple, Moorish-style, whitewashed quinta, which is more like a bed and breakfast than a hotel, is located on the main road, just on the outskirts of town.

Estremoz has always been famous for its ceramics, which are both functional and decorative. If you walk from the pousada down to the lower town (centered around the main Praça do Marques de Pombal), you will encounter numerous ceramic boutiques. On the way you will pass the **Luis de Camoes Square**, its marble pillory silent testimony to the trials of the Inquisition. On the south side of the main square is the 17th-century town hall, now housing the **Municipal Museum**, which has a good collection of popular art, as well as ethnographic and archaeological exhibits.

If you are fortunate or foresighted enough to be here on a Saturday, you can enjoy a lively market in and around the main square displaying everything from handicrafts, ceramics, and marble, to livestock, clothing, and old furniture.

Marvão

Port to Port

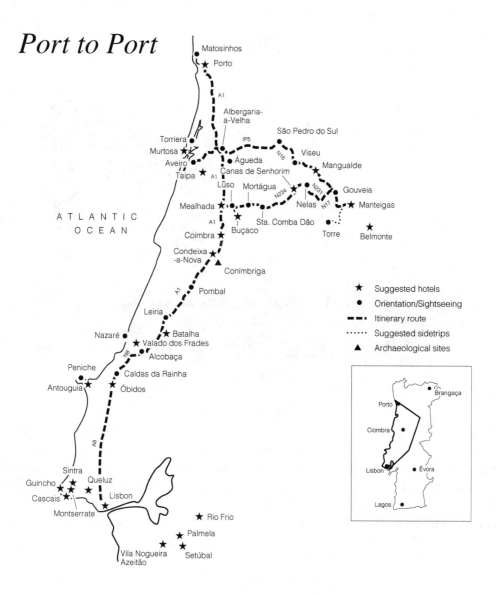

Matosinhos
★ Porto

A1

Albergaria-
a-Velha

São Pedro do Sul

IP5

Torriera
Murtosa ★
Aveiro
Taipa ★

Águeda
Canas de Senhorim
Lúso
Mealhada

N16

Viseu
Mangualde

Mortágua
Sta. Comba Dão

N234

Gouveia
Nelas
N231
Manteigas
N17

Buçaco
Coimbra ★

A1

Torre
★ Belmonte

ATLANTIC
OCEAN

Condeixa
-a-Nova

▲ Conímbriga

A1

Pombal

Leiria

Nazaré
★ Batalha
★ Valado dos Frades
Alcobaça
Peniche
★ Caldas da Rainha
Antouguia ★
Óbidos

N8

A8

Sintra
Guincho
Queluz
Cascais ★
Lisbon
Montserrate

★ Rio Frio

★ Palmela
★
Vila Nogueira   Setúbal
Azeitão

★ Suggested hotels
● Orientation/Sightseeing
▬ ▬ ▬ Itinerary route
· · · · · Suggested sidetrips
▲ Archaeological sites

Porto
Brangaça
Ciombra
Lisbon
Évora
Lagos

99

Port to Port

Canal at Aveiro

This itinerary takes you along the Atlantic shore of Portugal from Lisbon, the country's most important port, to Porto, the second in importance. You will often see Porto spelled Oporto, especially in the United Kingdom. That is simply a variant retaining the article "o" which means "the." Oporto simply means "the port." Porto is the Portuguese form, though, so we'll be using that. Porto is also the source of the word Portuguese, as it was the Porto dialect that King Diniz proclaimed to be the national language in the 13th century.

Recommended Pacing: If you do not want to rush, spend a night in Óbidos before continuing to Buçaco or Coimbra for a night. From there either go straight up the coast to Porto or follow our itinerary to spend the night in Manteigas before concluding the itinerary in Porto.

This itinerary follows the coastline known as the Costa da Prata (the silver coast). This is one of the less-developed coasts and rather less spoiled by modern high-rises. Quaint fishing villages with pretty beaches are more the rule than the exception.

The trip is not all sea coast, however, since we detour inland to visit three of the country's most compelling sights: the romantic forest of Buçaco, the old university city of Coimbra, and the spectacular mountain scenery of the Serra da Estrâla—Portugal's highest range.

We wind up in Portugal's second city, Porto, situated at the mouth of the River Douro, second in size only to the River Tagus. Although considerably smaller than Lisbon, Porto is a very cosmopolitan city with strong historical and commercial bonds with Britain. Here the British discovered, and acquired a taste for, the local wine known as port, and port has been a booming business ever since.

Leave Lisbon on the A8 (blue toll road) to **Óbidos**. We recommend three hotels here—the **Pousada de Óbidos–Castelo**, located within the town walls; the **Estalagem do Convento**, situated just outside the gates; and the charming **Casa d'Óbidos**, which is located just below the walled town. See the itinerary *Medieval Monuments* for suggestions on what to see and do in Óbidos.

Leaving Óbidos, head north on IC1, which bypasses **Caldas da Rainha** (formerly the mineral baths of Queen Leonor, wife of João II) and continue on to **Alcobaça**. See the itinerary *Medieval Monuments* for sightseeing suggestions. There is such a rich history in Alcobaça that you must not miss it.

From Alcobaça, continue north on N8 to Batalha, where you need to stop to see another of Portugal's jewels, the **Monastery of Batalha**. See the itinerary *Medieval Monuments* for sightseeing suggestions.

From Batalha follow the N1 to Leiria and then take the connecting road to the A1. Continue north on the A1 and turn off to Condeixa. Just beyond Condeixa is **Conimbriga**, one of the most impressive Roman ruins on the Peninsula, dating from the 1st to the 3rd centuries AD. On the right after you enter are some beautifully preserved mosaic floors edged by gardens. There is also a very nice, small museum at the site containing the artifacts (jewelry, glass, bronze, ceramics, sculpture, etc.) discovered in the excavation. There's a small shop where some rather good replicas are sold.

Return to the A1 and head north. Take the first exit beyond Coimbra marked to Mealhada. Follow signs to Mealhada and then continue east on N234 to Luso where you see on your left a sign to one of our places to stay, a lovely private mansion, the **Vila Duparchy**. If you want to live like royalty, continue on for a short distance and watch on your right for **Buçaco**, and the magnificent **Bussaco Palace**. This elaborate hotel is reminiscent of a grand English country estate, situated in the awesome Buçaco Forest at an altitude of about 365 meters above sea level. In the late 19th century a summer palace was built for the royal family. When the Republic was proclaimed in 1910, the royal family quietly left the country and the palace was converted into a private hotel (though the government owns the building). This is one of Portugal's most magnificent hotels, and a remarkable place to stay while you explore the site's natural beauty. Long a protected area, the Buçaco Forest was taken over by the Discalced Carmelites in the 17th century. The meditative order added to the number of distinct species of flora during their residence and constructed a continuous wall around the area. A papal bull in 1643 forbade the cutting of the trees and threatened excommunication for those who did. In 1834 all church property was secularized and the forest passed to the state, when even more species of trees were planted until today the total exceeds 600 specimens from around the world.

Bussaco Palace

Numerous marked trails leave the hotel in all directions, taking you through the dense forest to the viewpoints, tiny hermitages, springs, and pools that dot the area. The Via Sacra, or Way of the Cross path, twists up to the highest peak, the Cruz Alta, which has spellbinding views of the surrounding area and of several other mountain ranges. This peak may also be reached by road if you aren't up for a three-hour hike, and there are other appealing points that require less effort.

Buçaco was the scene of an important battle between General Wellington and the Napoleonic invaders in 1810. Wellington and a combined British and Portuguese contingent occupied the high ground and won the encounter. The French were forced to retreat and had to console themselves with the sacking of Coimbra. Wellington and his troops retired to the area defended by the lines of Torres Vedras.

The very lively old university city of **Coimbra** deserves an all-day visit. You can either use the Bussaco Palace hotel or the Vila Duparchy as a base and visit Coimbra from there or, if you want to really immerse yourself in sightseeing, there is an excellent place to stay in Coimbra, the romantic, historically fascinating **Quinta das Lágrimas**.

Coimbra was the capital of Portugal from the 12th to the 13th centuries. The first Portuguese university was established here in the 14th century, but was moved to Lisbon for a time. It was permanently returned to this city in 1537, and Coimbra has been the intellectual center of the country—indeed, of the whole Portuguese empire—ever since.

The older town on the hill is the location of the majority of the sights. The original **university** buildings are here, alongside some rather prosaic newer structures. Retaining the old ways, some students can still be seen in traditional black capes bearing colorful ribbons corresponding to their faculty (medicine, law, etc.). The main university building has a large central patio, and the impressive library building is just outside.

Just down the hill to the north you will find the **Machado de Castro Museum** with admirable collections of painting, sculpture, ceramics, and furniture, as well as a display of Roman antiquities. Slightly behind the museum is the old **Cathedral** (*Se Velha*), a good example of the Romanesque style from the 12th century and containing a fine Gothic retable in the soaring interior.

A long walk down the hill past the old cathedral passes through the old part of the city, then the notable **Almedina Gate** and, beyond that, the lower town (the more modern part) along the Rua Ferreira Borges (on the north it becomes Visconde) where the main shopping area is situated. At the north end of the street is the **Monastery of Santa Cruz** (on the 8th of May Square), in whose church is the impressive tomb, among others, of Afonso Henriques, the first King of Portugal. A bit to the east of the monastery is the large, colorful central market, worth a short visit.

If you are traveling with children, you might enjoy a visit to the children's park called **Portugal dos Pequeninos** (Children's Portugal), a complex of miniature buildings representing the geographical styles of the whole country and of the former overseas empire. It is located across the Santa Clara Bridge over the River Mondego. In this same area is the Santa Clara-a-Nova Convent where the remains of Saint Queen Isabel (wife of King Diniz) lie in a silver tomb.

Leave Buçaco heading east on N234, bypassing Mortágua after 13 kilometers. Another few kilometers bring you to Santa Comba Dão. Continue on the N234, where you'll be greeted by a succession of tidy towns surrounded by olive groves and the vineyards that produce Dão wine. *Note*: There was a flurry of highway work in progress when we were last there so the roads might have changed a bit by the time you arrive.

Staying on the N234, you come to the quaint old town of **Canas de Senhorim**, crowded with stone-block houses with wooden or stone balconies. Soon thereafter is the little town of Nelas, where you turn right on N231. The snow-capped peaks of the Serra da Estrâla now lie on the horizon and, after 21 kilometers and a crossing of the River Mondego, you will reach **Seia**, a charmingly situated market town at the foot of the mountains. Bear left toward Gouveia through a number of picturesque hamlets and some extraordinary scenery. Also along this road are a number of *artesanato* (handicraft stores) specializing in leather goods (vests, jackets, fur-lined slippers, purses, etc.).

If time permits, the 70-kilometer round-trip excursion to the top of Torre Peak beyond Manteigas will guarantee unparalleled panoramas. (In winter the road is often closed by snow—enquire before you set out.) Along the way you pass through the unusual-looking, boulder-strewn glacial valley where the River Zezere is born.

From Gouveia take N232 toward Manteigas. This is a tortuously winding mountain road and requires a careful approach, but it also has some remarkable views of the Serra. Partway up is a sign saying "**Cabeca do Velho**" (Old Man's Head), and if you look to your right, following the arrow, you'll notice a rock outcropping resembling the title given it. Watch also for a sign indicating the Nascente do Mondego, or the origin of the

River Mondego, which flows east from here, then curls back west in a much larger form. Another 20 kilometers along this dramatic road brings you to **Pousada de Manteigas– São Lourenço**, perched high above the River Zezere with truly impressive views of Manteigas in the valley below and of **Torre**, Portugal's highest peak at 1,980 meters.

While in this scenic area don't fail to descend the switchback mountain road to the colorful town of **Manteigas**, set like a jewel amid one of the most striking settings imaginable. It's situated at the head of a narrow valley surrounded on all sides by terraced farms stepping their way up the steep hillsides. Just west of town, as you enter the valley, a 6-kilometer detour to the left leads to the **Poco do Inferno** (the Well of Hell) where a waterfall flows wildly into a deep cave.

Leaving Manteigas, wind your way back down to Gouveia toward Mangualde on N232. Notice the broadened Mondego as you cross. Join the N16 leaving town to the north, and another 15 kilometers brings you to the beautiful old red-roofed town of Viseu clustered around its cathedral on the banks of the River Pavia. You get a splendid view as you approach.

Center of a 16th-century school of painting, **Viseu** boasts a good art museum: the **Museu Grao Vasco**. O Grao Vasco, the Great Basque (Fernandes), was one of the founders of the school. The museum is housed in a 16th-century mansion and located on the large cathedral square in the center of the old town. The 13th-century (subsequently remodeled) cathedral with its Manueline vault is worth a visit, too. Stroll around the enchanting old town to see the impressive mansions dating from the 16th, 17th, and 18th centuries.

Continue on N16 through pretty countryside to **São Pedro do Sul**, near a mineral spa whose waters will cure, they say, almost anything that ails you. This is one of the most picturesque villages in the region, situated at the confluence of the Sul and Vouga rivers and surrounded by deep-green terraced hillsides.

Bear left, remaining on N16, to **Vouzela**. As you enter, note on your right the enchanting little church, its façade totally covered with blue-and-white tiles. In this area you begin to encounter *espigueiros*, the characteristic storage and smoking sheds set on stilts next to the stone houses or in the fields. They are typical of northern Portugal and Galicia in Spain (where they are called *horreos*).

From Vouzela go south for 8 kilometers to join the IP5, which you stay on all the way to **Aveiro**. The most notable feature of Aveiro is its large lagoon, formed by a long, thin sandbar, some 49 kilometers long and 2½ kilometers across at its widest. The average depth, outside the canals the ships use, is only a bit over 2 meters. The numerous canals crisscrossing the town itself add to its considerable charm.

Naturally enough, most activity in Aveiro centers around the water. The major products are salt from the surrounding salt pans, seaweed (used for fertilizer), and fish taken from the lagoon. Boat trips around the lagoon are sometimes available, depending on the time of year. They take you near the seashore lined with lovely houses and, although it's a fading practice, with a little luck you'll see the colorful, flat-bottomed boats called *moliceiros* collecting seaweed. Check with the tourist office on the Praça da Republica for current schedules and prices. One tour includes lunch at the **Pousada do Murtosa/Torreira–Ria** in Torreira on the other side of the lagoon (see hotel listings). If you prefer, you could visit the area by driving north on N109 to Estarreja then turning left on N109-5. Here you cross the bridge over the lagoon and join up with the N327, where you again turn left for the 20-kilometer trip along the water to **São Jacinto** beach at the tip of the bar. The whole trip will take about an hour each way, not counting stops.

In Aveiro there are worthwhile sights, mostly in the area to the south of the central **Humberto Delgado Square**, which is actually a wide bridge over the main canal. The **Art Museum**, in a former convent, has a good collection of Portuguese art from all periods. The convent itself contains the baroque tomb of Santa Joãna, daughter of King Afonso V, who died here in 1490. On the same street is the **Misericordia Church**, which has a striking baroque doorway and extensive azulejo decoration.

As you might expect, seafood is the main gastronomical fare around here. Two local specialties for the adventurous are eel stew (*caldeirada de enguias*) and an egg-based sweet called *ovos moles*. Aveiro has also long been a center of fine pottery and porcelain production, and you'll find both for sale around town. However, if you are a true potteryphile, you might want to make the 8-kilometer excursion (south on N109) to a little town called **Vista Alegre**, world-famous for its pottery works since 1824, which now has a museum depicting the history of developments in pottery manufacture. The porcelain made here is of an extremely fine quality and often hand painted with a faint Oriental flair.

From Aveiro, it's just a quick drive to

Porto and its many sights. Leave Aveiro and return to the A1 and then drive north to **Porto**. You approach the city over the **Arrabida Bridge**, the youngest, longest, and westernmost of the three spectacular spans across the River Douro. The one you see to your right is the **Dom Luis I**, built in 1886, and beyond that is the railway bridge, **Maria Pia**, built ten years earlier by Gustave Eiffel (before he built the tower in Paris). The finest city views are available from these vantage points.

Hotel Infante de Sagres, Porto

In Porto we recommend the **Hotel Infante de Sagres**. It is located downtown, so follow the *Centro* signs to find it. Set on a relatively quiet *praça* down a side street, it escapes a lot of the noise and traffic normally associated with such a convenient situation. Its namesake, and Porto's native son, is Prince Henry the Navigator, the driving force behind Portugal's monumental voyages of discovery, famous for his school of navigation in Sagres. His parents were King João I and Philippa of Lancaster, daughter of John of Gaunt. Their marriage in 1387 cemented the bond that Porto still maintains with the British. In the 18th century the British discovered port wine and the rest is history.

Porto is the second largest city in Portugal, with nearly half a million inhabitants, and the heart of the nation's most important economic region, accounting for well over 50% of the country's economic production. The city has a long history of relative autonomy (fiercely protected) and has frequently found itself at odds with Lisbon. Unaffected by the 1755 earthquake, Porto retains an old-world ambiance unmatched in the capital city.

Most of the important sights are reached easily on foot from your hotel. Just a block east is the bustling **Avenida dos Aliados** that runs from the Town Hall on the north to the busy **Liberdade Square** (the center of town) on the south. A few blocks to the west of the square on Rua dos Clerigos is Porto's landmark, the 75-meter **Clerigos Tower**, offering expansive views over the city and the river.

Continuing south along the Avenida Dom Afonso Henriques, you encounter the **Cathedral,** founded in the 12th century but subsequently considerably altered. It boasts several ornate altars, including an impressive one of silver. Just south of the cathedral is the **Guerra Junqueira Museum** with an assortment of pottery and tapestries. Across Dom Afonso Henriques is found the **Santa Clara Church**, elaborately decorated with carved wood. Northeast of here is a well-preserved section of the original town walls.

To the west and south of the cathedral area is the town's older quarter. A few blocks in that direction will bring you to the elegant 19th-century **Bolsa**, or Stock Exchange, with a gigantic neo-Moorish hall. Right behind it is the **São Francisco Church**, decorated in sumptuous baroque and rococo style with carved wood and gilt. East and a bit north of here is the **Museum of Ethnography** with a regional display illustrating the everyday life of the residents of northern Portugal.

Porto's most important museum is the **Museu Soares dos Reis** (named for the 19th-century sculptor), housed in an 18th-century palace. It has an extensive collection of Portuguese primitives and sculpture by Soares dos Reis, among other paintings, mostly by Portuguese artists.

The wine to which the city has given its name is mostly produced in the suburb across the river known as **Vila Nova da Gaia**. If you want to see the process and taste the results, take the Dom Luis I Bridge and go to the right as you reach the other side. You will see numerous wineries near the river where port wine is fermented in 25,000-gallon vats before being bottled and aged (15 years or more). Port officially comes only from the Douro river basin and is fortified with brandy to stop its fermentation and thus increase the sweetness. Most of these wineries may be visited, especially on weekdays during normal business hours.

If you turn left off the bridge instead of right you'll discover the 16th-century **Convent of Nossa Senhora da Serra do Pilar**, which has one of the best views of the city climbing up from the banks of the Douro.

If you have the time, an excursion up the coast north of Porto is a worthwhile trip. Take the Rua do Ouro along the river to the west of downtown through **São João do Foz**, a suburb sitting right at the mouth of the Douro with a 17th-century fort. Turn north along the Atlantic, past the old Castelo do Queijo, and continue to the new port of **Leixoes**, built at the mouth of the River Leca to circumvent problems with silt that plague Porto's channel. A few kilometers after crossing the river to Leca da Palmeira, join the N107, passing Porto's Pedras Rubras airport, and turn left on the N13.

After a pretty 15 kilometers you will reach **Vila do Conde**, an ancient fishing village that predates the Romans, but which is increasingly attractive as a resort. The town is known for its lace making and, if you happen to be there on a Friday, you will find an especially large selection at the weekly market. The **Santa Clara Convent** is worth a visit, if only to see the carved ceilings and the tombs of the 14th-century founders, Dom Afonso Sanche and Dona Teresa Martin. In the cloister is a fountain fed by a 6-kilometer-long aqueduct, which originates in nearby **Povoa de Varzim**. This neighboring town is also a popular resort due to its nice beach, casino, and colorful old fishermen's quarter.

 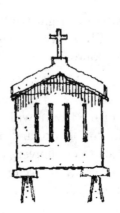 

Back to the Beginning

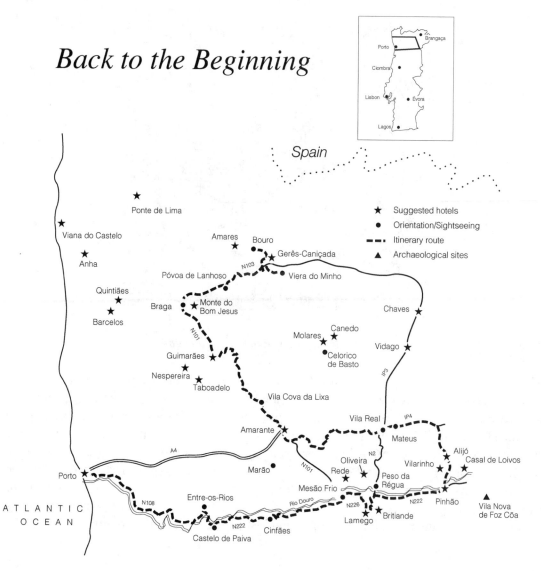

Spain

Suggested hotels ★
Orientation/Sightseeing ●
Itinerary route ▬ ▬ ▬
Archaeological sites ▲

Ponte de Lima ★

Viana do Castelo ★

Anha ★

Quintiães ★

Barcelos ★

Amares ★
Bouro ●
Gerês-Caniçada ●
N103
Póvoa de Lanhoso ●
Viera do Minho ●

Braga ★
Monte do Bom Jesus ★
N101

Guimarães ★
Nespereira ★
Taboadelo ★

Molares ●
Canedo ★
Celorico de Basto ●

Chaves ★
Vidago ★
IP3

Vila Cova da Lixa ●

Amarante ★

A4
Marão ●
N101

Vila Real ●
IP4
Mateus ●

Oliveira ●
Rede ★
Vilarinho ★
Alijó ★
Casal de Loivos ★

Porto ★

ATLANTIC
OCEAN

N108
Entre-os-Rios ●

Rio Douro
Mesão Frio ●
Peso da Régua ●
N2

N222
Pinhão ★
Vila Nova de Foz Côa ▲

N222
Cinfães
N226
Lamego ★
Britiande ★

Castelo de Paiva

Porto
Brangaça
Ciombra
Lisbon
Évora
Lagos

113

Back to the Beginning

Nossa Senhora dos Remedies, Lamego

This is a short itinerary, perfect for a few days' excursion out of Porto into the beautiful and intensively cultivated Douro Valley, where the grapes for *vinho verde* (green wine) are grown. Because the climate does not allow time for the grapes to ripen fully, the wine produced is quite light with a slight sparkle. The Douro is a swift river, dropping over 120 meters during its 160-kilometer journey across Portugal, and carving deep, precipitous canyons into the landscape. The unwieldy geography has not daunted the people who live on the steep but fertile slopes along its banks, however, and the sight of tiny white villages clinging to the hillsides, surrounded by narrow strips of fields stepping down to the river, ranks among the most picturesque in the country.

Recommended Pacing: Spend a night or two in Lamego, a historic town in the heart of the wine-growing region, and two nights in Pinhão overlooking the vineyards and the sweep of the Douro River. A long day's drive will find you at an impressive natural reserve known as the Peneda-Gerês National Park. You can break your journey in the historic town of Guimarães, just before the park, stay at one of the pousadas in either Gerês or Amares, or continue through the park and stay in the old spa town of Chaves, and then continue the loop back to Porto.

This itinerary begins in **Porto**: for sightseeing suggestions see the itinerary *Port to Port*. Head out of Porto by driving east along the river past the Maria Pia Bridge until you come to N108. Turn right and hug the riverbank until just before reaching the town of Entre-os-Rios, which means "between the rivers," so-named because it stands at the confluence of the Douro and the Tamega. Cross the Douro in the direction of **Castelo de Paiva**, a charming little wine town cozily sheltered by intensely green hills. Take N222 east toward Cinfães and, as you pass through the terraced slopes, you'll notice farmers working their fields by hand, just as it has always been done—the steep terrain isn't amenable to modern farm machinery. Most of the houses are on steep hillsides and appear accessible only on foot. Just before arriving in Cinfaes you pass the **Carrapatelo Dam** with what is said to be the largest navigation lock in Europe. Portugal's long-term goal is to make the Douro navigable from Spain to the sea, so the dams have all been built with locks for that eventuality. Besides being the commercial wine center of the *vinho verde* region, **Cinfães** is also known for its handicrafts: weaving, basketry, lace, and wood miniatures—a favorite model being the *barco rabelo*. These flat-bottomed sailboats were the traditional transporters of goods, especially wine, down the Douro (the shallow drafts were necessary because of the widely varying depth of the water). Today, tanker trucks and the railroad have largely replaced them.

Beyond Cinfães you continue to parallel the river through the neat little town of Resende. Another 15 kilometers brings you to Barro, with a good view of the valley. Beyond is Samodaes and, a bit farther, the **Miradouro da Boa Vista**, where you will surely want to stop for some picture taking—there is a first-rate view of the entire area.

Douro River Valley

From Miradouro da Boa Vista, continue on to **Lamego**, known as the "museum city" because it retains much of its original Visigothic flavor. Lamego is thought to have been settled first in 500 BC, and it was later destroyed then rebuilt by the Romans. It changed hands several times during the Moorish period and was finally retaken definitively in 1037. The first Cortes (loosely akin to a parliament) in the young Portuguese nation was held here in 1143 and proclaimed Afonso Henriques as King Afonso I, the first ruler of the Portuguese kingdom (although he had proclaimed himself king in 1139, the act confirmed his status). In later epochs its importance can be attributed to its situation on the main road connecting Braga and Guimarães in Portugal to Cordoba and Sevilla in Spain. Lamego is justly proud of its long history of national importance, and its early reconquest by the Christians is the reason for its surprising number of handsome churches and chapels.

A **castle keep** looms over the town of Lamego. The Romanesque structure dates from the 12th century, but the Moors built the encircling wall in the 11th century to shelter their castle, which was on the same spot. Its underground cistern is unique in Portugal and was probably also a Moorish contribution.

Lamego's **Cathedral** is also 12th century, but the square tower is all that remains of the original edifice—the rest was periodically remodeled in the 16th and 17th centuries. The cloisters were added in the 16th century, along with the lovely chapels of Santo Antonio and São Nicolau. Across the square and to the right of the cathedral is the former **Episcopal Palace**, now housing an attractive museum with early Portuguese paintings, Flemish tapestries, sculpture, and antique furniture.

A walk south from the cathedral leads to an area of town with numerous fine old mansions and palaces of 17th- and 18th-century vintage. At the end of Rua Cardoso Avelino is Lamego's most attractive church, **Nossa Senhora do Desterro**. It dates from the 17th century and is richly decorated with azulejos and carved wood. Just north of there is the **Church of the Holy Cross**, also well appointed inside. Lamego is also noted for its smoked ham, and of course its sparkling white wine. The city is appealing and typical of the older cities in the interior of Portugal. Just south of Lamego there is a delightful little inn, the **Quinta da Timpeira**.

On a hill southeast is the beautifully situated **Nossa Senhora dos Remedios**, an elaborate baroque sanctuary built in the 18th century and dedicated to the patron saint of Lamego. Approximately 700 stairs ascend the hillside, interrupted by landings, pavilions, statues, and fountains. If you consider hundreds of steps intimidating, note that the church can also be reached by car from the other side. The view over the town and countryside is spectacular from the terrace of the chapel. This serves as a pilgrimage church during Lamego's annual festival in late August and early September. The festival is one of the country's most famous and is marked by music of all types, parades, and a procession featuring religious figures traditionally drawn by oxen.

From Lamego take N2 north to Peso da Régua. Just before crossing the river, turn right and follow the N222 as it traces the south bank of the Douro. This is much less congested and far more scenic than the portion you took from Porto to Lamego. The river is wide and beautiful, and the road skirts it closely. On each side of the river the steep hills are covered with vineyards right down to the water's edge. It is an absolutely beautiful wine region and reminded me very much of the Mosel River Valley of Germany. A local vintner commented that the centuries-old task of clearing the steep hillsides of stone, using that stone to bank the man-made terraces, and then harvesting the vineyards should qualify as one of the wonders of the world! It does seem a daunting and incredible feat. Continue on to the small town of Pinhão. Set right on the riverbank, enjoying spectacular vistas of the sweeping river banded by terraced vineyards, is the recently opened **Vintage House**.

Continuing on from Pinhão, take N322 toward Alijó for 1 kilometer, then turn right at the sign for a lovely inn in **Casal de Loivos**. After 6 kilometers, the **Casa de Casal de Loivos** is on your right, a house with a dark-green door and fancy grillwork on the shutters. This charming small inn has the most dramatic setting of anywhere along the Douro: you can sit on the terrace and marvel at the untouched beauty of the gentle, vineyard-covered hills that drop down to the river looping through the valley far below.

The home has been in the family of your gracious host, Manuel Bernardo de Sampayo, for many generations and he has a wealth of information on what to see and do in the area. If he is full, you might want to stay with a close friend of his, Christina van Zeller, who has just recently opened her home, the **Casa de Vilarinho**, to guests in another wine village. (See listing under Pinhao.)

If you are at all interested in archaeological sites, be sure to take an excursion to see the prehistoric rock drawings discovered in 1992 by Nelson Rebanda near **Vila Nova de Foz Côa**. At this time there are two sites open to the public, but you need to make a reservation (usually from one to four weeks in advance) through the **Parque Arqueológico Vale do Côa.** From the Visitor Center a jeep takes you to the site where a guide takes you on a walking tour lasting about one and a half hours. For reservations and more detailed information contact Parque Arqueológico Vale do Côa—tel: 279.76.43.17, fax: 279.76.52.57.

Continuing your journey, go north to **Alijó** (where the **Pousada de Alijó–Barão de Forrester** is located) then continue for about 23 kilometers and turn west on IP4 toward Vila Real. From Vila Real, stay on IP4 to Amarante. You can look forward to a scenic but arduous 50-kilometer drive on the IP4, skirting the northern edge of the Serra do Marao and crossing the River Tamega near Amarante. About halfway, you traverse the **Alto do Espinho Pass**, 1,066 meters up in the Serra. This area was once heavily forested, but fire and an aggressive, if shortsighted, lumber industry has decimated the wooded slopes. **Amarante** is a pretty country town built up from the Tamega, which is spanned by an 18th-century bridge.

Follow IP4 to the junction with N101 and bear right toward Braga. After 9 kilometers you reach the nondescript village of **Trofa**, renowned for its lace making. A picturesque 17 kilometers later you'll arrive in **Guimarães**, known as the "cradle of the Portuguese kingdom" because Afonso Henriques was proclaimed the first king of Portugal here in 1139.

Guimarães has two pousadas—the **Pousada de Guimarães–Santa Marinha**, which sits magnificently above town on the site of a 12th-century convent, and the **Pousada de Guimarães–Nossa Senhora da Oliveira**, located in the center of town. You can't go wrong at either one—both are charming. The Pousada de Guimarães–Santa Marinha is housed in a convent founded in 1154 by the wife of Afonso Henriques, but evidence uncovered during the construction of the pousada suggests that there was a much earlier structure here—perhaps dating back as far as the 8th century. In the 17th century the convent was turned over to the Hieronymites and almost totally rebuilt in a later style.

As befits the first capital of the nation, Guimarães retains one of the best-preserved castles in the country, constructed in the 10th century, but extensively restored in the 1930s. Afonso Henriques was born here in 1110, so the **castle** has a symbolic significance for the nation. There are fine views from the narrow, multi-towered ramparts. At the foot of the hill is the 15th-century **Paço dos Duques**, built by the first Duke of Bragança, a member of the powerful Portuguese family that furnished the country with its monarchs after 1640. The seat of the ducal family was transferred to Vila Viçosa at a later point, and the palace was abandoned. It has since been restored (in the 20th century) and merits a visit for its superior antiques—paintings, furniture, tapestries, porcelain, weapons—and striking chestnut ceilings.

In the old quarter of town around the **Largo da Oliveira** is a network of ancient, picturesque streets and squares reflecting the town's medieval past. Also there is the church of **Nossa Senhora da Oliveira**, founded in the 12th century by Afonso Henriques. It was then expanded, and the Manueline tower was added in the 16th century. The adjoining building of the former Dominican monastery now houses the **Alberto Sampaio Museum** with an interesting collection of Portuguese art.

Follow now a circuitous route through some beautiful scenery to the Peneda-Gerês National Park. Leave Guimarães on N101 south back toward Amarante and then bear left on N206 toward Fafe. If you're paying attention to the map, you'll notice that this is not the most direct route to your destination, but it takes you through some unforgettable country. **São Romao de Aroes** has an early-13th-century Romanesque church, and the picturesque little village of **Fafe** has some handsome 18th- and 19th-century mansions built by families who returned after making their fortunes in colonial Brazil. Another 28 kilometers through beautiful landscape brings Arco de Baulho into view, where you turn left on N205, coming next to the ancient settlement of **Cabeceiras de Basto**, with a large monastery built mostly in the 18th century (though founded much earlier). Soon you arrive at the Nossa Senhora do Porto Reservoir on the River Ave, after which you pass through several quaint villages before reaching **Póvoa de Lanhoso** where there is a ruined 12th-century castle with stellar views from its hilltop perch.

Santa Maria do Bouro

Take N103 east to begin your approach to the park through wooded hills. After about 20 kilometers watch for the sign directing you left toward **Caniçada** and **Pousada do Gerês–São Bento,** a cozy lodge majestically situated on the edge of the nature park. The pousada is delightfully appealing and overlooks the giant blue Caniçada Reservoir far below, set like an aquamarine in the valley.

Not far away is another superb place to stay, the **Pousada de Amares–Santa Maria do Bouro**, located directly west of Caniçada on the N308. Built into the ruins of a 12th-century monastery, this idyllically located pousada is one of our favorites.

Whichever pousada you choose, you are close to **Braga,** the impressive **Monte do Bom Jesus** (see page 129 for more information), and the **Peneda-Gerês National Park** where you will be surrounded by great natural beauty. This is an ideal spot for relaxation, free of the seduction of sights other than peaceful forest and cool, blue mountain lakes. If hiking in an untamed forest brimming with wildlife piques your interest, plan to spend some time here. Almost every conceivable outdoor recreation is a possibility in the park: horseback riding (and horse-drawn carriage rides for the less hearty), aquatic sports on the reservoirs, mountain climbing, etc. Guided tours of the park are available, and in one day you can easily make the drive from the pousada to the little spa of **Gerês**, which retains a faded glamour. It used to be quite the "in" place to go and even King Luis I came here to "take the cure," although it doesn't say much for the medicinal merits of the spa as he died the next year!

Depending on where you are headed, if you continue north, we suggest the picturesque river town of Ponte de Lima with its wealth of gorgeous bed and breakfasts as your next stop. Alternatively, you might consider following the N103 as it travels through the serras, weaves a journey high above the mountain lakes, and leads you to the old spa town of **Chaves**. Here we recommend staying at the **Forte de São Francisco Hotel**, an historic monument, embraced by the walls of a castle fortress that commands an imposing position above the old town and its river, or in the countryside looking back to the city at the charming **Quinta da Mata**. While in Chaves you will want to visit the citadel, the old streets of the main town, the spa, and the thermal waters, and there is a wonderful half-hour walk along the River Tâmega and the Roman bridge.

From Chaves the N2 weaves a scenic journey south to **Vidago**, where the former palace of the Portuguese kings now offers luxurious accommodation as the **Vidago Palace Hotel**. Carry on to Vila Real and the E82, which travels west back to Porto and the coast.

Romantic River Routes

Spain

Rio Minho

Monção

Valença do Minho

N101

N101

Extremo

Vila Nova
da Cerveira

N13

Spain

Caminha

▲ Dolmen

Vila Praia
de Ancora

N101

Rio Lima

Ponte de Barca

N13

Rio Lima

Ponte de Lima

Viana de Castelo

Anha

N201

ATLANTIC
OCEAN

Amares

Bouro

Quintães

Monte do
Bom Jesus

Gerês Caniçada

Barcelos

N103

Braga

Vieira do Minho

Citânia de Briteiros

N204

Vila Nova
de Famalição

Nespereira

Guimarães

Toboadelo

A3

Porto

★ Suggested hotels
● Orientation/Sightseeing
▬ ▬ Itinerary route
· · · · · Suggested sidetrips
▲ Archaeological sites

Brangaça

Porto

Ciombra

Lisbon

Évora

Lagos

Romantic River Routes

Dolmen at Vila Praia da Ancora

This itinerary takes you through the extreme northwest corner of Portugal, the verdant area near the River Minho known as the "Verde Minho." It is indeed an apt description: its intensely cultivated fields and heavily forested mountain slopes envelop the visitor in green. Culturally, the area shares a great deal with its Spanish neighbor to the north, Galicia. The Galician language and the dialect of northern Portugal resemble each other, and the similarity of other characteristics—architecture, folk dances, music, traditional dress, food, wine—is striking. This is the most densely populated section of the country and also the coolest and the rainiest. The economy is primarily agricultural—the majority of the small family farms are still cultivated and harvested in much the same way as they have been for generations. Once off the beaten path, you slip back in time, occasionally even passing families in wooden carts drawn by a team of oxen.

Recommended Pacing: Spend two nights in a charming property belonging to Solares near the quaint town of Ponte de Lima. Conclude your itinerary with a night at Viana do Castelo.

The Verde Minho also encompasses what is technically the oldest part of Portugal: the part that was declared a separate kingdom by Afonso Henriques in 1139. As a result there are a large number of Romanesque monuments. There are also many churches, attesting to the Minhotos' reputation as extremely pious people who are renowned for their gay religious festivals and popular pilgrimages. It's one of the last areas where you may see local citizens in traditional dress even when it's not festival time. Local handicrafts run the gamut from lace to knife blades. The town markets, therefore, offer a wide variety of interesting possibilities for your shopping pleasure. Local food specialties include a hearty dish, *caldo verde*, a creamy cabbage and potato soup. *Bacalhau*, or dried cod, is perhaps even more ubiquitous here than in the rest of the country.

Porto occupies a privileged location at the mouth of the River Douro and serves as the economic hub of northern Portugal. However, the area north of the city to the Spanish border presents some very attractive contrasts to the cosmopolitan air of the country's second-largest city. It is a region sprinkled with quaint villages set in a verdant landscape of vineyards and fertile river valleys (the Ave, the Cavado, the Lima, and, of course, the Minho), an intriguing mixture of an ancient society and young wine.

Leave Porto heading north through the suburbs on A3 toward Braga. Take the turnoff to **Barcelos**, center of a thriving handicraft region. You cross the River Cavado on an interesting 15th-century bridge as you enter town. If you happen to be here on Thursday, you will see everything from pottery to basketry to linen displayed at the open **market** in the huge main square called the Campo da Republica in the center of town. On any other day you should visit the **Centro de Artesanato** in the Largo da Porta Nova, just off the southwest corner of the square, which sells a wide variety of local handicrafts. It is housed in a tower remaining from the 16th-century town fortifications. Nearby is the 18th-century **municipal garden** with pretty baroque fountains and ornate walls.

By far the most famous folk-art ceramic around here (and perhaps in all of Portugal) is the **Galo de Barcelos**, or Barcelos cock, a multicolored rooster, available in all sizes, which you'll find for sale throughout the country. The cock symbolizes this ancient legend: A Galician passing through Barcelos on his way to Santiago de Compostela in Spain was accused and convicted of a crime. During his final plea at the judge's house, he exclaimed in frustration, "As certainly as I am innocent, it is equally certain that that cock will rise up and crow when I am hanged." The chicken in question was a roasted one on the judge's dinner table, and the pilgrim's claim provoked much laughter among those present. And, of course, at the proper moment the roasted chicken arose and crowed. The judge managed to get to the gallows before the poor fellow met his fate and released him. He returned to Barcelos many years later and built a monument to Saint James, which is now in the Archaeological Museum of the city.

The **Archaeological Museum**, partially in the open air, is housed in the former Palace of the Dukes of Bragança, as is the **Regional Ceramics Museum**, a collection of colorful native pottery. The palace is located a few blocks southwest of the main square, near the bridge across the Cavado, where you can also see the parish church with its fine azulejos.

Convento da Franqueira, Barcelos

Opposite the palace is the **Solar dos Pinheiros**, a 15th-century granite mansion that is very representative of other admirable old mansions in the vicinity.

If you want to stay in the Barcelos area, an excellent choice is the outstanding **Quinta do Convento da Franqueira**, beautifully housed in a lovely convent a few kilometers from town. Another lovely bed and breakfast is the **Casa dos Assentos**, nestled in the shadow of the village church of Quintiães.

When you are ready to continue, return on N103 across the Cavado and remain on it to **Braga**. This is one of the country's oldest cities and was once the seat of the Portuguese monarchy. We have two recommendations for places to stay here—sister hotels—at the heart of the village of Monte do Bom Jesus, on a hill overlooking Braga. The hotels are located near the church of Bom Jesus do Monte: the **Hotel do Elevador** and the **Hotel do Parque**. To reach these hotels, from Braga follow signs for Chaves, then bear right toward **Monte do Bom Jesus**. The shady, switchback road winds up to a plateau on top of the hill 215 meters above the city with a spectacular view over the valley below. Here you find the **Church of Bom Jesus do Monte**, which was built in late neoclassical style by a local architect, Carlos Amarante, in the late 18th century.

Bom Jesus was designed as a pilgrimage church. An elaborate, 265-step staircase that starts from the base of the hill and leads to its summit, represents the Stations of the Cross, with chapels at each landing. One segment is called the Stairway of the Five

Senses, and another the Stairway of the Virtues, with the senses and virtues represented by tiled fountains. You might want to take the stairs down, then return by the *elevador* (funicular) back up. In the wooded hills behind the pilgrimage church there is a beautiful park laced with trails leading up to a small lake. This is a favorite spot for families to come and relax on weekends.

Monte do Bom Jesus makes a delightful place to stay, but you must also go down the hill to visit **Braga**, which was probably settled by the Celts long before the Romans arrived in 250 BC. It was an important Roman town, subsequently occupied by the Suevi, the Goths, and the Moors before being reconquered by the Christians in the 11th century. It became the center of the religious hierarchy in the area and maintained that status until the 18th century. This presence resulted in the great number of architectural monuments that now dot the town. Braga is Portugal's fourth-largest city (after Lisbon, Porto, and Coimbra) and, as such, has the inevitable urban development at the edge of town, but the older central area retains a great deal of its traditional charm and ambiance.

The **Cathedral** dominates the old town. Originally built in the 11th century, only the south doorway (Porta do Sol), the apse of the cloister, and some minor trim remain from that period. Other elements, including the numerous small chapels, were later additions, and the interior was redone in 18th-century baroque. The Anca-stone high altar is especially interesting. Reached from the courtyard, the Gothic Capela dos Reis contains the tombs of Henry of Burgundy and his wife—parents of the first king, Afonso Henriques—along with the mummified body of a former archbishop.

Across the street to the north is the former **Archbishop's Palace**, which has three separate wings dating from the 14th, 17th, and 18th centuries. One wing now houses one of the country's most important libraries. East of there is the **Torre de Menagem** (keep), which survives from the town's 14th-century fortifications. Behind the tower are formal gardens. To the south is the 16th-century **Capela dos Coimbras** whose interior is prettily decorated with azulejos and sculpture. If you continue east to the Avenida da Liberdade and turn right, then right again on Rua do Raio, you find the **Fonte do Idolo**, said to be of pre-Roman origin. At the end of that street is the **Palacio do Raio** (or do Mexicano), which typifies the numerous 18th-century mansions in Braga.

Braga is designed for wandering and savoring the old-world atmosphere of its colorful, landscaped squares and charming, narrow, cobblestoned streets. If you are in town at mealtime, you will have your choice of many restaurants with good, inexpensive regional food.

One excursion from Braga is to the pre-Roman ruins at **Citania de Briteiros**. The settlement, apparently of Celtic origin (3rd century BC), is about 10 kilometers southwest of town (watch for signs as you descend Monte do Bom Jesus). Drive through the gate up to the caretaker's house to buy your ticket. The ruins of three defensive walls encircle the village, consisting of some 150 large and small structures. Of particular interest are the circular houses. There are remains of fountains, aqueducts, and a funeral monument in the 10-acre site, the most impressive and largest in Portugal. The site also has a wonderful view over the surrounding valleys.

Leaving Braga, venture deeper into the Minho countryside. Take N201 northwest from Braga toward Ponte de Lima. Just as you leave town, you pass near the **Chapel of São Frutuoso dos Montelios**, one of Portugal's oldest Christian monuments. Although still the subject of controversy, it was apparently built in the 7th century, partially destroyed by the Moors, and rebuilt in the 11th century, thus incorporating a mixture of Byzantine (uncommon in Portugal) and Gothic influences. It seems to have originally had the form of a Greek cross, but parts of it were destroyed in the building of the adjacent Church of São Francisco, an 18th-century monastery church.

Return to N201 (or you can take the A3) and continue north. You traverse intensely green, wooded hills with vineyards for the next 27 kilometers until you reach **Ponte de Lima**, which means "Bridge over the Lima River." The Roman stone bridge has 15 large arches and 12 small ones. The town, one of our favorites in Portugal, is delightfully situated on the bank of the Lima amid lush, rolling hills and has a wonderful old-world ambiance. It has been settled since Roman times, as the bridge suggests, and traces of its medieval fortifications are interspersed among the more modern white houses near the end of the bridge. If you can arrange to be here on Monday, you will enjoy the famous **market** on the riverbank, which has taken place for several centuries. Numerous shops

Paço de Calheiros, Ponte de Lima, Calheiros

also display the varied handicrafts of the region, including blankets and baskets. The tourist office has a modest exhibit of regional handicrafts.

Ponte de Lima was the center of much wealth and consequently the area is dotted with gorgeous big estates and mansions, many of which have opened their doors to guests. Many of the most outstanding of these bed and breakfasts have formed an affiliation called **Solares de Portugal** to jointly promote their properties, and we feature a wonderful selection of these in our guide. There are too many concentrated in the region around Ponte de Lima to give you details of them here, but look in the back of the book under Ponte de Lima and you will see a description of each. There is certain to be one that will suit your fancy because they range from a delightful stone mill to an opulent palace. All of the Solares de Portugal properties require a minimum two-night stay and are often difficult to find. Our suggestion is to make your reservation before leaving home, then while sightseeing in Ponte de Lima, go by the Solares de Portugal office (which is in the middle of the town) and ask directions.

When it's time to leave the Ponte de Lima area, take the N202 and turn left past Refoios to Souto, where you bear right toward **Ponte da Barca**, another picturesque little country town on the River Lima. Head north from there on N101, being sure to look back toward town after crossing the 16th-century bridge for a splendid view. A few kilometers farther and you reach the lovely village of **Arcos de Valdevez**, straddling the River Vez.

As you continue north toward the border, you are treated to glorious landscapes and quaint little villages. After about 17 kilometers watch for a panoramic vista point toward the Serra de Peneda to the east and the Lima Valley to the south. Twelve kilometers later you pass the large 19th-century Palacio da Brejoeira on your left. Soon thereafter you reach the border town of **Monção**, on the bank of the Minho. Being on the border with Spain, Moncão is a fortified town with a long history of heroic defense of the Portuguese frontier. The town has two main squares, the Praça da República and the **Praça Deu-la-Deu**, named in honor of Senhora Deuladeu Martins who saved the town against the Spanish in the 14th century. She accomplished this feat by giving bread to the Spanish invader, Henry II of Castile, who thought that if the town had so much surplus food, it would never surrender—he called off his troops and left the town in peace. The ruins of a 14th-century castle also attest to Monção's strategic location. Be sure to pay a visit the pretty interior of the Romanesque **parish church**, which dates back to the 13th century. The town is also famous as a source of *vinho verde*, the youthful regional wine.

Remain on N101, which now continues westward, paralleling the mighty River Minho. After 5 kilometers you pass **Lapela**, a tiny town clustered around its ancient defensive tower. Continue through the intensively farmed riverbank with endless vineyards and cultivated terraces to **Valença do Minho**, a popular border-crossing town that faces the Spanish town of Tuy on the opposite bank. There is just one way into the old town, which sits perched on a hill overlooking the newer city below. Follow signs that lead you

Vila Nova da Cerveira

up the hill and through the thick fortified walls into the medieval city. Continue through town to the opposite end where, built next to the stone ramparts of the fort, you come to the **Pousada de Valença do Minho–São Teotónio**. This pousada, although in the old town, is not a historical building. It does not have great flair or style, but its location is super. If you decide to stay here, request one of the best rooms—these have breathtaking views of the river, the Eiffel-designed bridge, the town of Tuy, and the Galician Mountains beyond.

The northern fortified section of Valença do Minho was begun in the 13th century by Dom Sancho I and traces its origin to Roman times. The section to the south was added in the 17th century, after the Spanish monarchy had relinquished control over Portugal. This area is popularly called the "**Coroada**" (because of the crown-like shape of its layout) and is joined to the older part by a stone bridge. The stronghold consists of double curtain walls, numerous bastions, and watchtowers, all of which offer lovely vistas over the surrounding region. The well-preserved fortress retains a wonderful medieval atmosphere which will reward you for the time dedicated to strolling and shopping in the many souvenir shops along the narrow, winding, cobblestone streets. The ancient stone houses and fountains recapture the enchantment of a time long past.

A short excursion from here is to nearby **Monte de Faro** on N101-1 (7 kilometers). Ascend through forested slopes to a parking area, then walk up to the top for unforgettable views.

Leave Valença do Minho going southward on N13, which generally parallels the broad, beautiful Minho to its end with the river gradually widening as it nears the sea. After 15 kilometers you come to **Vila Nova de Cerveira**, a quaint small town with character built near the banks of the river.

Located in the center of town is the delightful **Pousada de Vila Nova de Cerveira–D. Diniz**. This hotel makes a good place to stop for lunch or, if you would prefer to spend the night here rather than in Valença do Minho, it is an excellent hotel choice. The inn occupies an entire fort with the rooms located in reconstructed old houses. The streets inside the pousada constitute a tiny village, including a beautiful 18th-century chapel, with the restaurant rising from the castle ramparts and overlooking the river. Dom Diniz constructed the original fort in the 14th century, but much of it was added later. It was inhabited as late as 1975. You find the pousada in the plaza just a couple of blocks off the highway. There is also a nice handicraft shop next door with local ceramics, lace, and needlework.

Continue south on scenic N13 along the Minho through several small villages to the ancient town of **Caminha**, once a defensive bastion opposing Monte Santa Tecla across the river in Spain. Today a simple fishing village (although the old town is not on the banks of the river), it has retained a lovely medieval atmosphere apparent in the main square with its old clock tower. The 15th- to 16th-century parish church, found on the street leading from the arch under the tower, has a particularly fine carved ceiling. The town is clustered about a large central plaza where there are tables under jaunty umbrellas inviting you to stop for a coffee or cold drink.

Still heading south on N13, you skirt the beaches of the Atlantic and pass a number of seaside towns, some wonderful old beach homes, and a few modern beach developments.

In **Vila Praia da Ancora** there is an extremely well-preserved dolmen, a solitary testament to settlement here as long as 4,000 years ago. To find it, take the turn to the left for Ponte de Lima to the sign V. P. Ancora, then take another left. About 30 meters toward town look for a small, hard-to-see plaque in a stone wall saying

Monumento Dolmen da Bairrosa and enter the courtyard behind the wall.

Back on N13, another 15 kilometers brings you to **Viana do Castelo,** the largest city in the Minho region north of Braga. Although apparently of Greek origin, Viana do Castelo became a boom town in the 16th century when Portuguese sailing skills paved the way for fishing the Newfoundland cod area. That period of prosperity is reflected in one of the town's most attractive features: the fine old mansions in the central section near the **Praça da Republica**. There is also a nice 16th-century fountain in the square and several handsome public buildings. A bit south of the square is the 14th-century **parish church,** which contains some fine woodcarving. A few blocks west of the square is the **Municipal Museum** with a worthwhile collection of antique furniture from the once-far-flung Portuguese Empire and colorful azulejos on the interior walls. At the west end of town near the river you find a 16th-century fort built by Phillip II of Spain during his reign on the Portuguese throne.

If the timing of your trip is flexible, try to be here around the middle of August when Viana is the site of one of the country's most famous religious pilgrimages. Folk dancing, fireworks, and parades characterize the celebration.

If you want to spend the night in Viana do Castelo, there are excellent places to stay. Perched serenely on a hill called **Monte Santa Luzia** (located at the north end of town) you'll find the classic **Pousada de Viana do Castelo–Monte de Santa Luzia**. This is a luxurious, turn-of-the century, resort-style hotel commanding spectacular views of the city and the river where it meets the sea. In a residential setting, just a short distance from the heart of town, is a lovely bed and breakfast, the **Casa do Ameal**.

If you are looking for less expensive accommodations, another choice is **Quinta do Paço d'Anha**, one of the properties that belongs to the Solares de Portugal affiliation. This 17th-century wine-producing estate is in a small town called Anha, which is across the river and south of Viana do Castelo.

Hotel Descriptions

The Pousada de Alcácer do Sal–D. Afonso II is an imposing castle-hotel. Its origins go way back—archaeologists have discovered that Phoenicians, Romans, and Moors all occupied this strategic site during its rich history. The massive stone fortification is built on a hillside with the River Sado flowing by below. Also below the castle is a patchwork design of salt flats (salt—sal—gave its name to the ancient village next to the castle). The shell of this pousada is indeed very old, but the interior shows little trace of its colorful heritage. You enter into a very modern reception area beyond which is the central courtyard where a modern sculpture holds center stage. The lounges are decorated with modern sofas and chairs, though Oriental carpets give a pleasant flavor of the past. The restaurant, which is bright and sunny with large windows overlooking the terrace, has modern, black-lacquered chairs. There is an inviting swimming pool well positioned on a terrace at the side of the hotel, enclosed on one side by the characterful crenellated castle walls. One of the nicest aspects of this pousada is the guestrooms, sporting built-in headboards with excellent reading lights and large bathrooms with walls of marble. Most of the rooms have the added bonus of a small balcony. *Directions:* From Lisbon travel south on the A2 and take the Alcácer do Sal turnoff, following the pousada signs. The pousada is 70 km south of Lisbon.

POUSADA DE ALCÁCER DO SAL–D. AFONSO II
7580 Alcácer do Sal, Portugal
Tel: 265.61.30.70, Fax: 265.61.30.74
35 rooms, Double: €164–€287
Open: all year
Credit cards: all major
Region: Costa de Lisboa
www.karenbrown.com/portugal/pousadaalcacer.html

The Convento de São Paulo is a very special place to stay. Although a hotel, it feels more like a private home where you are at ease to enjoy yourself without any formal structure, yet quietly in the background is a very professional staff to anticipate your needs. A convent, dating back to 1182, the hotel setting is sublime: snuggled up against a heavily wooded hill and facing an idyllic view of gently rolling hills decorated with groves of lemon, olive, and cork trees. There is utter tranquility—just the sound of birds and an occasional cowbell. Privacy is guarded as to enter you must first be announced at the gate and then ring a bell at the front door. Once inside you feel very lucky to be one of the special few with a reservation. En route to your room you will be in awe of the incredible azulejos—on one side of the hallway depicting the story of Jesus and on the other side, the life of Joseph. These 50,000 glazed tiles are a treasure, representing the largest private collection in Europe. The guestrooms are built into the monks' cells, but don't worry, you will not be roughing it—the rooms are attractively decorated with antiques and all have marble bathrooms (superior rooms are larger). Dining here is truly a treat, with all the produce and even the meat fresh from the convent's own farm. *Directions:* From Redondo, follow hotel signs to Aldeia da Serra. You will see the hotel on the hill at the far end of town.

HOTEL CONVENTO DE SÃO PAULO
Host: Julia Leotte
Aldeia da Serra, 7170-120 Redondo, Portugal
Tel: 266.98.91.60, Fax: 266.99.91.04
27 rooms, 7 suites, Double: €115–€225
Open: all year
Credit cards: AX, VS
Region: Planícies
www.karenbrown.com/portugal/saopaulo.html

The Pousada de Alijó–Barão de Forrester is named in honor of the Englishman, Baron James Forrester, who came to Portugal as a young man in the early 1800s to live with his uncle. He is credited with spreading the fame of port wines around the world—a deed so important to the economy that the King bestowed upon him the title of baron. The Barão de Forrester, situated in a small town in the Douro Valley, was purpose-built as a pousada. It has neither historical architectural interest nor special appeal when you first see it, but on stepping through the door you will be most pleasantly surprised. Everything is fresh and pretty and there is an air of comfortable good taste throughout, with no feeling of stiffness or formality. The living room, bar, and dining room are all color-coordinated with lovely fabrics and the tall windows are dramatized by beautiful tieback draperies. The guestrooms are spacious and maintain the same mood of quality and good taste. With some pousadas beginning to grow tired and show their age, it is very satisfying to see what an excellent transformation has been accomplished here. The Barão de Forrester also offers a lovely swimming pool and a tennis court. *Directions:* From Vila Real, take IP4 west. After about 25 km, there is a turnoff to Alijó. Just after leaving the highway, follow the sign to the pousada, which is about 23 km south of the turnoff.

■🗄 P ⊪ ≈ 🏃

POUSADA DE ALIJÓ–BARÃO DE FORRESTER
5070-031 Alijó, Portugal
Tel: 259.95.94.67, Fax: 259.95.93.04
21 rooms, Double: €126–€132
Open: all year
Credit cards: all major
Region: Montanhas
www.karenbrown.com/portugal/pousadaalijo.html

The Pousada de Almeida–Senhora das Neves was a wonderful surprise. Although photos depicted this new building as contemporary and a bit sterile, the hotel, in fact, has lots of charm. The ambiance is somewhat like a lodge with large rooms flowing from one to another. The furniture is not frilly—mostly comfortable leather-upholstered chairs and sofas. One area is especially inviting, with a cozy grouping of sofas and chairs around a large granite fireplace and a couple of square tables ready for a game of cards. The dining room also has a fireplace for chilly evenings and some old guns and a boar's head over the mantle. For those who like a friendlier touch, there are also displays of colorful plates on the walls, and well-tended plants to soften the rooms. The bedrooms are all similar in decor and exceptionally attractive, with handsome wooden four-poster beds and cream-colored bedspreads of fine quality. Above the beds there are handmade wall hangings in pretty pastel colors. The pousada is in a remote, windswept area of Portugal, right at the Spanish border, but even though off the beaten path, the fortified town is outstanding—really worth a detour. If you are interested in well-preserved walled towns, you will be fascinated by Almeida with its walls in the shape of a star. *Directions:* Pousada de Almeida-Senhora das Neves is within the fabulous fortified walled town of Almeida.

POUSADA DE ALMEIDA–SENHORA DAS NEVES
6350 Almeida, Portugal
Tel: 271.57.42.83, Fax: 271.57.43.20
21 rooms, Double: €115
Open: all year
Credit cards: all major
Region: Montanhas
www.karenbrown.com/portugal/pousadaalmeida.html

The Pousada do Alvito is an appealing 15th-century buff-colored castle conveniently located smack in the center of a village of whitewashed houses. A tall square keep dominating the center of one wall and round crenellated towers rising from each of the four corners reinforce the reality that this was in its heyday a proper fortress. When the castle was converted to a hotel, the architects took care not lose too much of the original character. Because it is so old, the castle shows varied influences including some intricate Moorish windows and handsome Gothic ceilings. The hotel is built around a large, cobbled courtyard which has three tall, slender cypress trees to soften its austerity. To the left of the reception area there is a small, sedate lounge beyond which you find the dining room with its arched windows opening onto the square. As in many of the pousadas, the dining room is one of the Castelo de Alvito's most attractive rooms, with a high vaulted ceiling, white walls accented with antique plates and oil paintings, and handsome armchairs upholstered in a colorful tapestry-like fabric. The spacious bedrooms are also winningly decorated. If you want to pay a little more, room 301, a deluxe twin tucked on the top floor with views out over the town to the countryside, is a real winner. There is a large swimming pool in the back garden. *Directions:* The hotel is easy to find. Once you arrive in Alvito, just follow the pousada signs.

❄ ☕ 💳 ☎ ♿ 🐎 ⅄ P 🍴 🏊 🖼 🚣 🐕 ⛷

POUSADA DO ALVITO–CASTELO DE ALVITO
7920-999 Alvito, Portugal
Tel: 284.480.700 or 284.480.701, Fax: 284.48.53 83
20 rooms, Double: €164–€244
Open: all year
Credit cards: all major
Region: Planícies
www.karenbrown.com/portugal/pousadaalvito.html

The Pousada do Marão–São Gonçalo, which began operation in 1942, was the second hotel in the Pousada affiliation. It was not built within a historical monument, but was constructed to provide lodging for travelers taking the twisting high road from Amarante to Vila Real. There is now a new highway, so access is much easier, but the setting remains dramatic, with the hotel perched on the hillside overlooking the steep valley below. The hotel's exterior, which is an eccentric hodge-podge of stone and wood, is very dated and could use some cosmetic assistance. The interior too is showing its age and is probably due for a total refurbishment before long, but the hospitality of the staff is excellent and there is a nice air to the hotel, with many fresh plants and flowers accenting the rooms. The most attractive room by far is the dining room with its fireplace in one corner, three walls paneled with wood, and, best of all, one wall of windows with a sweeping view. The bedrooms are adequate, but fairly small. Each has a similar decor, with printed cotton bedspreads and matching curtains. Ask for one of the bedrooms with a view. *Directions:* Although the address of the pousada is Amarante, it is actually in Marão, which is about halfway between Amarante and Vila Real. It is well marked on the left side of the IP4, approximately 20 km east of Amarante.

▨▤ 🚶 🍴

POUSADA DO MARÃO–SÃO GONÇALO
Amarante, 4604-909 Marão, Portugal
Tel: 255.46.11.13, Fax: 255.46.13.53
15 rooms, Double: €107–€144
Open: all year
Credit cards: all major
Region: Montanhas
www.karenbrown.com/portugal/pousadamarao.html

The Pousada de Amares–Santa Maria do Bouro is a stunning addition to the Pousada affiliation. Built into the ruins of a 12th-century monastery, the hotel is definitely worth a detour. The beautiful structure of the monastery has been lovingly preserved: massive stone walls, carved fountains, arched doorways, soaring ceilings, and a cloistered courtyard remind you hauntingly of the Cistercian monks who once lived and worshiped here. The interior makes no pretense to recreate a religious ambiance but is a pleasing blend of old and new, with a distinct leaning toward the modern. The walls are either of exposed stone or painted a pastel creamy yellow. Huge modern paintings and a few exquisite antiques highlight the spacious public rooms. Three-meter-wide hallways with light-pine flooring lead to the guestrooms, which have stainless-steel doors. The use of light-toned wood continues in the bedrooms, incorporated into the built-in headboards, desks, and chairs. Enormous windows let in streams of sunlight and views of beautiful wooded hills. If you are very lucky, you might get number 201—a corner room with windows and balconies on two sides. Behind the hotel is a massive herringbone-tiled terrace flanked by ponds, and on a lower terrace, a lovely oval swimming pool. This pousada is truly an architectural masterpiece with a glorious setting. *Directions:* The pousada is not in the town of Amares, but about 12 km southeast in Bouro.

POUSADA DE AMARES–SANTA MARIA DO BOURO
4720-688 Amares, Portugal
Tel: 253.37.19.71, Fax: 253.37.19.76
32 rooms, Double: €159–€216
Open: all year
Credit cards: all major
Region: Costa Verde
www.karenbrown.com/portugal/pousadaamares.html

The Quinta do Paço d'Anha is rich in history. Amazingly, it has been in the d'Alpuim family since 1503, at which time the property was given to them by the Duke of Bragança. The family had strong ties to the monarchy and when King Dom António Pior de Crato was persecuted by Spanish soldiers, he hid here in 1580. Vineyards surround the estate and the family continues the tradition of the production of fine vinho verde wine and brandy, both of which have received many awards. The estate is made up of various buildings. The family lives in a characterful, whitewashed, 17th-century manor house. Nearby, several of the old stone buildings have been totally renovated inside and converted into apartments accommodating from two to five people. Although these have kitchenettes, breakfast (which is brought to the apartments each morning) and daily housekeeping are included in the very reasonable price. The apartments are attractively furnished, using many of the family antiques that have been handed down through the generations. Because of the individual quarters, guests are afforded much privacy. *Directions:* From Viana do Castelo, take the N13 bridge south from the center of town. Follow N13 (the old bridge) toward Porto. About 2 km after leaving the city, you will see a Turismo de Habitação sign and a Paço d'Anha sign on the right. Follow the old wall down to the left and then right to the main entrance.

QUINTA DO PAÇO D'ANHA
Host: Eng. António Júlio d'Alpuim
Anha, 4900 Viana do Castelo, Portugal
Tel: 258.32.24.59, Fax: 258.32.39.04
6 apartments (€100–€138)
Minimum nights required: 2
Open: all year
Credit cards: AX, VS
Region: Costa Verde
www.karenbrown.com/portugal/pacodanha.html

The fabulous Pousada de Arraiolos brings much-needed accommodations to Arraiolos, one of Portugal's jewels, a walled town and center for colorful handmade carpets. The beautiful hotel has a spectacular setting just outside town amidst rolling hills dotted with olive trees. It is a stunning complex of glistening white buildings nestled in the valley. Dominating the picture is the beautiful church with its square bell tower next to the convent, which houses the pousada. The heart of the hotel is the cloister whose columned walkway is now enclosed with glass. On the ground level, most of the lounges and the dining room are accessed by strolling past this tranquil inner garden, while on the second floor the corridors to the bedrooms also look onto the cloister. The architects have kept the original structure, but inside everything has been redone in a simple, modern style, with a color scheme in the public rooms of blue and white, which mimics the color seen so frequently in the houses and lovely tiles of this region of Portugal. The guestrooms are very big and extremely attractive, with large balconies for enjoying the view. There is a lovely swimming pool in the garden. The most outstanding feature of this pousada— is the church, which is part of the convent. It is incredibly beautiful with walls completely covered with blue tiles depicting biblical scenes. *Directions:* Outside Arraiolos on the road to Pavia.

POUSADA DE ARRAIOLOS–
NOSSA SENHORA DA ASSUNÇÃO
7044-909 Arraiolos, Portugal
Tel: 266.41.93.40, Fax: 266.41.92.80
32 rooms, Double: €159–€216
Open: all year
Credit cards: all major
Region: Planícies
www.karenbrown.com/portugal/pousadaarraiolos.html

Atouguia, whose name derives from the ancient word for a bull, was once a great center for bullfighting. The town crest proudly displays a bull with horns topped with crowns. Bulls are patterned into the old cobbled streets. On the edge of town is Casa do Castelo, built as an extension to the ruins of the medieval walls that once encircled a 12th-century Moorish castle. A garden terrace and distinctive arched stained-glass windows dress the front façade. On the ground floor is a lovely living room and a dining room, where a delicious breakfast is served, with French doors opening onto the light and beauty of the garden. A back corner room with stained glass windows serves as a bar-salon. Four guestrooms are found upstairs in the main house. We enjoyed the "red" room with its king bed, a spacious tiled bath, and lovely back-garden views. Step down to my favorite, the "green" room, an end room whose windows on two sides overlook the pretty side garden and lovely, protected swimming pool, and which opens onto its private terrace. Three small poolside bedrooms (Fleur, Star, and Boat) are considered prime in summer. The Casa do Castelo radiates the warmth of the charming family who has always lived here. *Directions:* Travel west from Óbidos towards Peniche along the 114. Look for the B&B sign on the right side of the road when the village is on the left, 5 km before Peniche.

CASA DO CASTELO
Host: Maria Helena Horta Gama d'Almeida Baltazar
Estrada Nacional 114, #16
Atouguia da Baleia, 2520 Peniche, Portugal
Tel: 262.75.06.47, Fax: none
7 rooms, Double: €75
Minimum nights required: 2
Open: all year, Credit cards: all major
Region: Costa da Prata
www.karenbrown.com/portugal/casadocastelo.html

The 16th-century Quinta do Convento da Franqueira is an absolute dream—it is no wonder that the father of the current owner, your gracious host Piers Gallie, was immediately captivated by the property. He bought it on first sight and brought his family from England to live here over 30 years ago. Captain Gallie restored the convent with loving care, meticulously retaining its wonderful architectural features while adding all of the modern amenities. The inn wraps around the adjacent cloister, testimony that in years gone by, this was the convent for the adjacent church. A flight of stairs leads to an exceptionally elegant, yet extremely comfortable living room where guests can relax, fix themselves a drink, and study the many books available about what to do and see in the region. There is an appealing ambiance throughout of an English country home. Each of the bedrooms is spacious and beautifully furnished with antiques. Utter tranquility prevails, with only wooded hills and vineyards as far as the eye can see. A path leads through the gardens to a spring-fed swimming pool nestled on the hill with a magnificent view of the convent and the church. Quinta do Convento da Franqueira is one of our favorites—truly a very special hideaway. *Directions:* The quinta, located about 6 km southwest of Barcelos, is very tricky to find. When you make your reservation, ask Piers Gallie to send you a map and instructions.

QUINTA DO CONVENTO DA FRANQUEIRA
Host: Piers Gallie
4755-104 Barcelos, Portugal
Tel: 253.83.16.06, Fax: 253.83.22.31
3 rooms, Double: €90–€95
Minimum nights required: 2
Open: May to Nov
Credit cards: AX, VS
Region: Costa Verde
www.karenbrown.com/portugal/quintadoconvento.html

The Pousada da Batalha–Mestre Afonso Domingues, although lacking in historical ambiance, offers modern convenience as well as an excellent location. The pousada is just off the main Lisbon-Porto highway, and opposite the 15th-century Batalha monastery (Abbey of Santa Maria da Vitória), which was built to commemorate King João's victory again the Spaniards (whose forces outnumbered his by 5 to 1) at the great battle of Aljubarrota. The monastery is one of Portugal's highlights, so it is a tremendous advantage to be able to park your car at the pousada and walk across the square to the cathedral. The hotel is pleasant with comfortable, mostly modern wood furnishings throughout. The flooring in the front lounge and the dining room is a distinctive pattern of black and white mosaic tiles. The bedrooms are of average size, with high ceilings and relatively spacious bathrooms. Some of the bedrooms (such as 104) have a remarkable view out to the abbey. At night the vista is especially magical, with the lights from within illuminating the stained-glass windows. The restaurant also overlooks the abbey and features an outdoor terrace, which is especially enjoyable in fine weather. Though likely to be remembered more for its convenience than its atmosphere, the Mestre Afonso Domingues provides an ideal base for numerous sightseeing excursions. *Directions:* Located just off the N1, 11 km south of Leira.

❄ ☕ 💳 🍴

POUSADA DA BATALHA–
MESTRE AFONSO DOMINGUES
2440-102 Batalha, Portugal
Tel: 244.76.52.60, Fax: 244.76.52.47
21 rooms, Double: €115–€159
Open: all year
Credit cards: all major
Region: Costa da Prata
www.karenbrown.com/portugal/pousadabatalha.html

Batalha is a town not to be missed—its monastery (Abbey of Santa Maria da Vitória) is one of Portugal's highlights. At the Quinta do Fidalgo, just a few minutes' drive from the monastery, you can enjoy a leisurely breakfast and still have time for an early start before the swarm of tour buses arrives. The inn's setting, just outside town, is peaceful and the history of the home adds its character and charm. For over 300 years the estate has been in the family of your charming hostess, Maria Adelaide, who is the essence of refinement and good taste. As you approach the manor, you realize there are actually two houses—Maria Adelaide lives in one while the other is dedicated to her guests. On the ground floor is a handsome, large living room filled with family heirlooms and dominated at the far end by a fireplace surrounded by comfortable brown leather chairs and sofas. Four of the guestrooms are up the stairs from the living room. As I toured, each room soon became my favorite! Some have twin beds and others have doubles, but otherwise all are equally attractive with beautiful antique headboards and gorgeous antique chests or desks. All the rooms look out through shuttered windows to a large park studded with graceful old maple trees. *Directions:* In Batalha follow signs to the pousada. Pass the pousada and take the road that travels back underneath the IC1—the second lane on the left leads to the quinta.

☕ P

QUINTA DO FIDALGO
Host: Maria Adelaide Oliveira Simòes
2440 Batalha, Portugal
Tel: 244.76.51.14, Fax: 244.76.74.01
5 rooms, Double: €91–€101
Open: Mar to Nov
Region: Costa da Prata
www.karenbrown.com/portugal/fidalgo.html

The mood is set before you even enter the doors of the Pousada de Beja—the hotel, which is painted white with accents of red and ochre, has a distinctly dignified look. You enter through an arcaded entrance into a grand square lobby with gray marble floors and white walls stretching to high ceilings. The pousada dates back to the 13th century when it was built as a monastery and architectural details from its earlier life lend romance and charm. The core of the pousada is the cloister with its pretty garden, and the surrounding promenade, which used to be open, is now enclosed with glass, letting sunlight stream into the hallways leading to the public lounges and the guestrooms. Without exception, all the rooms are splendidly decorated, absolutely decorator-perfect. The use of opulent fabrics, quality antiques, and beautiful works of art achieves a refined elegance. The most dramatic room of all is the dining room, which has high-backed chairs upholstered in hunter green and sumptuous swag draperies which must be 9 meters long. The bedrooms are spacious, decorated with great style, and have large marble bathrooms. If you want to splurge, the suite, decorated in lovely yellows, is outstanding. Although in the city, the hotel has parklike grounds containing tennis courts and a spectacular swimming pool. *Directions:* Once in Beja, there are many pousada arrows to direct you to the hotel, located in the old part of the city.

❄ ☕ 💳 🛗 🍽 ≈ 🏃

POUSADA DE BEJA–SÃO FRANCISCO
7801-901 Beja, Portugal
Tel: 284.32.84.41, Fax: 284.32.91.43
35 rooms, Double: €159–€279
Open: all year
Credit cards: all major
Region: Planícies
www.karenbrown.com/portugal/pousadabeja.html

Set against a beautiful backdrop of the Serra da Esperança mountain range, near Manteigas and Covilhã, the Convento de Belmonte pousada is a relatively new member of the pousada organization. It is situated near the northeastern border and we found it convenient to spend our last night in Portugal here before continuing on to the northern coast of Spain. While guestrooms are housed in a modern extension, the heart of the hotel is the renovated Convent of Nossa Senhora da Esperança and its intimate 13th-century chapel. The hotel's ambiance and decor complement the wonderful old convent and public areas are quite dramatic, with handsome furnishings set against the old stone walls under old wooden beams, offering lovely views of the surrouding countryside through thick stone portals and windows. The pousada organization was very respectful when restoring the convent and took great care and expense to preserve the historical architecture as well as the wonderful old amphitheater set in a neighboring woodland. Accommodations encompass one dramatic suite and thirty guestrooms, which are attractive with a comfortable, simple, uncluttered decor and enjoy the benefit of modern bathrooms. This is an area that is known for its great fishing and the chef often includes seafood on the menu, the grilled codfish being a house specialty. *Directions:* Belmonte is located north of Covilhã off the IP2, KH192-A23, southeast of Manteigas off the EN232.

POUSADA DE BELMONTE–
CONVENTO DE BELMONTE
6250 Belmonte, Portugal
Tel: 275.91.03.00, Fax: 275.91.03.10
25 rooms, Double: €137–€248
Open: all year
Credit cards: all major
Region: Montanhas
www.karenbrown.com/portugal/pousadabelmonte.html

Historic Braga is a "must-see" city, filled with tourist attractions. Just a few kilometers from Braga, atop the Monte do Bom Jesus—a religious sanctuary dating back to 1722—you find the Hotel do Elevador, named for its proximity to the 19th-century water-powered funicular that transports sightseers who lack enthusiasm for climbing the elaborate but long staircase up and down the mountain. Opened over 100 years ago, the two-story hotel has a magnificent setting. It terraces down the wooded mountainside facing Braga. When we visited in October 1997, the hotel was to reopen after being closed for long time for a total face-lift. On our latest visit, we were thrilled to find that the renovation has enormously upgraded the facility, which is now bright and cheerful with light streaming through large windows highlighting beautiful creamy-beige marble floors that you find throughout. The most outstanding feature of the hotel is its glass-enclosed dining room, which juts out over the hillside overlooking a sculpted garden and beyond to Braga. The view is especially romantic at night when the lights of the city twinkle in the distance. The majority of the bedrooms are downstairs—all have panoramic views. *Directions:* From Braga, take N103 east for 6 km, following signs for Monte do Bom Jesus. The hotel is on the hill, below the church of Bom Jesus, next to the funicular.

HOTEL DO ELEVADOR
Manager: Albino Viana
4710-455 Braga–Monte do Bom Jesus, Portugal
Tel: 253.60.34.00, Fax: 253.60.34.09
22 rooms, Double: €74–€90
Open: all year
Credit cards: MC, VS
Region: Costa Verde
www.karenbrown.com/portugal/elevador.html

Hotel do Parque is perched high on the side of a hill, overlooking Braga and next to Bom Jesus do Monte, a marvelous baroque 18th-century church. The attractive hotel was originally a private mansion, dating back to the end of the 19th century. It is a handsome, three-story white building with red-tiled roof and tall windows accented by stone trim. You enter into a spacious hall, which evokes the Victorian era with velvet sofas trimmed in a wine-color that complements the color of a row of floor-to-ceiling columns that form a line across the room. An old-fashioned, traditional air prevails. There are several dignified, quiet sitting areas, a comfortable bar, and a pretty dining room. The hallways are nice and light since they have windows opening onto two inner atriums with skylights. Guestrooms are pleasantly furnished with an old-world look and have nice large bathrooms. Some of the rooms look out across the garden to the church. The hotel backs up to the park of Monte do Bom Jesus where a path weaves romantically up through a forest to a small lake snuggled in the trees. On summer weekends the lake, which has colorful rowboats for rent, is a popular destination for families from Braga. *Directions:* The hotel is located 6 km southeast of Braga on Monte do Bom Jesus.

HOTEL DO PARQUE
Manager: Albino Viana
4710-455 Braga–Monte do Bom Jesus, Portugal
Tel: 253.603.470, Fax: 253.603.479
45 rooms, Double: €74–€130
Open: all year
Credit cards: MC, VS
Region: Costa Verde
www.karenbrown.com/portugal/parque.html

The Pousada de Bragança–São Bartolomeu was purpose-built as an inn to fill a vacuum—a hotel was desperately needed in this remote, hauntingly lovely niche of northeastern Portugal. From photos I'd received, I was not expecting much pizzazz—the pousada looked nice but nothing special. I was wrong—this is a super place to stay. With no pretensions to antiquity, the hotel is modern throughout, with pale-wood furniture, light-pine floors, and large windows, which let in lots of light, creating a cheerful ambiance. The upkeep seems very good—no worn or tired look here. An added bonus is a round pool set in the terrace below the hotel. However, what makes this hotel very special is not the physical appearance, but the setting: the hotel faces the stunning 12th-century Bragança Castle, which crowns the knoll of a hill just across the ravine from the pousada. Still-intact medieval walls wrap around the hill, enclosing the castle along with its pretty white church and quaint houses clustered within its embrace. Happily, each of the pousada's bedrooms has a balcony, which captures this romantic sight. At night the castle is softly illuminated, which further enhances its magic. All of the bedrooms are very nice, but in the left wing they are exceptionally large—ask for one of these. *Directions:* From the IP4, follow signs to the city center where you will find pousada arrows guiding you to the pousada.

❄ ☕ 💳 🛗 🚶 🍴 ≈

POUSADA DE BRAGANÇA–SÃO BARTOLOMEU
5300-271 Bragança, Portugal
Tel: 273.33.14.93, Fax: 273.32.34.53
28 rooms, Double: €126–€132
Open: all year
Credit cards: all major
Region: Montanhas
www.karenbrown.com/portugal/pousadabraganca.html

This is a beautiful, ivy-covered home set behind its own stone wall and gates. Inside, new materials provide a lovely complement to old stone and exposed woods. Beyond the attractive entry is a handsome dining room. Upstairs is a guest sitting area, which boasts the wonderful ceilings of Douro, thickset windows, and a magnificent oil painting. Just off the sitting area is a small room that overlooks the connecting 17th-century chapel with its very ornate carvings, paintings, tiles, and sculptures and a carving of Saint Anthony. The Casa offers four guestrooms. The Room of the Chapel is lovely, with shuttered widows opening to garden views. Across the hall, Donna Maria is more ornate with its 18th-century dark-wood furniture regally paired with rich-blue fabrics. An end room, the Iron Bed Room, overlooks the side road and garden parking, while the Martyr is a handsome room with twin beds, and fabric of rich red and creams. The garden is captivating, with gorgeous wisteria-covered walkways, landscaping and a lovely pool. *Directions:* On the outskirts of Lamego turn off on the N226 towards Monimenta de Beira. When the N226 cuts through the town of Britiande do not turn right to the center of town but continue on for just a short stretch and turn at the sign for the Igreja Matriz and Turismo de Habitação. Drive down the narrow passage. The gated entry to the Casa is just opposite the square and stone obelisk.

CASA DE S. ANTONIO DE BRITIANDE
Hosts: Mr & Mrs Antonio Carlos Sobral Pinto Ribeiro
Britiande, 5100-360 Lamego, Portugal
Tel & fax: 254.69.93.46
4 rooms, Double: €100
Dinner available upon special request
Minimum nights required: 2
Open: Mar 1 to Oct 31, Credit cards: all major
Region: Montanhas
www.karenbrown.com/portugal/casadesanantonio.html

This hotel is aptly named, as it is indeed housed within an ornate, 19th-century royal palace—the last palace built by the Portuguese kings. Before its politically expedient exit in the early 20th century, the royal family enjoyed luxury, tranquility, and hunting in this retreat, encircled by elegant gardens and thick pine forest. The hotel is private, though the space is leased from the government. Alexandre de Almeida's collections of magnificent antiques are displayed in the public rooms, each of which resembles a museum exhibit, creating the impression of a collector gone crazy. The bedrooms vary in size and grandeur—many have 5-meter-high ceilings and are opulently furnished with gilded antiques (some original to the palace). The choice bedrooms overlook the lovely sculpted gardens, laden with flowers in the spring and summer. The restaurant is the pièce de résistance, with elaborately carved arched windows, gleaming multi-hued wood parquet floor, and a three-dimensional painted wood ceiling, which sparkles with pinpoints of light. To this beautiful setting add fine food, an extensive wine list, and attentive service. The Bussaco Palace's enchanting location, sumptuous atmosphere, and fine food provide you with an unforgettable stay. *Directions:* From Coimbra take N1 north to Mealhada. Go east on N234 for about 8 km. A sign on your right indicates the road that winds up the hill through the thickly wooded Buçaco park to the hotel.

BUSSACO PALACE
Manager: Paulo Mesquita
Buçaco, 3050-261 Luso, Portugal
Tel: 231.93.79.70, Fax: 231.93.05.09
60 rooms, 4 suites, Double: €170–€200
Open: all year
Credit cards: all major
Region: Costa da Prata
www.karenbrown.com/portugal/bussaco.html

The Solar Abreu Madeira has a prime setting facing a tiny square in the sleepy little town of Canas de Senhorim, which used to be well known for the raising of cattle but which is now famous for fine cheeses and delicious Dáo wine. The house is so long that it stretches across one whole side of the square, while on another corner of the square sits a church whose bells were sweetly tolling mass the day we visited. The two-story, 18th-century white manor is flanked at one end by a crenellated tower and at the other by its own beautiful little chapel. You might be puzzled as to which is the proper door to use, but you can tell because there is a discreet tourism sign near the bell, then you enter into a museum-like hallway where there are two antique carriages on display. The dining room is very dramatic, with a large table around which sit handsome antique, high-back wood-and-leather chairs. A large crystal chandelier adds the final touch of grandeur. All of the bedrooms are spacious and nicely decorated with antiques. To the side and behind the house is a garden where a swimming pool beckons on hot summer days. Everything throughout the manor is neat and tidy—this is obviously the home of a meticulous owner. *Directions:* Canas de Senhorim is on the N234 6 km southwest of Nelas. When you reach the village, follow the turismo signs.

SOLAR ABREU MADEIRA
Host: D. Maria Luisa Abreu Madeira
3525 Canas de Senhorim, Portugal
Tel: 258.74.28.29, Fax: 258.74.14.44
3 rooms, Double: €75
Minimum nights required: 2
Open: all year
Region: Montanhas
www.karenbrown.com/portugal/madeira.html

I adore the Casa de Canedo—from the extremely warm welcome from Gloria and Marissa, to the absolutely gorgeous and meticulously groomed grounds, to the handsome and very commodious guestrooms. A rugged dirt road delivers you to its entry. Park and then walk under a canopy of wisteria, glimpsing a gorgeous pool and flower-filled grounds. Everything about the Casa de Canedo is divine, from the display of earthenware jugs, to the walk-in fireplace, to the priceless antiques, to the gorgeous artwork. The feeling is country, not formal, and with each room I kept thinking, "If only I could replicate this at home!" My favorite guestrooms are the elegantly furnished Patio Room, with its beautiful country tiles in the bathroom and its own patio terrace looking out over the vineyards and countryside, and the Lake Suite, which overlooks the courtyard pond and has a lovely bedroom and separate living room with red sofas before a fireplace. Guests enjoy lots of public areas—a library, piano room, sitting room, and game room with billiard table. Definitely ask to see the elaborate chapel. Dinner, offering regional specialties à la carte, either in the cozy dining room or at the outdoor barbecue, is a treat. *Directions:* From either Arco de Bauhle to the north or Celorico de Basto to the south, take the N210 to the village of Canedo. Watch for a small sign off the road pointing to the Casa de Canedo (6.6 km south of Arco, 11.7 km north of Celorico).

CASA DE CANEDO
Hosts: Rodrigo & Maria José Rau
Barreiro P, Canedo
4890-140 Celorico de Basto, Portugal
Tel: 255.36.12.93, Fax: 255.36.17.65
9 rooms, Double: €100
Dinner available upon special request
Minimum nights required: 2
Open: all year, Credit cards: all major
Region: Costa Verde
www.karenbrown.com/portugal/casadecanedo.html

Built in 1962, the Pousada do Caramulo–São Jerónimo fills a gap for travelers wanting to be a bit off the beaten path. Caramulo is small town in the hills that attracts not only travelers looking for a retreat in the sweet clear air, but also auto enthusiasts who come to visit the vintage car museum located here. Approaching Caramulo on road N230 from Águeda, you go over a low mountain pass studded with eucalyptus trees whose fragrance perfumes the air. When you reach Caramulo, the pousada is on the main road. It is a simple, rather plain building. The exterior is modern, with a façade of stucco and stone without much architectural embellishment. The guestrooms are small, but fresh and clean, with built-in headboards, good reading lights, mini bars, and TVs. Many have a balcony with a table and chairs so you can enjoy the fresh air. Looking out over the road there is a sweeping view of the valley spread out below. The restaurant is the most attractive room in the pousada, with an open fireplace at one end and carved-wood chairs and tables. The food is especially tasty, featuring regional specialties with cod usually on the menu. The the dining room has a glorious view—large picture windows capture the panorama of trees and valley. An added bonus is a kidney-shaped swimming pool prettily set in a wooded glen in the front garden. *Directions:* Located in Caramulo on the N230, well marked with pousada signs.

❄ ☕ 💳 🚶 🍴 🏊

POUSADA DO CARAMULO–SÃO JERÓNIMO
3475-031 Caramulo, Portugal
Tel: 232.86.12.91, Fax: 232.86.16.40
12 rooms, Double: €107–€113
Open: all year
Credit cards: all major
Region: Montanhas
www.karenbrown.com/portugal/pousadacaramulo.html

Just a half-hour from Lisbon, the Albatroz is a delightful discovery, combining the charm of a country inn with the luxury of a five-star hotel. Originally a villa built in the 19th century for King Dom Manuel II, it has since been enlarged and renovated to provide its guests with quiet, understated elegance amid the bustle of old Cascais. The hotel is perched on a rocky outcropping that juts out into the beautiful Bay of Cascais. Small beaches snuggle below the rocks to each side of the hotel. In the original villa there are eleven bedrooms, a bar with a terrace overlooking the sea, and the excellent Albatroz restaurant—which is especially famous for its seafood. It is elegantly decorated in pale beige and white, and has a marble-and-wood floor. The bedrooms in the original villa have a charming old-world flavor, with high, sculpted ceilings and carved-stone windows—no two are alike in size or décor, but all are lovely and decorated with antiques. There are also bedrooms in the newer wing, which overlooks the oval swimming pool and beyond to the sea. These bedrooms are spacious and tastefully appointed, though more contemporary in style, decorated in soft colors and furnished in warm wood. They all have balconies so that you can step outside and enjoy the fresh air. There are also two suites and four superior rooms (all facing the sea) in a charming old villa just across the road. *Directions:* Located in the center of Cascais.

❋ ⬛ CREDIT ☎ ⛎ 🏇 Ⴤ P ⏁⏁ ≈ 🖼 ᒪ ⟡ ♿ ❦

HOTEL ALBATROZ
Host: Dr. Carlos Simões de Almeida
Rua Frederico Arouca, 100
2750-353 Cascais, Portugal
Tel: 214.84.73.80, Fax: 214.84.48.27
47 rooms, Double: €220–€479*
*Breakfast not included
Open: all year, Credit cards: all major
Region: Costa de Lisboa
www.karenbrown.com/portugal/albatroz.html

The Casa da Pérgola offers an incredible value and a superb location in the heart of colorful Cascais with an easy commute to Lisbon by train. The house next door is almost a twin to the Casa da Pérgola—hostess Patricia Corrêa Gonçalves's great-grandfather gave both of his daughters a matching house, side by side, though only the Casa da Pérgola has remained in the family. The front garden is enticing, with neatly clipped hedges outlining colorful flower beds and a pretty little fountain. The house has a wonderful whimsical look—it is a sparkling-white three-story home with a red-tile mansard roof, blue-and-gold azulejos framing the windows, and accents of bright Chinese red. You enter into a small foyer with a handsome floor of black-and-white marble. To the left is the intimate breakfast room. Straight ahead, a marble staircase with a wrought-iron-and-brass banister leads upstairs to the bedrooms and to the living room, which oozes old-fashioned elegance—Oriental carpets, a huge chandelier, ornate wood-paneled ceiling, a wine-red velvet sofa, walls tiled halfway up with beautiful blue-and-white tiles, and many oil paintings. All of the guestrooms are nicely decorated, mostly with family heirlooms. The choice bedroom is 14, "Cinzento." This was Patricia's grandparents' room and has beautiful antique twin beds and a large balcony overlooking the garden. *Directions:* The hotel is on a small street off the Alameda da Grande Guerra.

CASA DA PÉRGOLA
Host: Corrêa Gonçalves family
Avenida Valbom, 13
2750 Cascais, Portugal
Tel: 214.84.00.40, Fax: 214.83.47.91
11 rooms, Double: €80–€100
Open: all year
Region: Costa de Lisboa
www.karenbrown.com/portugal/casadapergola.html

The Senhora da Guia is a captivating inn on the seaside road between Cascais and the Praia do Guincho. Set in a pine-studded property just across the road from the sea, it offers very special accommodations combined with personalized service. The inn has enjoyed such popularity that rooms have been added throughout the years. A large annex with bedrooms arranged in a U shape around a central lawn is built on the slope above the original hotel. This section is very attractive and continues the same traditional architectural style of white-stuccoed walls, dark-green shutters, and red-tiled roof. The focal point of the public rooms remains in the original part of the house, which has a welcoming lounge with polished hardwood floor, Oriental rugs, marble fireplace, and cozy antiques. There is a gleaming wood bar at one end and sliding glass doors lead out to a shady verandah with a terrific view looking over the pretty saltwater swimming pool and beyond to the sparkling sea. There is also an intimate dining room downstairs. A spectacular crystal-and-wood stairway leads upstairs to the high-ceilinged, whitewashed bedrooms—comfortably old-fashioned, well proportioned, and tastefully decorated. Take advantage of the setting and request a bedroom with a lovely sea view. *Directions:* From Cascais take N247, which hugs the coast going west toward Guincho. The hotel is on your right, about 3 km from Cascais.

※ ⚓ ☕ ▦ ☎ 🚶 🐎 🏇 ⍟ P ⑂ ≋ 🖼 ⚓

SENHORA DA GUIA
Host: Carlos Ornelas
Estrada do Guincho
2750 Cascais, Portugal
Tel: 214.86.92.39, Fax: 214.86.92.27
42 rooms, Double: €125–€330
Open: all year
Credit cards: all major
Region: Costa de Lisboa
www.karenbrown.com/portugal/senhoradaguia.html

The Pousada de Castelo de Bode–São Pedro, perched above the Castelo de Bode dam on the Zêzere River, attracts water-sports enthusiasts who come to enjoy such activities as water-skiing, sailing, motor-boating, and fishing. Originally built in 1945 to house the dam construction engineers, the building was converted to a pousada in the early 1950s. Unfortunately the view is not outstanding (unless perhaps you are an engineer) because instead of overlooking the reservoir, the inn faces the rather uninspiring concrete back of the dam. The whitewashed building with its yellow trim, green shutters, and red-tiled roof has a somewhat Moorish feel. The smallish, high-ceilinged bedrooms are plain, but pleasant, with simple wood furniture and flowery drapes and spreads. Not all of the rooms look toward the dam: our favorite was a corner room that looks onto the water and the woods. A small bar downstairs opens onto an outdoor stone terrace. The wood and red-tiled sitting room is cozily furnished and features a stone fireplace, making it a gathering spot on cool mountain evenings. The green-and-white dining room is particularly pretty, and overlooks the dam through big picture windows on three sides of the room. *Directions:* From Tomar take the N110 south toward Entroncamento and after 7 km turn left toward Castelo de Bode. The pousada is well marked overlooking the dam.

❄ ☕ 💳 🏃 🍴 ⚓

POUSADA DE CASTELO DE BODE
2300 Castelo de Bode, Portugal
Tel: 249.38.11.59, Fax: 249.38.11.76
25 rooms, Double: €108–€156
Open: all year
Credit cards: all major
Region: Costa da Prata
www.karenbrown.com/portugal/pousadadebode.html

Looking for a place to break our journey from Portugal to Spain, we felt fortunate to discover the Forte de São Francisco Hotel. The hotel, an historic monument, is embraced by the walls of a castle fortress and its interior public areas incorporate the old cloister of a recently restored 16th-century convent. The fortress commands an imposing location above the old town of Chaves, the river, and surrounding hillside. Be sure to visit the citadel, the old streets of the main town, the spa, and thermal waters, and there is a wonderful half-hour walk along the River Tãmega and the Roman bridge. The hotel is a great place to settle in its own right. The pool is beautifully positioned up against the castle ruins and enjoys unobstructed views. The cozy tavern, its ceiling hung heavy with sausages (a regional specialty), serves light meals, while the elegant dining room is enclosed by glass so as not to obstruct the view. There is also a disco-bar. The 58 guestrooms are modern in their appointments, traditional with reproduction furnishings, and offer a very comfortable night's sleep. Breakfast is offered as a buffet in the dining room or will be delivered to the privacy of your room. *Directions:* Chaves is located at the junction of N103 and N2 just south of the Spanish border in northeastern Spain. Once in town, look up and navigate towards the castle walls and you will arrive at the gated entry to the hotel.

FORTE DE SÃO FRANCISCO HOTEL
Manager: Antonio dos Ramos
5400-435 Chaves, Portugal
Tel: 276. 33.37.00, Fax: 276.33.37.01
58 rooms, Double: €140–€165
Open: all year
Credit cards: all major
Region: Montanhas
www.karenbrown.com/portugal/saofrancisco.html

Sitting on the hillside looking back at the city of Chaves, the Quinta da Mata is a lovely 17th-century farmstead set in meticulous, flower-filled grounds. Inside, wide, heavy wooden doors, thick stone walls, deep, shuttered windows, and dark Masseira ceilings create a backdrop for the handsome furnishings and cozy ambiance. From the reception a hallway banked in stone leads to the guestrooms and the main sitting room and dining room. Center stage in the sitting room is a large fireplace with a stone surround and plates hung as decoration above. The dining room is cozy with its beamed Masseira ceiling and handsome trestle table set in front a wonderful display of old plates. Ask to open the door at the end of the room, which opens to a balcony overlooking the home's own, ornate chapel! The Presidential Suite has lovely tiled floors, stone seats below deep-set windows, and views over the tennis courts and the city of Chaves. I also admired a very handsome bedroom with beautiful twin beds whose headboards complemented the old ceiling and built-in armoires. Other rooms were less dramatic but also very comfortable. A lovely pool is landscaped into a terrace garden with breathtaking views of the surrounding countryside. *Directions:* From the city of Chaves head towards the river and follow directions first to Vila Real and then Mirandela on the N213. Three km after leaving town, look for the sign for the Quinta da Mata.

QUINTA DA MATA
Hosts: Mr & Mrs Filinto Moura Morais
Apartado 194, 5401 Chaves, Portugal
Tel: 276.34.00.30, Fax: 276.34.00.38
6 rooms, Double: €75
Dinner available upon special request
Minimum nights required: 2
Open: all year, Credit cards: all major
Region: Montanhas
www.karenbrown.com/portugal/mata.html

The Quinta das Lágrimas is a stunning, small deluxe hotel. Not only is this exquisite palace of pale yellow with white trim located in one of Portugal's most interesting towns, but the furnishings are outstanding, the staff exceptionally friendly, the restaurant excellent, and—to add icing to the cake—the hotel is rich in historical romance. If you recall the ill-fated love story of Inês and Pedro I (whose tombs you visited in the Alcobaça), it was in the royal wooded park behind the quinta where the 14th-century lovers secretly met and where Inês was subsequently murdered. According to legend, her tears turned into a fountain—hence the name of the hotel, Quinta das Lágrimas (House of Tears). The Duke of Wellington frequently visited here as a guest of his aide-de-camp who owned the palace and was so captivated by its beauty that he dedicated a plaque and planted two majestic sequoias in the garden. As you might suppose, the gardens are still remarkable, dotted with centuries-old trees, fountains, and romantic twisting paths. Also in the garden the more modern era is represented by a dramatic, large swimming pool. This property has been in the same family since 1730, so it is no wonder that pride of ownership has made it so remarkable. *Directions:* Quinta das Lágrimas is located across the river from the center of Coimbra, next to the Portugal dos Pequenitos and the Convent of Santa Clara.

QUINTA DAS LÁGRIMAS
Host: Jose-Miguel Alarcão Júdice
Director: Mário Stromp Morias
Santa Clara
3041-901 Coimbra, Portugal
Tel: 239.80.23.80, Fax: 239.44.16.95
39 rooms, Double: €149–€375
Open: all year, Credit cards: all major
Relais & Châteaux, Region: Costa da Prata
www.karenbrown.com/portugal/lagrimas.html

The Pousada de Condeixa-a-Nova–Santa Cristina was opened as a base for travelers wanting to visit this richly historic area of Portugal—including, of course, the not-to-be-missed Roman ruins of Conímbriga, just a few-minutes' drive away. From the outside, the pousada maintains the ubiquitous theme of white stucco with wrought-iron and red-tiled roof. Inside, the hotel cleverly incorporates the best of the old and the new. A contemporary two-story wall of glass fills the hotel with sunshine and lets guests enjoy a sweeping view out over a lawn and beyond to rolling hills. The decor is exceptionally attractive: everything is light and airy, yet an old-world ambiance is created by the architectural details used. Throughout the pousada you find rich wood paneling, sumptuous carved ceilings, beautiful painted wall panels, and ornate chandeliers (all from a palace in Lisbon). The lounges and dining room are tastefully furnished with lovely fabrics and quality furniture. Some antiques add to the ambiance. The bedrooms are all spacious and have large marble bathrooms and lovely furnishings which basically just vary from room to room by the color scheme used in the fabrics. In the garden is a large swimming pool—a refreshing respite after a day of sightseeing. *Directions:* From A1 follow signs for Conímbriga and Condeixa-a-Nova. When the road splits, turn left toward Condeixa. Soon you see a pousada sign where you turn left.

POUSADA DE CONDEIXA-A-NOVA–
SANTA CRISTINA
3150-142 Condeixa-a-Nova, Portugal
Tel: 239.94.40.25, Fax: 239.94.30.97
45 rooms, Double: €126
Open: all year
Credit cards: all major
Region: Costa da Prata
www.karenbrown.com/portugal/pousadacondeixa.html

As you walk through the impressive portals into the Pousada do Crato-Flor da Rosa, as a guest, you are supporting the marvelous preservation program undertaken by the Pousada affiliation. Tourism has made it possible to assume some monumental projects, which are rescuing a number of irreplaceable historical buildings. The Pousada do Crato is one of the such endeavors, a hotel created within a 14th-century monastery. The shell of the building still stands in all its original glory and the cloisters are incorporated into the design, as are the graceful vaulted ceilings and ornate windows. To the old is married the best of the new, with state-of-the-art bedrooms displaying every modern nicety. There is an understated elegance to the bedrooms, all of which are extremely large-the three suites in the tower are even bigger! There is an immensity to the pousada, with cavernous rooms opening one onto the other. One of my favorites is the lounge-bar, which has elegant columns bracing a soaring vaulted ceiling of great beauty. History buffs relish the tale of António, one of the monastery's priors, who in 1580 briefly became King of Portugal. Claiming to be an illegitimate son of King João III's brother, he laid claim to the throne, but was only able to sustain his sovereignty for one day. *Directions:* Easy-once in Crato, follow signs to the pousada, which is located just north of Crato in the village of Flor da Rosa.

❄ 🍺 CREDIT 🛗 🚶 🍴 ≈

POUSADA DO CRATO–FLOR DA ROSA
7430-999 Crato, Portugal
Tel: 245.99.72.10, Fax: 245.99.72.12
24 rooms, Double: €159–€216
Open: all year
Credit cards: all major
Region: Planícies
www.karenbrown.com/portugal/pousadacrato.html

The Pousada de Elvas–Santa Luzia, facing onto a busy street on the edge of town, opened its doors in 1942 and has the honor of being the first hotel in the pousada chain. It is located in Elvas, a historical town that still maintains much of its rich Roman heritage. The exterior of the pousada with its whitewashed walls and red-tiled roof is not especially inspiring, but the kitchen is very well known and offers an excellent menu highlighting delectable regional specialties such as bacalhau dourado, carne de porco à alentejana, and the wonderfully sweet dessert sericaia, all served in abundance and with a smile. Be sure to go with a big appetite. As it is just a dozen kilometers from the border, neighboring Spaniards have discovered the large, bustling restaurant and, on Sundays in particular, you are likely to hear more Spanish than Portuguese. When the crowds of diners disperse, a cozy atmosphere prevails in the bar and the lounge with their dark wood and leather furniture. Note: The pousada has been renovated since our last visit. *Directions:* Located outside the town walls, at the east end of town near the junction of N4 and the road to Ajuda, on the way to Spain.

❄ ☕ 💳 🚶 🍴 🏊 🕴

POUSADA DE ELVAS–SANTA LUZIA
7350-097 Elvas, Portugal
Tel: 268.63.74.70, Fax: 268.62.21.27
25 rooms, Double: €115–€121
Open: all year
Credit cards: all major
Region: Planícies
www.karenbrown.com/portugal/pousadaelvas.html

Unlike most hotels in the Algarve which were built to accommodate the great influx of tourists, the Monte do Casal, a country house dating back to the 18th century, is a wonderful exception. The inn reflects the style of the region, with white walls, brown shutters, and heavy tiled roof. Eight acres with almond, olive, and fruit trees surround the small hotel and bougainvillea highlights the white walls, while in the garden is a lovely swimming pool. There are nineteen guestrooms-five suites, five deluxe rooms, three twin-bedded rooms and six, recently added garden rooms-all with en-suite bathrooms. All of the rooms have terraces where your breakfast is served, each with a view out over the countryside to the sea. You will probably hear a lot of English accents, as many British have been drawn to your gracious host, Bill Hawkins, who hails from England. It is no coincidence that he runs the hotel so professionally since he trained in both the Savoy and Claridges in London and worked at hotels in Switzerland and Bermuda. Mr Hawkins is also a trained chef and his meals (served outside on the terrace in summer and in the old coach house when days are nippy) are outstanding. However, the greatest attribute of this simple inn is Bill Hawkins himself-he has natural warmth and takes great care of his guests. *Directions:* From the IP1 take the Faro exit number 5 and follow signs to Estói. Once in Estói, follow the yellow Monte do Casal signs for 3 km to the hotel.

MONTE DO CASAL
Host: William Hawkins
Cerro do Lobo
Estói, 8000-661 Faro, Portugal
Tel: 289.99.15.03, Fax: 289.99.13.41
19 rooms, Double: €206–€288
Open: Feb 6 to Nov 20
Credit cards: all major
Region: Algarve
www.karenbrown.com/portugal/montedocasal.html

Located just a few kilometers outside the walled town of Estremoz, the Monte dos Pensamentos has a Moorish flavor—a one-story, whitewashed building with an arcade of arches forming a series of open porches across the front and minaret-like towers accenting the entrance. Dating back to the early 19th century, the home has been in Cristóvão Leitão's family for three generations. He and his charming wife, Teresa, completely renovated it and offer two apartments, two suites, and one double guestroom. Teresa has excellent taste and everything is beautifully decorated using pretty fabrics and attractive furnishings. Everything is appealing and of superior quality, including the modern bathrooms. If you are traveling with children, the apartments, with their well-equipped kitchenettes, would be a perfect choice. However, whichever room you choose, you will be pleasantly surprised at the exceptional value. Throughout the house are many family antiques—of special interest is the fabulous collection of antique plates that decorate the walls. To the left of the house is one of its most inviting features, a cobblestone terrace with little tables set out under the umbrella of shade trees. Adding to the charm are red geraniums in bright-blue pots and red bougainvillea lacing the white walls. A swimming pool sits in the grounds. *Directions:* It is on a small road behind the Galp gas station and has a Turismo Rural sign at the entrance.

P ≋

MONTE DOS PENSAMENTOS
Host: Cristóvão Leitão
Estrada da Estação do Amexial
7100 Estremoz, Portugal
Tel: 268.33.31.66, Fax: 268.33.24.09
5 rooms, Double: €60–€95
Meals upon special request
Open: all year
Region: Planícies
www.karenbrown.com/portugal/pensamentos.html

The Pousada de Estremoz has a rich history: In 1259 King Dom Afonso III, recognizing the strategic importance of the site near the Spanish border, commissioned the castle. In 1497 Dom Manuel I met Vasco da Gama here and entrusted him with the command of the armada that took him to India. In 1698, after a fire destroyed all but the Tower of the Three Crowns, João V had an armory built over the ruins. From the mid-19th to mid-20th century, the castle was a military barracks, then briefly a School of Industry and Commerce before being converted into one of Portugal's most outstanding pousadas. The enchantment begins as you cross the drawbridge and drive through the fortified portal into the picture-perfect walled village of Estremoz. It is just a bit farther up the hill to the castle. A grand marble staircase leads to high, wide hallways lined with beautiful antiques and an impressive collection of contador chests. The bedrooms are regal, each one unique, but all spacious, decorated in rich colors and sumptuously furnished with antiques and handsome reproductions. Views are either of the countryside and town, or over the interior garden courtyard. There is an inviting swimming pool snuggled in the pretty garden, sheltered by ancient stone walls. The restaurant, with its massive stone pillars and arched ceiling, offers excellent fare in a romantic setting. *Directions:* After entering Estremoz, follow well-marked signs to the pousada.

POUSADA DE ESTREMOZ–RAINHA SANTA ISABEL
7100-509 Estremoz, Portugal
Tel: 268.33.20.75, Fax: 268.33.20.79
33 rooms, Double: €182–€293
Open: all year
Credit cards: all major
Region: Planícies
www.karenbrown.com/portugal/pousadaestremoz.html

A captivating city, Évora rises clean and white from the Alentejo plains. Within its walls nestles the sumptuous Pousada de Évora-Lóios, originally a 15th-century private mansion, which was built on the ruins of the old Évora castle. Over the course of the centuries the mansion has been enlarged and embellished, at one time serving as a monastery for the Lóios monks, whose chapel (now privately owned) can still be seen flanking the pousada. The building was falling into ruin when it was rescued and restored to its former glory by converting it into an elegant pousada. Cool granite and marble arches around which are nestled the cozy sofas and chairs of the spacious lounge support soaring Gothic ceilings. An ornately carved, wide marble staircase leads upstairs to broad hallways and diminutive red-tiled bedrooms (the original monastic cells), charmingly furnished with hand-carved chestnut armoires and beds topped with crisp linen and white bedspreads. There is an extraordinary sitting room upstairs, intricately hand-painted from floor to ceiling and furnished with beautiful antiques. The glassed-in dining room, arranged around the interior garden cloister and whispering fountain, has tables tucked amidst slender, carved pillars. *Directions:* The way to the pousada is well marked within the city. It is just opposite the still-standing columns of the Roman Temple of Diana.

POUSADA DE ÉVORA–LÓIOS
Largo Conde de Vila Flor
7000-804 Évora, Portugal
Tel: 266.70.40.51, Fax: 266.70.72.48
32 rooms, Double: €177–€293
Open: all year
Credit cards: all major
Region: Planícies
www.karenbrown.com/portugal/pousadaevora.html

Évora is a stunning town of great charm and rich historical heritage with its many churches, mansions, palaces, and an exquisite Roman temple. The 16th-century mansion was the private home of a nobleman, but in 1892 it began to take paying guests, thus making it the first hotel in Évora. This handsome building is true to the Alentejan style with white walls and bright-yellow trim. After entering through a dark-green door, you climb a broad stone staircase bordered with yellow-and-blue-patterned tiles and accented by potted plants. The staircase sweeps up to a handsome gallery laced with wisteria, which looks out to the street through a cloister-like colonnade. Another door takes you into the reception area. The breakfast room is very attractive, with square tables and handsome wood-and-leather chairs, and guests also have the use of an old-fashioned-looking lounge and a cozy bar. Since this is an old mansion, the guestrooms vary in size and are located up and down a maze of hallways. All of the bedrooms have antique headboards and a few have recently been redecorated, but these are a bit smaller than some of those with the original furnishings. The Solar Monfalim is a simple hotel, but beautifully located, friendly, and an excellent value. *Directions:* Entering Évora, follow the green "Hotel" signs to the center of town then you will see signs for Solar Monfalim. Difficult to find, you will probably need to park and ask directions.

SOLAR MONFALIM
Manager: Ana Ramalho Serrabulho
Largo da Misericórdia, 1
7000-646 Évora, Portugal
Tel: 266.75.00.00, Fax: 266.74.23.67
26 rooms, Double: €60–€80
Open: all year
Credit cards: all major
Region: Planícies
www.karenbrown.com/portugal/solarmonfalim.html

The Pousada do Gerês-São Bento is a handsomely rustic, turn-of-the-century mountain lodge, tucked atop a hill overlooking the deep-blue waters of the Caniçada dam. Once a private hunting lodge, the ivy-draped, blue-shuttered, tan-stone building is now an exceptionally attractive pousada situated within the Peneda-Gerês National Park, one of Europe's most impressive nature reserves. Only the lounge and restaurant are to be found on the main floor, to either side of an open stone fireplace, which reaches up to a wood-beamed cathedral ceiling. The cozy lounge and tiny bar are furnished in wood and pale leather. The Swiss-style restaurant has fresh flowers on every table and floor-to-ceiling windows overlooking the lake surrounded by rich-green, terraced hillsides. An open stairway leads upstairs to the small, spotless bedrooms, with wood floors and four-poster single beds with leather headboards and brightly colored spreads. A few of the rooms also have handsome, varnished wood-plank ceilings. Most of the bedrooms overlook the courtyard and the tennis court, above which is a terrace with a large swimming pool and shaded tables. However, splurge and request one of the premium bedrooms that have small wood balconies and lovely views over the water. *Directions:* From Braga go east on N103. After about 28 km, turn left on N306 toward Caniçada and follow signs to the pousada.

❄ ☕ 💳 🏃 🍴 🏊 🏃

POUSADA DO GERÊS–SÃO BENTO
4850-047 Gerês–Caniçada, Portugal
Tel: 253.64.71.90, Fax: 253.64.78.67
29 rooms, Double: €126–€132
Open: all year
Credit cards: all major
Region: Costa Verde
www.karenbrown.com/portugal/pousadageres.html

Pousada de Guimarães–Nossa Senhora da Oliveira, built within in a series of renovated manor houses dating back to the 13th century, faces the cathedral in the enchanting heart of the old section of Guimarães, surrounded by narrow, pedestrian streets and stone-paved plazas. The main entrance—on a small lane to the side of the house—leads through the original granite-block-framed doorway and into the cozy wood-beamed and red-tiled reception area. The small inn is faithfully restored and the reception sets the tone for the decor throughout. The atmosphere is intimate and charmingly homelike with low, wood ceilings and handsome antique furniture lending authenticity to the feeling of going back several centuries in time. On the main floor are two sitting areas, a small bar, and a charming restaurant, which looks onto the cathedral square. The bedrooms are found on the two upper floors, each with a tiny lounge at the far end of the hall. The rooms have gleaming, dark hardwood floors and ceilings. The simple, regional-style furniture is of a natural wood, complemented by woven spreads, drapes, and rugs in natural colors. Wood-framed windows overlook the colorful, medieval streets lined with stone houses and flower-draped iron-and-wood balconies. If you're seeking comfort and historical ambiance in a central location, this pousada has it all. *Directions:* The pousada, located in the historic heart of Guimarães, is well marked.

POUSADA DE GUIMARÃES–
NOSSA SENHORA DA OLIVEIRA
Largo de Oliveira
4801-910 Guimarães, Portugal
Tel: 253.51.41.57, Fax: 253.51.42.04
15 rooms, Double: €126–€164
Open: all year
Credit cards: all major
Region: Costa Verde
www.karenbrown.com/portugal/pousadanossa.html

Pousada de Guimarães–Santa Marinha, a jewel, is romantically installed in the Convent of Santa Marinha da Costa, which dates back to the 12th century when the Saint Augustine order was founded by the wife of D. Afonso Henriques, Portugal's first king. This splendid whitewashed convent is flanked on one side by an exquisite twin-steepled stone church and on the other by a wing of rooms, carefully constructed to mimic the architecture of the original convent. The decor in the public rooms—an exciting blend of genuine antique and classy contemporary—results in elegant harmony. You can see premeditated concession to history in portions of the original stone wall that have been left exposed, and stone pillars, arches, and carved wood ceilings. The open interior cloister with its romantic stone fountain serves in warm weather as an enchanting bar. Behind the convent is a beautiful formal garden backing onto a wooded park. The bedrooms in the original convent, which have stone-framed windows and walls thick enough for window seats, offer more old-world ambiance than those in the newly constructed part of the hotel. Once cells for the monks, these are, however, rather small—although a few have been transformed into large, beautifully decorated suites. The newer bedrooms are spacious and attractive, with large blue-and-white tiled baths. *Directions:* Off the road to Penha, 3 km south of Guimarães, in the Penha National Park.

❄ ☕ 💳 🛗 🚶 🍽

POUSADA DE GUIMARÃES–SANTA MARINHA
4810-011 Guimarães, Portugal
Tel: 253.51.12.49, Fax: 253.51.44.59
51 rooms, Double: €159–€292
Open: all year
Credit cards: all major
Region: Costa Verde
www.karenbrown.com/portugal/pousadamarinha.html

A rocky headland overlooking a gorgeous stretch of beach and turquoise water on one side and out to the westernmost promontory in Europe on the other provided a strategic location for a fortress in times gone by and now an ideal setting for a hotel. This somewhat austere, amber-colored fortress dating from the 17th century stands bare against a backdrop of sea. A pair of canons flanks the heavy wooden door behind which is an open, central courtyard set with a clustering of sofas and chairs. A coat of arms designates the reception and sets the feudal theme. Down either side of the courtyard are the entrances to the ground-floor rooms, which are well appointed but small, with limited views through small windows and across a stretch of roof. Climb a turreted stair to the second-floor rooms, which enjoy small, enclosed terraces and better views. Based on your preference, request a view to the south over the beach or to the north of Cabo (Cape) da Roca. Three junior suites enjoy terraces and unobstructed ocean views. For a refreshment, settle into cozy leather chairs in the handsome bar or in the neighboring salon. The fort's most dramatic, elegant, and enticing room is its restaurant where tables set spaciously apart enjoy unobstructed ocean views out through large arched windows. The menu is superb—boasting French tradition and Portuguese specialties. *Directions:* From Cascais, leave town on the road that hugs the coastline, the N247.

FORTALEZA DO GUINCHO
Manager: Gabriel Lousada
Estrada do Guincho
Guincho, 2750-642 Cascais, Portugal
Tel: 21.48.70.491, Fax: 21.48.70.431
27 rooms, Double: €250–€385
Open: all year, Credit cards: all major
Relais & Châteaux
Region: Costa do Estoril
www.karenbrown.com/portugal/fortalezadoguincho.html

Quinta da Timpeira is a beautifully decorated, immaculately kept, skillfully run, reasonably priced bed and breakfast in a region brimming with fascinating sights. Your charming hosts, Isabel and Francisco, totally restored Francisco's mother's country home, adding rooms for guests. Isabel is an engineer, and I'm sure it was her skilled eye that gave the renovation such imagination. In the curved, contemporary wing added to the front of the house you find a cozy sitting nook where guests can relax before an open fireplace and a dining area with a handsome table set in front of a wall of windows. (There is a second, larger dining room in a separate house that used to be the caretaker's cottage.) Although prior reservations are needed, dinner is always available (and highly recommended). Handsome antique furniture, accented by pretty fabrics and bouquets of fresh flowers, soften and enhance all of the rooms. In addition to the main living room, there are several intimate parlors, a game room, and even a cute boutique selling handmade goods. In the garden are a swimming pool and tennis court. The price is excellent for the quality of accommodation and level of service—you will even enjoy evening turn down service. *Directions:* From the historic center of Lamego, take the old N2 south toward Viseu. After leaving town, go 2.5 km and turn left at the two signs indicating Quinta da Timpeira and Turismo Rural.

❄ ☕ ✗ 🏧 ☎ 🐴 P ≈ 🏃 ⚰ 🎨 🍇

QUINTA DA TIMPEIRA
Host: Francisco Parente
Lugar da Timpeira
5100 Lamego, Portugal
Tel: 254.61.28.11, Fax: 254.61.51.76
7 rooms, Double: €55–€75
Dinner available upon special request
Open: all year, Credit cards: all major
Region: Montanhas
www.karenbrown.com/portugal/quintadatimpeira.html

A beautiful 18th-century mansion, As Janelas Verdes is so personal, so homelike, it is hard to believe it is indeed a four-star hotel. You enter a tiny foyer with just a discreet reception area to your right to relieve your concern you might have accidentally entered a private residence. An arched doorway opens to a cozy parlor with a marble fireplace, an upright piano, walls an appealing whisper of pale yellow, and upholstered furniture in tones of deep wine-red. An old-fashioned, comfortable elegance abounds with nothing to disturb the feeling that you are an invited guest—even the bar is on the honor system. A house-party atmosphere prevails. In chilly weather, guests relax in the parlor, or in the library on the top floor with a view of the Tagus river, but on balmy days the favorite place to gather is on the romantic, cobblestoned patio with its high walls draped with ivy, a whimsical fountain with tiles of frolicking monkeys, and wrought-iron tables and chairs. No two guestrooms are alike, but each is handsomely decorated with antiques—the choice rooms are those overlooking the patio. Once the residence of the famous Portuguese novelist, Eça de Queirós, As Janelas Verdes today belongs to the talented Duarte Fernandes brothers who also own two other of Lisbon's most charming, intimate hotels—all are beautifully managed. *Directions:* The hotel is in the old part of the city— down from the Museum of Ancient Art.

AS JANELAS VERDES
Hosts: Cardoso & Fernandes families
Rua das Janelas Verdes, 47
1200-690 Lisbon, Portugal
Tel: 213.96.81.43, Fax: 213.96.81.44
29 rooms, Double: €165–€245*
*Breakfast not included: €12.50
Open: all year, Credit cards: all major
Region: Costa de Lisboa
www.karenbrown.com/portugal/asjanelasverdes.html

The intimate Hotel Britania has the same ownership as the Hotel Lisboa Plaza and also shares a similar, excellent location. It is just off the Avenida Liberdade, but on the opposite side of the tree-lined promenade from its sister hotel. Designed in 1944 by the famous Portuguese architect Cassiano Branco, the Hotel Britania was in its heyday quite grand (peek round from the lobby to see the original barber shop) but under past ownership had been "modernized" and the splendid marble columns in the lobby shrouded in dark wood paneling. Happily, the original ambiance has been restored. The dark paneling is now gone and the marble lobby is gently illuminated by a handsome, large, hand-blown glass chandelier. The lobby opens into a handsome bar. Gorgeous old parquet floors and beautiful ceiling murals have been uncovered and there is a wonderful and interesting display of historic, colonial heraldic shields. All of the guestrooms are similar in decor, and most have the same pleasing color scheme of deep rose and creamy yellow, which is repeated in the carpet, the bedspreads, and the draperies. All of the bedrooms have beautiful, marble tiled bathrooms. The cheerful breakfast room is especially attractive, with a skylight illuminating small tables surrounded by chairs upholstered in a pretty green pattern. The family-managed Hotel Britania extends a warm reception. *Directions:* In the heart of Lisbon, just off the Avenida Liberdade.

❄ ⚓ ✄ 💳 ☎ ♿ 🏃 🐎 ⛓ Y P 🖼 ⚓

HOTEL BRITANIA
Hosts: Alves de Sousa & Fernandes families
Rua Rodrigues Sampaio, 17
1150-278 Lisbon, Portugal
Tel: 213.15.50.16, Fax: 213.15.50.21
30 rooms, Double: €148–€225*
*Breakfast not included: €12.50
Open: all year, Credit cards: all major
Region: Costa de Lisboa
www.karenbrown.com/portugal/hotelbritania.html

For a delightful hotel in a fabulous location, the Lisboa Plaza is an excellent choice. It is not inexpensive, but its quality and service rivals, and its prices are lower, than Lisbon's deluxe hotels. The hotel is tucked on a small street, just steps from the Avenida Liberdade, Lisbon's premier promenade. From first glance the hotel is most appealing: the contemporary building has been given pizzazz and a traditional look by a row of green awnings running across the front, flowerboxes with clipped greenery, and windows with old-fashioned small panes instead of plate glass. You enter into a grand foyer which is elegant and serene, with light streaming through the windows and a beautiful cream-colored marble floor blending with walls of the same tone. Opening off this spacious foyer are the lounges, dining room, and bar. All the rooms are superbly decorated and maintain the same appealing ambiance of quiet, understated refinement. A relaxing, homelike ambiance is created by intimate sitting areas accented with beautiful fabrics, soft pastel colors, fine-quality furniture, handmade carpets, fresh flowers, and potted plants. Behind the bar a handsome bronze of a horse and jockey sets a sporting theme, which is continued by prints of racehorses on the walls. The guestrooms have all the amenities of a deluxe hotel and continue the same theme of good taste and pastel colors. *Directions:* In the heart of Lisbon, just off the Avenida Liberdade.

HOTEL LISBOA PLAZA
Host: Fernandes family
Avenida Liberdade/Travessa do Salitre, 7
1269-066 Lisbon, Portugal
Tel: 213.21.82.18, Fax: 213.47.16.30
106 rooms, Double: €148–€370*
*Breakfast not included: €12.50
Open: all year, Credit cards: all major
Region: Costa de Lisboa
www.karenbrown.com/portugal/hotellisboa.html

The Hotel Metropole is not a deluxe hotel, but its location, facing the Praça do Rossio, a beautiful square, can't be bettered at any price. The exterior is very attractive—a handsome, turn-of-the-century, five-story building with symmetrical windows on each floor opening to balconies accented with wrought-iron railings. You enter into a tiny foyer with solemn gray floors and walls, then a small elevator takes you up one floor to the reception area and the spacious lounge, which has a bar at one end and a row of windows opening onto the square. Also on this same floor is a breakfast room for guests. Throughout the hotel everything is neat and tidy, with a color scheme set by the attractive carpets, which are a deep rose with a subtle creamy-yellow pattern. The guestrooms have the same carpet and the same color scheme, which is repeated in the striped draperies. All the rooms have cream-colored walls and appealing, traditional-style headboards with matching dressing tables and bedside tables. Ask for one of the rooms on the second, third or fourth floor with a balcony facing the square—the view from these rooms is magical at night when the fountains dance under spotlights and the castle on the hill is gently illuminated. Some of the rooms at the end of the hallways (such as 58, but without a balcony) are larger and have especially dramatic views. *Directions:* In the heart of Lisbon, facing Praça do Rossio.

HOTEL METROPOLE
Manager: Clara Rodrigues
Praça do Rossio, 30
1100 Lisbon, Portugal
Tel: 213.46.91.66, Fax: 213.21.90.30
36 rooms, Double: €140–€160
Open: all year
Credit cards: all major
Region: Costa de Lisboa
www.karenbrown.com/portugal/metropole.html

The Fernandes family remodeled an 18th-century mansion, embraced by the gardens and stone walls of St. George's Castle, into an intimate 14-room hotel. This building was constructed on the site of the former Alcáçova Palace kitchens, which is why it is still known as the "Palacete das Cozinhas" (Kitchen Mansion). Solar do Castelo has an inviting courtyard entrance cooled by a fountain and the reception is reached by passing under a dramatic arched entry. The living room doubles as a breakfast room and bar and has an expanse of window overlooking the central courtyard. Of the fourteen guestrooms, eight are found in the old section and six in a newly constructed wing, which you reach along a windowed passageway over the entry. In the new part, four rooms enjoy balconies and overlook the courtyard. Air conditioning was installed at great expense, as it had to respectfully navigate the uncovered archeological foundations. Old tiles and stones were carefully removed, restored, and replaced for the traditional finishing touches. Classified as an Historic Building, the mansion has been beautifully restored and brought back to life by high-quality contemporary design and comforts. As parking is extremely difficult, management recommends taking a cab from the airport; picking up a rental car when you leave town. *Directions:* Located within the St. George Castle walls above the old town of Lisbon.

SOLAR DO CASTELO
Hosts: Cardoso & Fernandes families
Manager: Diogo Laranjo
Rua das Cozinhas, 2 (Ao Castelo)
1100-181 Lisbon, Portugal
Tel: 218.870.909, Fax: 218.870.907
14 rooms, Double: €165–€245*
*Breakfast not included: €12.50
Open: all year, Credit cards: all major
Region: Lisboa
www.karenbrown.com/portugal/solardocastelo.html

York House is a delightful hotel that exudes charm from the moment you enter to the last friendly smile on your departure. In between, you'll be treated to the hospitality that has been York's trademark for over a hundred years. Originally a 17th-century monastery, York House became the barracks of the Royal Guards when the Marquis of Pombal dissolved the monastic order. Since 1876, it has known French, British and, now, Portuguese ownership. At first glance, the simple façade doesn't hint at the cozy ambiance that awaits you within. From the street, a stone-paved, open staircase bound by ivy-covered walls leads up one floor. Here a romantic, pink-walled courtyard abounds with a profusion of flowers, trees, and plants—a refreshing contrast to the bustling street outside. From the courtyard you enter the hotel where—secreted off a maze of antique-lined hallways where handmade rugs accent polished floors—a very special bedroom awaits. Each of the tastefully decorated bedrooms varies in size and shape and has furnishings that lovingly preserve an old-world ambiance. The enchanting dining room, overlooking the garden courtyard, has walls accented with blue azulejos. Here you can enjoy set meals in a restaurant also open to the public. York is a popular oasis, so early reservations are advised. *Directions:* Located in an old, once-grand part of Lisbon, near the Museum of Ancient Art.

YORK HOUSE
Manager: Alda Leitao
Rua das Janelas Verdes, 32
1200 Lisbon, Portugal
Tel: 213.96.24.35, Fax: 213.97.27.93
31 rooms, Double: €190–€200*
*Breakfast not included: €14
Open: all year, Credit cards: all major
Region: Costa de Lisboa
www.karenbrown.com/portugal/york.html

The Estalagem Casa d' Azurara is a stately 18th-century manor that was built for the Earls of Mangualde—obviously a very prominent family since the medieval town carries its name. Because the entrance faces directly onto the road, it is a pleasant surprise to discover a beautiful large garden behind the house, which gives you the feeling of being in the country. From the moment you enter, there is the ambiance of a private home. Instead of one large lounge, there are several intimate, tastefully decorated parlors, conducive to chatting with friends. The bedrooms, continuing the same mood, are traditionally furnished with handsome wooden beds enhanced by matching bedspreads and draperies, and all offer direct-dial telephones, TVs with CNN, well-equipped bathrooms, and air conditioning. As an added bonus, the Casa d'Azurara has an excellent, cozy restaurant, renowned for its traditional cuisine. The decor here is extremely appealing, with small tables elegantly set with fine linens, and at the end of the room are floor-to-ceiling windows capturing the view of the lovely garden. *Directions:* Mangualde is located about 10 km east of Viseu. When you come into town, watch for signs to the hotel, which is located a few blocks from the center. If you get lost, anyone in town should be able to give directions.

ESTALAGEM CASA D'AZURARA
Host: José Maria A. Costa Cabral
Rua 78
3530 Mangualde, Portugal
Tel: 232.61.20.10, Fax: 232.62.25.75
15 rooms, Double: €87–€130
Open: all year
Credit cards: all major
Region: Montanhas
www.karenbrown.com/portugal/acurara.html

This is a rustic mountain retreat located in the heart of the dramatic Serra de Estrela. Constructed of austere native granite with a multi-level red-tile roof, the sturdy pousada strongly resembles a ski lodge and, indeed, the sport is pursued in the nearby Penhas da Saúde. In the summer, fishing and hiking are popular, due to the proximity of the River Mondego and the beautiful Vale do Rossim Lake. Inside, the pousada is unexpectedly pretty, with a charming Alpine flair. It seems fireplaces are strategically tucked in every nook and cranny—snugly flanked by comfy chairs and sofas upholstered in country fabrics. The attractive, casually inviting lounge has a cathedral ceiling of gleaming wood. The dining room, warmed by a central fireplace, is well known for its regional specialties and its fabulous panoramic view. When the weather is agreeable, guests also enjoy a stunning outlook from the terrace. The accommodations are appropriately simple and comfortable. The spotless, whitewashed bedrooms are attractively furnished with pale-wood four-poster twin beds. The second-floor rooms have tiny terraces with breathtaking views over the terraced, green mountainsides to the village below, while the main-floor rooms have windows overlooking the valley, although their vistas are not quite as dramatic. *Directions:* Located 13 switch-backed kilometers straight up from the picturesque whitewashed village of Manteigas.

POUSADA DE MANTEIGAS–SÃO LOURENÇO
Estrada de Gouveia
6260-200 Manteigas, Portugal
Tel: 275.98.24.50, Fax: 275.98.24.53
21 rooms, Double: €122–€124
Open: all year
Credit cards: all major
Region: Montanhas
www.karenbrown.com/portugal/pousadamanteigas.html

Marvão, with its narrow cobbled streets and sparkling white houses, is one of the most charming of the many such towns that cling to the tops of high hills overlooking the Spanish border. One of our favorite pousadas in Portugal is the Pousada do Marvão–Santa Maria, snuggled in the center of Marvão, but sometimes space isn't available there, so we were delighted to discover the reasonably priced Albergaria El Rei Dom Manuel. At first glance this white, two-story house with red-tiled roof seems of new construction, but photos on the walls in the reception area attest that indeed the shell of the hotel is, like its neighbors, very old, although inside everything is new. The floors are made of large squares of red tile and the white walls are decorated with many nicely framed pictures. There is no effort to make the interior look antique, yet the decor is most appealing. Good taste prevails throughout, with nothing flamboyant or modern—traditional, pretty fabrics and good-quality furniture provide a sweet country ambiance. The dining room is especially outstanding—a cozy room with pretty tablecloths that repeat the pattern of the drapes. The bedrooms are all similar with built-in headboards, good reading lights, pretty fabrics, and, of course, brand-new bathrooms. *Directions:* Easy to find—it faces directly onto the first small square (with parking available) that you come to after entering the gates of the town.

❄ ☕ ✄ 💳 ☎ ♿ 🚶 🐴 P ♙ ⛵ ♿

ALBERGARIA EL REI DOM MANUEL
Host: Manuel Joaquim Gaio
Largo do Terreiro
7330-122 Marvão, Portugal
Tel: 245.90.91.50, Fax: 245.90.91.59
15 rooms, Double: €60
Open: all year
Credit cards: MC, VS
Region: Planícies
www.karenbrown.com/portugal/elreidommanuel.html

Together with similar vantage points up and down the border, the hilltop town of Marvão, only 6 kilometers from Spain, was ringed with fortifications in the 14th century by King Dom Diniz. As you approach the village, rising like a fist from the Alentejo plains, it appears impregnable still. Within its ramparts is a sleepy pousada that, for over 20 years, has been offering travelers comfort, tranquility, and excellent meals in one of the most dramatic settings in Portugal. Inside, the decor imparts the flavor of a simple mountain lodge: the cozy lounge and restaurant have brick-red tile floors, wood-beamed sloped ceilings, and stone fireplaces. The pièce de résistance is the restaurant. Not only is it extremely attractively furnished, but also it is walled on three sides with windows capturing a truly awesome view. The endless panorama—stretching across the Serra de Marvão and into Spain—takes your breath away. All of the bedrooms are attractive with whitewashed walls, flowery bedspreads, and pretty wooden, regional-style furniture with decorative paintings. Only a handful of the bedrooms have a view, which is not nearly as dramatic as the vista from the public rooms. These "view rooms" are smaller as they are in the original part of the pousada, which was built into two very old houses. The rooms in the newer wing are more spacious. *Directions:* Drive into the walled village of Marvão and follow the arrows to the pousada.

❄ ☕ 💳 🚶 🍴

POUSADA DO MARVÃO–SANTA MARIA
7330-122 Marvão, Portugal
Tel: 245.99.32.01, Fax: 245.99.34.40
29 rooms, Double: €126–€172
Open: all year
Credit cards: all major
Region: Planícies
www.karenbrown.com/portugal/pousadamarvao.html

Vila Duparchy, nestled in a wooded park very close to the beautiful Buçaco Forest, makes an excellent choice for exploring this region so rich in military history. The manor was originally built by Jean Alexis Duparchy, a Frenchman involved in constructing the Beira Alta railroad, then purchased in 1895 by the Duarte de Figueiredo family who still own it today. You enter the property through a gate bound by two stone pillars then wind up the hill to the stately, salmon-colored manor with windows trimmed in white. The feeling is one of being in a private home—a mood enhanced by your gracious host family. The dining room is beautiful, with an intricately paneled ceiling and a crystal chandelier handsomely accenting an antique dining table. Breakfast is served in a sunny, glass-enclosed porch that stretches behind the house, overlooking the garden and pool. A graceful staircase with a pretty wood banister curves upstairs where the bedrooms open off a central hallway. Each bedroom is extremely attractive, with antique furniture, pretty fabrics, and large windows letting in plenty of light. Spacious room 2, with a four-poster bed and the only private balcony, and number 3, an equally large room with beautiful antique beds and an enormous bathroom, are favorites. *Directions:* From Coimbra take N1 north to the Mealhada exit #14 and then go east on N234 in the direction of Luso for 6 km. The entrance to the villa is on your left just before Luso.

VILA DUPARCHY
Host: Maria José Duarte de Figueiredo Principe Santos
Mealhada, 3050 Luso, Portugal
Tel: 231.93.07.90, Fax: 231.93.03.07
6 rooms, Double: €75
Dinner available upon special request
Minimum nights required: 2
Open: all year, Credit cards: AX
Region: Costa da Prata
www.karenbrown.com/portugal/viladuparchy.html

Perched on a hill overlooking the River Douro, the Pousada de Miranda do Douro is a contemporary square building made of blocks of granite. The river is quite interesting at this point because it is restricted by a narrow gorge, but just in front of the hotel it pools into a small lake formed by a dam. You are looking into Spain as you look across the river, which forms a natural border. Since this pousada is not set within a historical building, it does not offer any architectural interest, nor is there an antique ambiance within. However, the decor is pleasant and there is a nice lounge with a fireplace for nippy days. There is also a very appealing dining room with windows on two sides. Doors from the dining room open onto a terrace—a most inviting spot to have a drink while looking over to Spain. The bedrooms have the standard hotel look, with built-in headboards, good lighting, a writing desk, and, best of all, a balcony with a view of the river. The pousada is found in the newer part of town, but a few minute's walk takes you into another world. Part of Miranda do Douro is very old and many of the residents, whose families have lived here for generation after generation, speak their own language. Be sure to visit the gorgeous cathedral—well worth the stroll. *Directions:* As you drive into Miranda do Douro, the pousada is easy to find. It is located on the left side of the road just before it dips downhill toward the river.

❄ ☕ CREDIT 🚶 🍴

POUSADA DE MIRANDA DO DOURO–
SANTA CATARINA
5210 Miranda do Douro, Portugal
Tel: 273.43.10.05, Fax: 273.43.10.65
12 rooms, Double: €82–€119
Open: all year
Credit cards: all major
Region: Montanhas
www.karenbrown.com/portugal/pousadamiranda.html

Casa do Campo is a charming, 17th-century country manor in an unspoiled, beautiful area high up in the hills above the River Tâmega. This impressive two-story stone-and-stucco house is fronted by a wall enclosing a beautiful small Renaissance chapel where mass is still held. This is a very large estate and all the guestrooms are bright and inviting and each is individually furnished using handsome antiques. My favorite, a charming room with chairs upholstered in a pretty rose-patterned fabric that is repeated in the curtains, has windows on two sides overlooking the garden. However, even if the accommodations were not as lovely as they are, this country estate would be well worth a visit for its breathtaking gardens. I have never seen anything quite so unusual and quite so stunning. Terraced above the mansion is a fantasy land created by camellias, some dating back 200 years-it is said (and I believe it) that there is no other display of camellias quite like this anywhere in the world. Over the centuries the plants have been trained to form an intricate, magical world of covered pathways interspersed with lovely fountains and even whimsical houses whose roofs and walls are also made up of camellias. In another section of the garden is a splendid swimming pool. *Directions:* Located on the N210, about 2 km south of Fermil and 4 km north of Celorico de Basto. When making reservations, ask for a map.

CASA DO CAMPO
Host: Maria Armanda Meirles
Molares, 4890 Celorico de Basto, Portugal
Tel: 258.74.28.29, Fax: 258.74.14.44
8 rooms, Double: €75
Dinner available upon special request
Minimum nights required: 2
Open: all year, Credit cards: AX, VS
Region: Costa Verde
www.karenbrown.com/portugal/campo.html

Monsanto is considered one of the most authentic, unspoiled ancient villages in Portugal. Located on the fringe of the Spanish border it is tucked in a totally remote area that is accessible only (to be polite) by less-than-perfect roads. Archaeologists attest that man has been attracted here for thousands of years. It is no wonder, for Monsanto has both a mystical aura plus a fantastic, impregnable site. The town, full of narrow lanes and steep staircases, is built into a hillside that is scattered with unbelievably gigantic boulders, some of which seem to teeter precariously on narrow bases, ready to tumble down the hill at any moment. The homes, which are built of this same granite, seem to melt into the landscape. The top of the hill is dominated by the ruins of a 12th-century fortified castle, which offers a stupendous 360-degree view. One of the few new buildings in town is the Pousada de Monsanto. This is in no way a fancy hotel—in fact, it is very basic, but it is also very appropriate. A sophisticated hotel would seem to mock the simple nature of this unspoiled village. At the Pousada you will find friendly management, good, hearty food, modern bathrooms, comfortable, clean accommodations, and, best of all, a chance to explore Monsanto. *Directions:* Soon after you enter the town, there is a small parking area. The Pousada is just about a block up the hill from where you leave your car.

POUSADA DE MONSANTO
6060-091 Monsanto, Portugal
Tel: 277.31.44.71, Fax: 277.31.44.81
10 rooms, Double: €89–€94
Open: all year
Credit cards: all major
Region: Montanhas
www.karenbrown.com/portugal/pousadamonsanto.html

In the 14th century, King Dom Diniz had massive fortifications built on the hills bordering Spain, hoping to protect Portugal from her aggressive neighbor. The hilltop town of Monsaraz was one of these fortifications, and its walls still stand as testimony to the king's successful strategy. Now, with the threat of conflict long past Monsaraz lingers as a picturesque, sleepy, cobblestoned village, and the Estalagem de Monsaraz has a perfect location from which to explore its magic. Located at the entrance to the town, off a peaceful stone-paved square, the friendly estalagem offers the best accommodations in town. Though restored in 1970, the whitewashed inn—with its bright-blue-painted cornerstones, green door, red terra-cotta roof, and stone-framed windows—looks outside and in like a century-old house. All is dark and cozy within: low stone doorways lead to the wood-beamed lounge and appealing restaurant warmed by an open fireplace and decorated with cowbells and colorful antique plates. Some of the bedrooms are in the main building, up the back stairs, while others are behind the hotel, next to the swimming pool terraced against the rocks. Some of these have a pretty view overlooking the surrounding countryside. All are outfitted in rustic, carved regional wood furniture and have beds topped with woven spreads. *Directions:* Just at the entrance into the town, a sign to the right directs you to the hotel.

ESTALAGEM DE MONSARAZ
Largo de São Bartolomeu
7200 Monsaraz, Portugal
Tel: 266.55.71.12, Fax: 266.55.71.01
12 rooms, Double: €84–€172
Open: all year
Credit cards: all major
Region: Planícies
www.karenbrown.com/portugal/monsaraz.html

The Hotel Rural Horta da Moura is snuggled in the rolling hills that stretch below the stunning walled village of Monsaraz and at first sight looks like one of the charming small whitewashed villages that dot the Alentejo. It has been built in the regional style with crisp white buildings prettily accented around the door and windows with bright blue. The dining room is very attractive and rustically elegant, with tables set with fine linens, beamed ceilings, red-tiled floor, wooden chairs, and colorful plates decorating the walls. The food is excellent, featuring traditional regional specialties and the finest Alentejan wines. The bedrooms stretch out in wings on both sides of the reception area, and there are more near the swimming pool. They are especially attractive with whitewashed walls, red-tiled floors, handsome high-backed wooden beds, and bedspreads with a homespun look. Many rooms also have a fireplace. There is a sophisticated, rustic ambiance enhanced by all the deluxe comforts of a fine hotel. Request a superior room—these are exceptionally spacious. Tennis is available and there is a stable of horses on the property. A horse-drawn buggy for five persons can be rented by the hour—what fun it would be to explore this lovely countryside in such a leisurely manner! *Directions:* Starting from the gate of Monsaraz, drive down the hill. Where the road splits, turn right and follow the signs to the hotel.

HOTEL RURAL HORTA DA MOURA
Manager: Francisco Zambo Jinito
7200 Monsaraz, Portugal
Tel: 266.55.01.00, Fax: 266.55.01.08
26 rooms, Double: €85–€175
Open: all year
Credit cards: all major
Region: Planícies
www.karenbrown.com/portugal/moura.html

The Quinta da Capela is sheer enchantment—a superb opportunity to slip back many centuries in time. This fabulous quinta dates back to the 16th century, but was rebuilt in 1773 and became the farm of a wealthy nobleman. The home is magnificent, with thick white walls, vaulted ceilings, fine furniture, many superb oil paintings, and hand-loomed carpets accenting red-tiled floors. Fabulous antiques are used throughout, though nothing is stiff or contrived—there is a homelike ambiance and genuine warmth of welcome. The comfortable lounge, where guests gather in the evening after fixing themselves a drink at the honor bar, is especially inviting. Beyond the lounge is a lovely breakfast room, bright and cheerful with pink-and-black harlequin marble floors. The sun streams through windows on two sides. The bedrooms continue the mood of being in a private home and each is individual in decor and beautifully furnished in antiques. Seven of the bedrooms are in the main house, while the others are suites in separate cottages. Surrounding the house are magnificent gardens with clipped hedges and even swans floating gracefully on the pond. If you fall in love with the Quinta da Capela, you will be fascinated to know that your charming hosts have opened another bed and breakfast in Brazil. *Directions:* On the road to Monserrate, about 3 km from Sintra. The entrance is on the right, marked with the name and two stone columns.

QUINTA DA CAPELA
Hosts: Arthuro Pereira & Marc Zürcher
Road to Monserrate
Monserrate, 2710 Sintra, Portugal
Tel: 219.29.01.70, Fax: 219.29.34.25
10 rooms, Double: €150–€195
Closed: Christmas
Credit cards: all major
Region: Costa de Lisboa
www.karenbrown.com/portugal/quintadacapela.html

The Atlantic stretches a long finger of water inland at Aveiro, and it is after this lagoon, or ria, that this pousada is named. Pousada do Murtosa/Torreira-Ria opened with only nine rooms, but due its popularity, more were added. The small wood-and-stone inn has a modern flavor inside and out. It is built smack on the water's edge, so briny sea air and the sound of gently lapping waves are constant company. Its isolated location, between São Jacinto and Torreira on the opposite shore of the lagoon from Aveiro, ensures peace and quiet. The multi-leveled, expansive lounge and lobby are sleek and shiny. Next to the pousada is a small pool. Sliding glass doors lead from the dining room to a long, sunny outdoor terrace over the water, where colorful boats glide by bearing the products of the ria: salt, algae, and fish. All of the bedrooms share the view of the calm, blue inlet from balconies just large enough for a breakfast table. The rooms are neither spacious nor luxurious, but are comfortably and simply furnished in blonde, wicker-like wood and accented with flower-print spreads and drapes. The pousada is extremely popular and offers a tranquil refuge. *Directions:* From A1, take the Aveiro exit and go toward Aveiro. Turn right at the first road, N109. After 8 km, turn left at Estarreja and continue straight to where the road crosses over the lagoon and turn left. The pousada is on the main road south of Torreira.

※ ⚓ ▣▦ 👫 ¶ 🏊 🏃

POUSADA DO MURTOSA/TORREIRA–RIA
Murtosa, 3870-301 Torreira, Portugal
Tel: 234.86.01.80, Fax: 234.83.83.33
19 rooms, Double: €135–€185
Open: all year
Credit cards: all major
Region: Costa da Prata
www.karenbrown.com/portugal/pousadamurtosa.html

Casa de Sezim is conveniently located near Guimarães, and although urbanization is slowly advancing, the property is surrounded by a large estate and thus exudes a tranquil country ambiance. The handsome salmon-colored, 16th-century mansion is owned by António Pinto de Mesquita, and it has been in his family "forever." The house was used primarily in the summer, but when Mr Pinto de Mesquita retired from his travels with the diplomatic service, he returned to his estate and made many improvements, including the installation of central heating. He also returned to the family tradition of wine production and today his two sons carry on the business (one of his sons is now also in the foreign service). Each of the bedrooms, eight with private bathrooms, is individually decorated with antiques that have been passed down through the generations. Nothing is contrived or decorator-perfect—instead, Casa de Sezim has the feeling of a friend's home. Downstairs there is a series of parlors with so many paintings and murals that it is almost like a museum—however, Mr Pinto de Mesquita quickly corrected me that this is no museum, but a home to be lived in and enjoyed. *Directions:* From Guimarães take the N105 toward Santo Tirso. Two kilometers after leaving Guimarães, turn right at a tiny sign marked Santo Amaro. In about 2.5 km the casa is on your left.

CASA DE SEZIM
Host: António Pinto de Mesquita
Santo Amaro
Nespereira, 4800 Guimarães, Portugal
Tel: 258.74.28.29, Fax: none
9 rooms, Double: €100–€120
Dinner available upon special request
Minimum nights required: 2
Open: all year, Credit cards: all major
Region: Costa Verde
www.karenbrown.com/portugal/sezim.html

This beautiful inn, set against a backdrop of the crowning castle, is a welcome haven from the crowds that this picturesque village attracts. Casa d' Óbidos is a charming complex: white-stucco buildings with orange-tiled roofs are blissfully surrounded by gorgeous gardens and a delightful pool. Guestrooms are housed in three buildings: the main building, the loft, and the cottage. In the main building off a lovely high-ceilinged corridor, doors open onto guest salons, a spacious breakfast room, and guest accommodations. The cottage, a complete house with two charming bedrooms, kitchenette, and living rooms, would be a perfect retreat for families or traveling friends. The loft, a spacious apartment with its own kitchen, can accommodate two people. Settle in and make Casa d'Óbidos your home base for exploring the region. This is not a typical bed and breakfast—the Sarmentos are gracious hosts and they also employ a staff to anticipate your needs. The property is large enough that one feels one can come and go with some anonymity. While Mrs Sarmento speaks wonderful English, Fernando communicates with a smile. *Directions:* From Óbidos look down to the equally dramatic, six-sided, 18th-century Sanctuary of Our Lord Jesus of the Stone. Follow the road to the sanctuary and just past it turn left, following signs to the Casa d' Óbidos.

CASA D'ÓBIDOS
Hosts: Fernando & Helena Campos Sarmento
Quinta de San José
2510-135 Óbidos, Portugal
Tel: 262.95.09.24, Fax: 262.95.99.70
6 rooms, Double: €75–€120, 2 apartments
Minimum nights required: 2
Open: all year
Credit cards: all major
Region: Costa da Prata
www.karenbrown.com/portugal/casadobidos.html

Our favorite hotel inside the walls of medieval Óbidos, the Estalagem do Convento, was originally an early-19th-century convent. It was converted in the 20th century to a modest hostelry. It enjoys a relatively peaceful street-front location slightly removed from, but within easy walking distance of, the center of town. It also boasts the only really good restaurant in Óbidos, whose charming decor—heavy wood-beamed ceiling, red-tile floor and open stone fireplace—promises a pleasurable dining experience whether or not you are a guest in the hotel. As the popularity of Óbidos has grown, more rooms have been added to meet the needs of more tourists. Several of these have fabulous views of the city and castle. Although every room guarantees traditional flavor, only five are found in the original convent building, their beautifully preserved wood ceilings and unusual dimensions making them the most appealing. All of the bedrooms have high ceilings, textured whitewashed walls, tile floors, painted wrought-iron beds, and traditional dark-wood furniture. There is a sitting room upstairs with fireplace, a cozy bar open to the public, and an interior garden patio where guests can dine in fine weather. For simple, old-fashioned comfort and exceptionally friendly management, this inn offers an excellent value. *Directions:* Located just outside the walls on a small street that traces the eastern edge of the village.

ESTALAGEM DO CONVENTO
Host: Luis de Sousa Garcia
Rua Dom Joao de Ornelas
2510 Óbidos, Portugal
Tel: 262.95.92.17, Fax: 262.95.91.59
31 rooms, Double: €85–€114
Open: all year
Credit cards: all major
Region: Costa da Prata
www.karenbrown.com/portugal/doconvento.html

The enchanting hilltop white town of Óbidos rises from the plains and is crowned by a massive stone castle, which was constructed in the 13th century by King Dom Diniz on top of a Moorish site. In the 15th century a palace was installed within the castle walls, but in 1755 both palace and castle were severely damaged by an earthquake. After extensive restoration, a pousada now stands on the site of the ruined palace, surrounded by ancient ramparts interspersed with dramatic crenellated towers. The public rooms are distinctly medieval in decor, with high stone ceilings, burnished red-tile floors, and dark antiques—even a suit of armor. On the main floor are a wood-beamed lounge and a bar with worn, comfortable armchairs. Upstairs another sitting room with open stone fireplace and an elegant dining room overlook the courtyard through arched, stone-framed windows. Narrow hallways lead to six small, wood-ceilinged bedrooms with surprisingly uninspired furnishings, the beds topped with brightly flowered spreads. However, the three suites, installed in the dark rampart towers, are richly decorated with antiques and loaded with historical ambiance. These are more expensive and have somewhat inconvenient floor plans. *Directions:* Inside the village walls at its north end. Signs direct you to the parking outside the castle walls—from there walk through an interior stone courtyard to check in and send someone back for luggage.

POUSADA DE ÓBIDOS–CASTELO
Paço Real
2510 Óbidos, Portugal
Tel: 262.95.91.05, Fax: 262.95.91.48
9 rooms, Double: €177–€237
Open: all year
Credit cards: all major
Region: Costa da Prata
www.karenbrown.com/portugal/pousadaobidos.html

Many of the quintas in the Algarve are simple farmhouses, but not the Quinta das Barradas—this enchanting white home features many extra adornments such as handsome balustrades and carved stone embellishments above the doors and windows. As you approach, the structure looks like one very grand home enhanced by beautiful gardens, but you soon realize that actually this is a complex of farm buildings renovated to create a harmonious small hotel brimming with charm. What is so special is that the buildings have been integrated so cleverly that many terraces and secret hideaways have been formed where guests can relax in seclusion. Many of the guestrooms have a terrace or a balcony looking out across the countryside. The bedrooms are very charming and true to the nature of the house with simple, attractive wooden furniture appropriate for a country home. Another bonus is that wonderful meals, using organic produce fresh from the garden, always available. It is no wonder that this quinta is so outstanding—it is owned by the extremely warm and gracious Wild family, professional hoteliers who also own the deluxe Romantik Hotel Vivenda Miranda a few kilometers away. *Directions:* From the center square of Odiáxere, turn north. A road goes off to the left toward Barragem, but keep to your right towards Arão. Go over a small bridge and take the first road to your left, which ends at the quinta.

QUINTA DAS BARRADAS
Hosts: Vera & Urs Wild
Odiáxere, 8600 Lagos, Portugal
Tel: 282.77.02.00, Fax: 282.77.02.09
16 rooms, Double: €98
Meals available for guests only
Open: all year
Region: Algarve
www.karenbrown.com/portugal/barradas.html

Casa das Torres de Oliveira is a splendid manor, dating from the early part of the 18th century, gloriously positioned on a hillside in a narrow valley that winds down to the River Douro. Vineyards lace the countryside as far as the eye can see, with nothing commercial or modern to disturb the idyllic setting. This was obviously an estate of great importance, undoubtedly dedicated to the production of port wine, which made many landowners wealthy. There are two square towers flanking the beautiful two-story mansion—thus the name "das Torres." As you wind down from the street and park your car, you will immediately notice that everything is neat and well kept and you see down to your left a gorgeous swimming pool snuggled amongst fields of grapes. You enter into a large reception hall with massive stones used for the flooring. Stairs lead up to the bedrooms, each large and decorated with antiques. All of the rooms are inviting, but one is truly stunning—the romantic room in the tower which is exceptionally large and has windows looking out in two directions over the vineyards. *Directions:* From Peso da Régua, take N108 west along the north bank of the Douro. Soon after passing the village of Caldas de Moledo (before arriving at Mesão Frio), turn inland at a blue Turismo de habitaçao sign and also a sign with the name of the hotel. Go 3 km and the house is on your left.

■▬ ▣ P ≈

CASA DAS TORRES DE OLIVEIRA
Host: José António Sousa Faria Girão Herdeiros
Oliveira, 5040 Mesão Frio, Portugal
Tel: 254.33.67.43, Fax: 254.33.61.95
4 rooms, Double: €100
Dinner available upon special request
Minimum nights required: 2
Open: Apr to Oct, Credit cards: AX
Region: Montanhas
www.karenbrown.com/portugal/oliveira.html

Climb the winding road up from the town of Ourém to its castle and inside its walls to the Conde de Ourém. Accommodation is in three buildings with 15th-century origins, commissioned by Dom Alfonso, the 4th Count of Ourém. The Pousada's reception is set behind whitewashed walls and wrought-iron gates, off a cobbled courtyard adorned with an artistic assortment of clay pots. The interior decor uses clean, modern furnishings and appointments that contrast with whitewashed walls and tile floors, and plain windows that frame the surrounding countryside and village rooftops. Regardless of location, guestrooms all have built-in pine headboards with complementing side tables and side chairs. However, in the main building, be sure to request either 213, 214, or 215—rooms that enjoy their own private terrace balcony (at no extra charge). The ground-floor rooms embraced within the walls of the old church are a bit more spacious and in the pool building the nicest rooms are those whose views drop off to the valley below. Public areas in the main building include a first-floor bar-salon and outdoor terrace set with tables shaded by white umbrellas, and an attractive, modern restaurant. In the church building a sitting area is dramatically set under the old arched entry and in the pool building you can settle at a small bar next to the pool where views stretch endlessly over the countryside. *Directions:* From Ourém follow signs to the castle above.

❄ ☕ CREDIT ♛ ‖ ≋

POUSADA DE OURÉM–CONDE DE OURÉM
2940 Ourém, Portugal
Tel: 249.54.09.20, Fax: 249.54.29.55
30 rooms, Double: €115
Open: all year
Credit cards: all major
Region: Costa da Prata
www.karenbrown.com/portugal/pousadaourem.html

The Quinta da Alcaidaria-Mór offers genuine warmth of welcome and a quinta brimming with charm and history. Amazingly, the home has been in the same family for over 300 years. The original owner was the king's personal physician and, as thanks for his years of loyal service, the king gave him the property and also a noble title. Your gracious hostess, Sra. Vasconcelos, raised seven children and—as might be expected with her experience—is an expert in managing a household with gentle efficiency. She is ably assisted by her daughter, Rosário, and together they make a great team, welcoming guests as visiting friends. There are six guestrooms, two garden suites and a cottage, all prettily decorated in a fresh, uncluttered style, with beautiful antique beds and a few fine pieces of furniture. My favorite bedrooms are upstairs, just off the guest sitting room, which have an appealing English-country look with shuttered windows accented by sheer white curtains, and pretty rose-patterned fabric repeated on the bedspreads, drapes, and upholstered chairs. There is a also a lovely pool in the garden. *Directions:* From the A1, follow signs to Ourém. Go through town and continue for about 2.5 km to where the road splits (the left branch is marked to Seiça and the right to Tomar). Almost in the middle of the intersection, on the left side of the road, there is an entrance that leads through a row of trees to the house.

QUINTA DA ALCAIDARIA–MÓR
Host: Vasconcelos Alvaiàzere family
2490 Ourém, Portugal
Tel: 249.54.22.31, Fax: 249.54.50.34
6 rooms, Double: €90–€115, 2 suites & 1 cottage
Dinner available upon special request
Open: all year
Region: Costa da Prata
www.karenbrown.com/portugal/alcaidariamor.html

The Pousada de Palmela, built within the walls of a dramatic fortification of Moorish origins, has a terrific hilltop setting. Installed in the 15th-century Monastery of Saint James (commissioned by King João I) and facing Palmela's enchanting 12th-century castle, the pousada is the essence of elegance and serenity. Verdant cultivated countryside surrounds its 250-meter-high position, guaranteeing panoramic vistas from every room. Inside, the focal point is its sun-drenched central cloister, enclosed by a symmetrical parade of stone arches. Light falls through the arcade onto broad, pale-stone hallways, furnished with natural leather armchairs for lounging beneath the vaulted ceilings. Upstairs you find the large, airy bedrooms, their decor a perfect mingling of old and modern. The floors are richly tiled in wine-red, the deep stone windows wood-framed and shuttered. The bedspreads and floor-to-ceiling drapes are cream-colored with subdued earth-tone accents, and woven from rough native material. A soft-leather armchair and simple, regional wood furniture round out the picture of comfort. The spacious bathrooms are colorfully tiled. Quite popular, room 109, is a corner room with sensational views. As for dining, the kitchen has a reputation for fine regional cuisine, and the restaurant occupies the former refectory. *Directions:* Take the Palmela exit from the A2. After leaving the expressway, the route to the pousada is well marked.

POUSADA DE PALMELA–CASTELO DE PALMELA
2950-997 Palmela, Portugal
Tel: 212.35.12.26, Fax: 212.33.04.40
28 rooms, Double: €159–€216
Open: all year
Credit cards: all major
Region: Costa de Lisboa
www.karenbrown.com/portugal/pousadapalmela.html

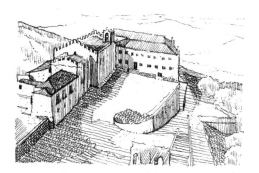

Casa de Casal de Loivos is an absolute treasure. It is more like an enchanting small hotel than a bed and breakfast, expertly run with three maids to pamper the guests, plus a full-time cook. Although there is no restaurant guests can enjoy a delicious dinner, (upon request) using old family recipes. The meal is often like a house party, served family-style around an antique table, sharing outstanding food and wines. Light lunches are graciously served to those who wish to take a day off from sightseeing (very tempting with the gorgeous swimming pool on the terrace). Manuel Bernardo de Sampayo, whose family has owned the house since the 17th century, speaks excellent English and is the epitome of the perfect host, exuding a sophisticated gentility and a genuine welcome. The attractive guestrooms are prettily furnished and have excellent bathrooms, marvelous views, and French doors opening out onto terraces. Perhaps the most outstanding feature of this house is its setting: perched in the hills above the River Douro, it has a panoramic view of vineyards in intricate patchwork designs terracing steeply down the hillside to the river, which loops through the canyon far below. *Directions:* From Pinhão, take N322 toward Alijó for 1 km, then turn right at the sign for Casal de Loivos. After 6 km, you will recognize the house on the right by the fancy grillwork on the windows and the dark-green door.

CASA DE CASAL DE LOIVOS
Host: Manuel Bernardo de Sampayo
Casal de Loivos
5085 Pinhão, Portugal
Tel & fax: 254.73.21.49
6 rooms, Double: €90
Dinner available upon request: €23
Closed: Jan
Region: Montanhas
www.karenbrown.com/portugal/casadecasal.html

The Douro River Valley is absolutely gorgeous: steep hillsides terraced with vineyards and dotted by white villages reflect in the sweeping, broad river below. Set right on the river's edge you find Vintage House, a first-class hotel cleverly constructed so that all the rooms enjoy the water views. The first building off the parking lot is the Lodge, and serves as a tasting room. Continue on as the reception area is found down the cobbled drive. The hotel has two restaurants. The first, located beneath the lodge, is where breakfast and set-menu dinners are served. The second is quite elegant and is where one would settle for lunch or an à-la-carte meal. Spacious public rooms include the library bar, found in oldest part of the hotel. This is very attractive, with lovely furnishings set against old stone walls and under old beams. Climb a circular stair from the library to the bedrooms, which are all very similar in their traditional, elegant decor and luxurious appointments. While all rooms enjoy balconies, the suites are lovely with their own separate sitting areas and double the terrace area of the other rooms. Of the standard guestrooms there are three that are exceptional: on the third floor, topping the original core of the hotel, rooms 301, 302, and 303 all enjoy the best views and their own rooftop terraces. *Directions:* Vintage House is on the River Douro in the shadow of the bridge in the small riverside village of Pinhão.

❄ ☕ ✂ CREDIT ☎ 👫 🚶 👫 P ⑪ ≈ 🚶 🖼 🚤 🐾 🎿 🍇

VINTAGE HOUSE
Manager: Manuel Marques
Lugar da Ponte
5085-034 Pinhão, Portugal
Tel: 254.73.02.30, Fax: 254.73.02.38
43 rooms, Double: €155–€284
Open: all year, Credit cards: all major
Relais & Châteaux
Region: Montanhas
www.karenbrown.com/portugal/vintagehouse.html

This family home is a very elegant manor house that is a wonderful example of the finer homes of the Minho area. The oldest part of Casa da Lage dates to the 16th century, with the more dramatic towers and spanning wing having been added in the 18th century. Each of the grand public rooms is lavishly furnished and has very ornate ceilings, typical of the region, with magnificent carvings including the family coat of arms. Advance reservations are required for the very elegant dining room. The breakfast room, on the ground level of the main house, is a large room with tables set under stone arches and wood beams. Guestrooms are found on the first floor of the main house and in the pool annex off the side lawn. In the main house the rooms are referred to as Tower Rooms I, II, III, and IV, the most dramatic being I, which opens onto the garden terrace and has a handsome, antique, exquisitely ornate four-poster bed. The other three are attractive and more traditional. The six rooms in the pool house, which are more standard in furnishings, enjoy a spacious and very pretty living room with a door opening onto the lawn. *Directions:* Cross the bridge from Ponte de Lima on the N202 in the direction of Viano do Castelo. After passing the town of Bertiandos and a small bridge over the River de Estoraos, turn right at a road sign for Arcos and travel 1.5 km to the entrance of Casa da Lage on the right.

CASA DA LAGE
Host: José Adolfo Coelho da Costa Azevedo
4990 Ponte de Lima–Arcos, Portugal
Tel: 258.73.14.17, Fax: 258.73.39.08
10 rooms, Double: €100
Dinner available upon special request
Minimum nights required: 2
Open: all year, Credit cards: all major
Region: Costa Verde
www.karenbrown.com/portugal/casadalage.html

For a convenient location, the Casa do Arrabalde wins the prize, just steps from the superb Roman bridge that spans the river in the heart of the colorful town of Ponte de Lima. For dinner you don't need a car at all, just walk across the bridge and you have a good selection of places to eat. This town is still graced by many fine old manor houses and the Casa do Arrabalde is typical of these, with a white exterior, black wrought-iron trim, and red-tiled roof. The main home, where the three bedrooms are located, faces directly onto the street with just a hedge separating it from the road. However, the property is much larger than it looks at first glance: it has a very large garden filled with fruit trees which stretches back to a second house, also owned by the Maia e Castro family. The house is rich in history and the present owners are direct descendents of the Abreu Maia family who built the house in 1729. As in many of these wealthy homes, the estate had its own private chapel, which is still in use-the current owners were married and their child baptized here. The three bedrooms and the two apartments are all very attractive and furnished in antiques. *Directions:* From the main part of town, cross the Roman bridge and turn left. The house is in the first block on your right. When making reservations, ask for a map.

CASA DO ARRABALDE
Host: Francisco Maia e Castro
4900 Ponte de Lima–Arcozelo, Portugal
Tel: 258.74.24.42 or 96.251.86.09, Fax: 258.742.516
3 rooms, Double: €75–€100, 2 apartments
Minimum nights required: 2
Open: all year
Credit cards: AX
Region: Costa Verde
www.karenbrown.com/portugal/casadoarabalde.html

The Casa do Outeiro (the first manor in the area to open its doors to tourism by taking in guests) is an especially lovely property. Although it is only 2 kilometers from Ponte de Lima, once you drive through the stone gateway, you enter an oasis of peace and tranquility. In summer the front of the home is partially hidden behind the lacy leaves of a magnificent stand of massive chestnut trees that dot the front terrace. The house is a two-story white building with giant granite pillars forming a porch in front. Dating back to the 16th century, the home has a colorful history, including a period in the early 1800s when it was confiscated by the French army and used as their headquarters. The bedrooms, all furnished in family antiques, are large and very attractive. My favorites were the two bedrooms on the ground floor with windows opening out to a lovely side garden. One of the most outstanding features of the house is its magnificent kitchen, which looks as though it should be featured in Architectural Digest. The kitchen is original to the house and has a massive, walk-in fireplace dominating one complete wall, copper and brass cookware on the walls, a beautiful antique dining table accenting a stone floor, and a lovely wood ceiling. *Directions:* When making reservations, ask for a map.

☕ 💳 P

CASA DO OUTEIRO
Host: João Gomes d'Albeu e Lima
4900 Ponte de Lima–Arcozelo, Portugal
Tel: 258.74.28.29, Fax: none
3 rooms, Double: €75
Dinner available upon special request
Minimum nights required: 2
Open: all year
Credit cards: AX, VS
Region: Costa Verde
www.karenbrown.com/portugal/outeiro.html

The Quinta do Sabadão is an enchanting 17th-century manor house located only about a 20-minute walk from the heart of Ponte de Lima. You will be captivated both by the charm of the accommodations and your gracious hostess's genuine warmth of welcome. A whimsical white wall, accented by windows with handsome stone trim, separates the mansion from the road. The entrance is through a fancy carved-stone gateway, which was "newly" added in the 18th century and still bears the family coat of arms (the property has been in the same family forever). You step through the gate into an inner courtyard romantically shaded by a leafy canopy of grapevines. Family-owned vineyards stretch out in the surrounding well-kept fields. Mrs Lima e Fonseca lives in one section of the mansion and has turned the facing wing into guest accommodations. Each of her three bedrooms is lovingly furnished with antiques and is as pretty as can be-my favorite was the one with an incredible antique sleigh-style double bed. In addition to the three double rooms, there are also two apartments in an old water mill. *Directions:* Quinta do Sabadão is located 2 km north of Ponte de Lima, signposted off N202 in the direction of Arcos de Valdevez. When making reservations, ask for a map.

QUINTA DO SABADÃO
Host: Maria Eulália Abreu Lima e Fonseca
4900 Ponte de Lima–Arcozelo, Portugal
Tel: 258.74.28.29, Fax: none
3 rooms, Double: €75, 2 apartments
Minimum nights required: 2
Open: all year
Credit cards: AX, VS
Region: Costa Verde
www.karenbrown.com/portugal/sabadao.html

Set amongst vineyards within the sound of church bells, the Casa da Várzea is a simple and appealing country farmer's home. On the first floor, behind thick stone walls, the entry, bar, and four guestrooms are invitingly cool in the summer heat. The honor bar is intimate and guests are welcome to taste the local vinho verde. Guestrooms, simply furnished with small beds and minimal seating areas, are found in rooms that were once associated with the harvest: crushing room, premier cellar, second cellar, and granary. Climb the stairway off the entry, handsome under its Minho ceiling and hung with the family coat of arms, to two sitting rooms, one very casual with books and a television, the second a bit more formal under another Minho ceiling, with views across the hills to Spain. Off the sitting room is an attractive front corner room with a cherry sleigh bed and off the hallway is a pretty room with a double bed whose shuttered windows open onto vineyard views. A pleasant dining room with a handsome trestle table, grandfather clock, and fireplace is used both for breakfast and as the place to gather on winter evenings. *Directions:* From the A3 take the Ponte de Lima exit and travel towards Ponte da Barca for about 8 km. After the square in Sao Martinho da Gandra turn right on the road signed to Beiral do Lima. Follow this road, winding upwards past a church, and after about 100 meters you find a small sign to the Casa da Várzea.

CASA DA VÁRZEA
Host: Inãcio Barreto Caldas da Costa
4990 Ponte de Lima–Beiral do Lima, Portugal
Tel: 258.94.86.03, cellphone: 968.202072
Fax: 258.94.84.12
6 rooms, Double: €75
Minimum nights required: 2
Open: all year, Credit cards: AX, VS
Region: Costa Verde
www.karenbrown.com/portugal/casadavarzea.html

The Paço de Calheiros is one of the most spectacular noble homes in the region of Ponte de Lima, which abounds with fabulous old mansions. You will see the imposing stone-and-plaster palace encircled by grapevines as you ascend approximately 2 kilometers up a tree-lined lane to its grand stone entrance gate. The property has been in the same family since 1336 when King Dom Diniz granted it to them. The present owner, Count Francisco Lopes de Calheiros, was one of the first to open his home to guests and is now president of the Solares association (a membership of some of Portugal's finest bed and breakfasts). His stunning property is exquisitely restored and maintained. A fountain plays in front and elegant sculpted gardens grace the back lawn, which offers a commanding view of the surrounding countryside. On a terrace above the palace is a swimming pool. Each of the bedrooms is a gem, having thick stone walls (some with windowsills) and all being simply appointed with family antiques. The dark-wood beds are exceptionally lovely, no two alike, and all topped with sparkling white spreads. All have gleaming modern bathrooms. Family heirlooms abound throughout the striking public rooms, many of which have elaborate fireplaces—one a walk-in stone hearth. *Directions:* Located 7 km from Ponte de Lima on the road to Arcos de Valdevez (N202). Watch for a sign to Calheiros and Brandara. When making reservations, ask for a map.

≡ CREDIT P ≈ 大

PAÇO DE CALHEIROS
Host: Conde de Calheiros
4990 Ponte de Lima–Calheiros, Portugal
Tel: 258.74.28.29, Fax: none
9 rooms, Double: €100, 6 apartments
Dinner available upon special request
Minimum nights required: 2
Open: all year, Credit cards: AX, VS
Region: Costa Verde
www.karenbrown.com/portugal/calheiros.html

Moinho de Estorãos is an absolute dream. I can't imagine a more idyllic hideaway-and the price is amazingly low for the charming accommodations. Do not expect a grand home with fancy furnishings-the Moinho de Estorãos is a rustic mill that has been authentically restored, retaining the old water wheel and grindstone. The setting is incredibly romantic: the quaint stone mill snuggles on the banks of the River Estorãos next to an ancient Roman bridge. Inside, the fairy-tale ambiance continues. The living room, as cozy as can be, has exposed stone walls providing a backdrop for simple furnishings that are carefully chosen to suit the mood of the mill. From a small window with white embroidered curtains you can peek out over the stream below. In the corner is a cute kitchen where you can fix yourself a light meal. There is one small, comfortable bedroom, while an armoire in the living room hides a rollaway bed, perfect for a family sharing the mill. Because the owners do not live on the premises, you will need to time your arrival carefully so that one of them can meet you with the key. Even though this is an apartment, breakfast is brought to you each morning. Plan to come and stay a while, making this your base for exploring this interesting niche of Portugal. *Directions:* On the banks of the River Estorãos, 7 km northwest of Ponte de Lima. When making reservations, ask for a map.

☕ P

MOINHO DE ESTORÃOS
Host: Eng. Octaviano Martins
4990 Ponte de Lima–Estorãos, Portugal
Tel: 258.74.28.29, Fax: none
Double: €75, 1 apartment
Minimum nights required: 2
Open: mid-May to mid-Oct
Region: Costa Verde
www.karenbrown.com/portugal/estoraos.html

Casa das Torres is a grand manor dating from the 18th century. You can spot it easily from quite a distance because it holds a prominent position just below the road, overlooking the valley below. The source of the name Torres (towers) is immediately self-explanatory as the long, narrow, two-story building is flanked at each end by an imposing tower. It is an appealing home with a white exterior highlighted by tall, carved stone, windows looking out across the valley below. You enter through stately gates into an inner courtyard. The house is large and the Malheiro family has renovated three bedrooms and two apartments for guests. Our favorite bedrooms are the two on the lower level that open out to the very large terrace stretching behind the mansion. These spacious guestrooms are furnished with lovely antiques and have pretty tiled bathrooms. A room has been set up for ping-pong, another for billiards, and there is a swimming pool on the terrace. Mr Malheiro speaks some English and French and his wife teaches German and English, so language should not be a problem. *Directions:* The Casa das Torres is one of the easier of the elusive quintas to find—it is located directly on the main road N306 from Ponte de Lima to Barcelos. It is on the right side of the road, about 6 km from Ponte de Lima. When making reservations, ask for a map.

CASA DAS TORRES
Manager: Manuel Correia Malheiro
4990 Ponte de Lima–Facha, Portugal
Tel: 258.74.28.29, Fax: none
3 rooms, Double: €75–€120, 2 apartments
Minimum nights required: 2
Open: all year
Credit cards: AX, VS
Region: Costa Verde
www.karenbrown.com/portugal/torres.html

In the region of Ponte de Lima, between the extremes of the grand manor estates of powerful landlords and the simple farmsteads of the workers you find some gorgeous country farm estates like Casa do Barreiro, which I feel offer the most charming and cozy accommodation. A vine-arbored drive winds through the estate up to this handsome mustard-colored complex and a path from the parking area weaves up through pools, gardens, and fountains to a handsome side entry. Before you climb the first stair, take note of the lovely, poetical passage preserved in scripted tile that pays tribute to the relationship of this home and the family it has sheltered since it was built in 1643. A backdrop of animal sounds and the upper fountain with its impressive carved pheasants and family coat of arms all attest to the home's farm heritage. Inside, the house is charming, with the real ambiance of a family home made cozy with time: worn tile floors, low ceilings, fireplaces, built-in cupboards, deep-set, shuttered windows, old wooden doors, gorgeous, intimate furnishings, and mementos all add to the atmosphere. When offered, evening meals are a wonderful family dinners served in the cozy, handsome dining room. *Directions:* From the A3 take the Ponte de Lima exit but travel in the direction of Ponte da Barca. The Casa do Barreiro is signed off the road from the town of S. Tiago da Gemiera, 2 km after leaving the A3.

CASA DO BARREIRO
Host: Maria Teresa Malheiro Barbosa
4990 Ponte de Lima–Gemieira, Portugal
Tel: 258.94.81.37, Fax: 258.94.86.65
6 rooms, Double: €75, 1 apartment
Dinner available upon special request
Minimum nights required: 2
Open: all year, Credit cards: AX, VS
Region: Costa Verde
www.karenbrown.com/portugal/barreiro.html

Casa de Covas is a charming country home completely dedicated to accommodating guests. The lovingly restored, 17th-century stone farmhouse offers, instead of individual bedrooms, three apartments, each with bedroom (or bedrooms), living room, kitchen, and private terrace. The one-bedroom suite on the ground floor is a real winner: both the large living room and the bedroom are tastefully furnished in beautiful antiques. Unbelievably, you can stay here for the same price as a simple double room, plus have all the privacy and convenience of your own home. Because you have a kitchen, you can enjoy a hearty lunch while sightseeing then fix yourself a light supper at night. Even though the owner does not live in the same house, breakfast is delivered daily to your door. What more could you ask for? (Because Mrs Lemos is not in residence, time your arrival carefully so that one of the family can meet you and show you your accommodations.) The setting is truly romantic: the house sits in the middle of a field of grapes completely enclosed by a high stone wall and you can stroll through paths that wind through the fragrant vineyards. *Directions:* Casa de Covas is located 6 km northwest of Ponte de Lima. When making reservations, ask for a map.

☕ P

CASA DE COVAS
Host: Maria Fernanda Mimoso Lemos
4900 Ponte de Lima–Moreira do Lima, Portugal
Tel: 258.74.28.29, Fax: none
Double: €60–€100, 3 apartments
Minimum nights required: 2
Open: all year
Region: Costa Verde
www.karenbrown.com/portugal/covas.html

This quinta, although it is on one of the main roads, feels delightfully secluded because it is nestled on the hillside with a small lane leading down to it through the woods. As with so many of these grand old mansions, it is walled with a gated entrance. Once into the courtyard, you will notice that the crest embellishing the side of the house is scripted in English, not in Portuguese, and indeed the romantic history of the house involves an English nobleman by the name of Norton who fell in love with and married a Portuguese lady. The beautiful 17th-century home, which has been in the same family since it was built, has survived many crises including several attacks by the French. There are three guestrooms and two apartments. One of the bedrooms is in a separate cottage with its own terrace, but I prefer the two bedrooms in the main part of the house because their bathrooms are more commodious. The bedrooms are not large, but very attractive—each with matching bedspreads and curtains. There is also a nicely appointed kitchen for guests' use. Part of the charm of this estate is the setting: well-kept gardens surround the house, which enjoys a view of vineyards, orchards, and chestnut trees. Steps from the garden lead up to a swimming pool. *Directions:* Take the A3 from Porto towards Braga. Located on N201 in the direction of Braga, 7 km south of Ponte de Lima.

QUINTA DO BAGANHEIRO
Manager: Luís Norton de Matos
4990 Ponte de Lima–Queijada, Portugal
Tel: 258.74.28.29, Fax: 258.74.14.44
3 rooms, Double: €75–€120, 2 apartments
Dinner available upon special request
Minimum nights required: 2
Open: all year
Credit cards: AX, VS
Region: Costa Verde
www.karenbrown.com/portugal/baganheiro.html

The Casa de Crasto is a private manor dating back to the 17th century, when its history was entwined through a scandalous marriage with that of the nearby Paço de Calheiros (which is also a guesthouse featured in our guide). Since then, the property has changed hands several times, currently being owned and occupied by the Pimente Lopes family, whose uncle acquired it in 1917. A tiny sign on the way to Ponte da Barca points across the road to the stone and whitewashed farmhouse. It has three double-bedded rooms, two twin-bedded rooms, an apartment, and one suite—each charming in its simplicity. Be sure to ask for one of the twin-bedded rooms, as these are more commodious. Throughout this well-kept home the walls and thresholds are made of thick stone, the wood floors creaky, the ceilings high, and the furnishings a variety of plain, handsome antiques. The dining room (in which dinner will be served if there's a full house) has one long antique table, a fireplace at one end, and a marvelous old kitchen with a stone oven and open hearth at the other. The setting is bucolic, yet the inn is just moments from historic Ponte de Lima. *Directions:* Located about 500 meters from Ponte de Lima. When making reservations, ask for a map.

CASA DE CRASTO
Host: Gracinda da Conceição Pimente Lopes
4990 Ponte de Lima–Ribeira, Portugal
Tel: 258.74.28.29, Fax: none
6 rooms, Double: €75–€120, 1 apartment
Dinner available upon special request
Minimum nights required: 2
Open: all year
Credit cards: AX, VS
Region: Costa Verde
www.karenbrown.com/portugal/crasto.html

The luxurious Hotel Infante de Sagres is a haven in the heart of Porto, Portugal's second-largest city. Although the hotel has a rich, old-world ambiance, it is actually rather new-having been built in 1951 by textile magnate Mr Delfim Ferreira to accommodate his foreign customers. Now owned by his son, Alexandre Ferreira, it has been elegantly converted to a hotel and is a showcase for some of the antiques and exquisite tapestries he has collected over the years. The style is grandiose, with large, plush public rooms, a gracefully carved staircase overseen by stained glass, wide hallways, and high, sculpted ceilings. The dining room, which is especially sumptuous with a massive crystal chandelier and ornate wall sconces, is renowned for fine food and unparalleled service. The attention to detail throughout is remarkable, as can be noted in the gleaming woodwork, rich fabric walls, the velvet settee in the elevator, and the charming small bar with its curious original ceiling depicting the towns of Portugal. The bedrooms are generously proportioned, with high, scalloped ceilings, and each features a television and mini bar. All are furnished with handsome wood pieces. You may choose to overlook the rooftops of Porto (request a top floor away from street noise) or the colorful courtyard solarium. *Directions:* Located in the heart of Porto. Ask for a map when making reservations.

HOTEL INFANTE DE SAGRES
Manager: Victor Nunes
Praca D. Filipa de Lencastre, 62
4050-259 Porto, Portugal
Tel: 223.39.85.00, Fax: 223.39.85.99
72 rooms, Double: €200–€1000
Open: all year
Credit cards: all major
Region: Costa Verde
www.karenbrown.com/portugal/sagres.html

As you explore the Algarve, it seems that massive high-rise condominiums have sprung up along every stretch of oceanfront, but fortunately, you can still find a few secret, intimate little resorts. A prime example is the idyllic Vivenda Miranda, nestled on a bluff above the sea. You enter into a reception area decorated in tones of pastel-peach and turquoise, a color scheme repeated in the lounge and dining room, which has picture windows looking out to the terrace and beyond to the sea. You will be captivated by the view from the terrace—it is gorgeous. A foreground of green shrubbery, tidy pathways lined with rocks, colorful beds of flowers, carefully planted trees, and lush green lawn enhance the blue of the water even further. A path along the bluffs brings you to a trail down to a wide, white-sand beach. Every spacious, nicely decorated guestroom has an ocean view and a private deck or terrace from which to enjoy it. This paradise is owned by your gracious Swiss host, Urs Wild, who for many years worked for Sheraton. When Urs found this fantastic property, it was a private home, owned by a British lord who had let it fall into disrepair. After much work Urs opened it as a hotel and has continued to expand the facilities. *Directions:* From Lagos take the coastal road west, following signs to Porto de Mós, just a few kilometers from the old city. When you reach Porto de Mós you will see signs to the hotel.

ROMANTIK HOTEL VIVENDA MIRANDA
Hosts: Vera & Urs Wild
Porto de Mós, 8600 Lagos, Portugal
Tel: 282.76.32.22, Fax: 282.76.03.42
26 rooms, Double: €137–€290
Minimum nights required: 2
Open: all year
Credit cards: MC, VS
Region: Algarve
www.karenbrown.com/portugal/vivendamiranda.html

Just south of Portimão is Praia da Rocha, a gorgeous expanse of broad beach flanked by colorful rocky cliffs. Here you find the Vila Lido, which offers one of the best values along the Algarve. This tiny hotel sits on a slight knoll just across the road from the beach, with lovely views and easy access to the sea. This is not a deluxe hotel, but is fresh and pretty, immaculately kept, and exceptionally friendly. Like so many houses in the south, the bright-blue-shuttered villa is whitewashed, with quaintly carved chimneys jutting from its red-tile roof. A low stone-and-plaster wall surrounds the property and broad stone steps lead to the arched entryway where a tiny plaque gives the only indication that this is other than a private residence. A sunny sitting room with polished parquet floors opens onto a verandah at the front of the house, both ideal for coffee or cocktails while sea-gazing. French doors lead from there into a charming breakfast room with hand-painted tile walls, carved ceiling, massive fireplace, and delicate furniture. A few of the bedrooms have decorative fireplaces, and all retain a genuine old-world flavor with their sculpted ceilings, tall windows, spacious dimensions, and solid chestnut doors, although the furnishings are relatively modern. Some premium rooms (such as 21, 22, and 25) have terraces and ocean views. *Directions:* Located at the south end of Praia da Rocha, opposite a stone fortress.

ALBERGARIA VILA LIDO
Hosts: Mette Hallas-Møller &
Jamildo Tavares Conserva
Praia da Rocha, 8500 Portimão, Portugal
Tel: 282.42.41.27, Fax: 282.42.42.46
10 rooms, Double: €75–€90
Open: Mar to Nov 15
Credit cards: MC, VS
Region: Algarve
www.karenbrown.com/portugal/lido.html

The Vila Joya, one of the Alrgarve's most deluxe hotels, sits on a wooded bluff overlooking an unspoiled stretch of sand called Praia de Galé. There is a Moorish flair to the hotel, although it is not painted the typical Moorish white, but instead is a pretty shade of honey-tan. Its waterfront location is outstanding and its gardens are glorious. A large oval pool, surrounded by a lawn dotted with white lounge chairs, nestles on a terrace below the hotel. Beyond the pool, a private gate opens to a path leading down to the beach where giant sand formations lend a whimsical look and create secluded hideaways. The restaurant is definitely worth a mention. Michelin gives it two stars—a much-coveted award. The dining room is intimate with a vaulted brick ceiling and open fireplace. This, combined with meticulous service and fine cuisine, is an unbeatable recipe for those to whom money is no object (the quality of the dining is particularly important since breakfast and dinner are included with the room rate). The owner of the Vila Joya is not on site, so although the management is professional, it is less personal than some of the owner-managed properties. However, for guests whose prime concern is location, excellent food, and beautiful surroundings, the Vila Joya is unique. *Directions:* Located 6.5 km west of Albufeira. From N125, take the Albufeira exit. Soon after exiting, turn right, following discreet signs for Praia de Galé.

VILA JOYA
Manager: Petra M. Sauer
P.O. Box 120
Praia de Galé, 8200 Albufeira, Portugal
Tel: 289.59.18.39, Fax: 289.59.12.01
17 rooms, Double: €400–€980*
*Includes breakfast & dinner
Closed: mid-Nov to mid-Feb
Region: Algarve
www.karenbrown.com/portugal/joya.html

The view from Casa Três Palmeiras will take your breath away. This beautiful home is perched on the bluffs above the sea. From the terrace there is a sweeping view of the ocean that is made all the more dramatic by gigantic red rocks in all sorts of fantasy shapes rising up from the blue water. A path leads down to the endless beach where you can walk for hours. Thank heavens for readers' suggestions—we would never have found this paradise on our own, for it is secreted away on a tiny private lane that weaves up beyond some of the Algarve's fanciest mansions. Casa Três Palmeiras looks like a private home, as indeed it was, designed and built in 1960 by Dolly Schlingensiepen and her husband who had honeymooned along the Algarve and returned frequently for holidays. When her husband died, the property was so large that Mrs Schlingensiepen decided to welcome guests into her home, running it like an exquisite small hotel. All of the bedrooms have their own private entrances, are fully air conditioned, and four of them face the large solar-heated seawater swimming pool, while the other opens onto the pretty garden. The rooms are beautifully decorated and the bathrooms superb. Add to all of this the genuine hospitality of your hostess and you will agree that this is indeed paradise. *Directions:* Very tricky. Mrs Schlingensiepen will send you detailed instructions.

CASA TRÊS PALMEIRAS
Host: Dolly Schlingensiepen
Praia do Vau, 8501-909 Portimão, Portugal
Tel: 282.40.12.75, Fax: 282.40.10.29
5 rooms, Double: €194
Open: Feb to Nov
Region: Algarve
www.karenbrown.com/portugal/casatrespalmeiras.html

The Pousada de Queluz–Dona Maria I is a real stunner. As you leave the highway at Queluz, you pass modern housing developments dotting the hills, a reminder that Queluz is a suburb of Lisbon. But you won't be disappointed when you reach the pousada, which faces the imposing 18th-century Queluz National Palace. The pousada is instantly appealing—a charming pink building with white trim and a red-tiled roof accented by a whimsical white bell tower. It is surprising that the building has such architectural splendor, for it was used to house the staff who tended to the royal entourage spending their summers at the palace. The interior of the pousada is tasteful in every respect. The attractive guestrooms are almost identical in style, with traditional furnishings, handsome rose-colored spreads and drapes, and every modern convenience including TVs, direct-dial telephones, mini bars, and beautiful marble bathrooms. Breakfast is served at the pousada, but in the evening guests dine across the street at the palace in the gorgeous Cozinha Velha, a real knockout of a restaurant. Originally the kitchen for the royal palace, it still incorporates in the center of the room the gigantic open fireplace where meats were roasted and an enormous table where food was prepared. *Directions:* From Lisbon take the IC19 in the direction of Sintra. About 18 km from Sintra, take the Queluz exit and follow signs to the Palácio Nacional and the pousada.

POUSADA DE QUELUZ–DONA MARIA I
Opposite Queluz Palace
2745-191 Queluz, Portugal
Tel: 214.35.61.58, Fax: 214.35.61.89
26 rooms, Double: €159–€207
Open: all year
Credit cards: all major
Region: Costa de Lisboa
www.karenbrown.com/portugal/pousadaqueluz.html

Nestled in the protection of the church, the Casa dos Assentos enjoys the sounds of the church bells by day and their blessed silence at night. A complex with extensive grounds, this was once the place where agreements concerning local rents were kept (assentos means "house of rents"). We arrived midday as many guests were leaving. Based on the warmth of embraces and the sentimental farewells, I assumed that the guests were family, but was proven wrong as they then settled their bills. The manor house, a beautiful two-story, ivy-covered 17th-century building, houses three traditional guestrooms upstairs above guest salons and a lovely, large apartment on the first floor. Two stone cottages provide the traveler with complete privacy and luxury with their own entrances, living rooms, kitchens (notice the wonderful tiles that date to the origin of the home), bedrooms, and numerous bathrooms. Located in a small country town in the heart of the countryside, this is a wonderful place to escape to or use as a base for exploring the region. *Directions:* From Barcelos take the road signposted for Ponte de Lima, the N204. At a stone marked 14 km (on the right) and a small chapel (on the left) turn left and follow signs to Quintiães and Casa dos Assentos. Follow the road round its curves then after 2 km veer left following the sign to Centro and look for the church tower. Turn right and you will see the entrance to the house.

CASA DOS ASSENTOS
Host: Julia dos Santos Alves Araújo Novais Machado
Quintiães, 4750 Barcelos, Portugal
Tel & fax: 253.88.11.60
6 rooms, Double: €75–€157
Dinner available upon special request
Open: all year
Credit cards: AX
Region: Costa Verde
www.karenbrown.com/portugal/assentos.html

The Pousada de Mesão Frio–Solar da Rede, located in the heart of Portugal's finest wine region, has a superb setting in 27 hectares of terraced fields of grapes, offering a sweeping view out over the vineyards to the River Douro winding its way through the steep hills. As you drive up the tree-lined lane, your heart will be immediately captivated by the superb 18th-century mansion that magically appears behind a gated entrance, framed by two massive stone pillars. The two-story white manor has traditional stone trim and ornate wrought-iron balconies, and is fronted by a terrace. Below is another terrace, a real dazzler with neatly trimmed box hedges outlining beds of colorful flowers. To one side of the pousada is a swimming pool shaded by fragrant orange trees. Inside, the promise of grandeur is fulfilled. Leading from the spacious reception hall is a handsome stone staircase that divides on the landing and continues up to a series of antique-filled parlors, a billiard room, a charming dining room, and the guestrooms. The ambiance throughout is that of a sumptuous private home, which of course this was. *Directions:* From Peso da Régua, take N108 west along the north bank of the Douro. Before you come to Mesão Frio, you pass through a tiny hamlet with a sign saying "Rede" and soon you come to the entrance of the pousada, which is marked on the right side of the road by a row of flags.

POUSADA DE MESÃO FRIO–SOLAR DA REDE
Santa Cristina
Rede, 5040 Mesão Frio, Portugal
Tel: 254.89.01.30, Fax: 254.89.01.39
29 rooms, Double: €109–€230
Open: all year
Credit cards: all major
Region: Montanhas
www.karenbrown.com/portugal/pousadamesaofrio.html

It is hard to capture the unique magic of Pallácio de Rio Frio: the bedrooms are not particularly large, nor does the decor reflect the latest trend, but these are the very factors that make a stay here so special. Inside the gates you step back in time, for the home is exactly as it was 100 years ago—except for the addition of modern plumbing. Your gracious hostess, Maria de Lourdes, was born here—as were her father, her grandfather, and her great-grandfather. The house is an enormous mansion with a two-tiered porch stretching across the front, the lower porch framed with arches and the top floor with columns. This huge, ornate home was once the center of an estate of great wealth, though most of the land has now been sold—with 17,000 hectares of property, the Pallácio de Rio Frio was the largest farm in Portugal and had the greatest wine production in the world. It is worth a stay here just to see the incredible tiles. The walls of the living room are completely covered in ceramic murals depicting hunting scenes, cowboys tending their cattle, and horses, with the people in the murals all being related to the family. The dining room is even more special, its walls tiled with the typical blue-and-white azulejos showing the pallácio and scenes of the wine harvest. *Directions:* Follow the Michelin map to Rio Frio. Once there, look for the mansion—if you get lost, ask anyone in the village for directions.

PALLÁCIO DE RIO FRIO
Host: Maria de Lourdes Lupi D'Orey
Rio Frio, 2955 Palmela, Portugal
Tel: 258.74.28.29, Fax: none
4 rooms, Double: €100
Dinner available upon special request
Minimum nights required: 2
Open: all year, Credit cards: AX, VS
Region: Costa de Lisboa
www.karenbrown.com/portugal/riofrio.html

Located within hailing distance of Cabo São Vicente is a tiny stone 17th-century fortress. Perched on a rocky promontory overlooking the craggy coast and the sea, this very special small inn offers only four guestrooms. Most of its traffic is a result of its restaurant's reputation—most visitors don't even realize there are guestrooms available. In fact, the inn is actually owned by the Pousada affiliation, but because there are so few accommodations, they feature it only as a restaurant. The stone walls of the old fortress stretch out to the high bluffs where from the ramparts you have a spectacular view of the turquoise-colored sea and waves crashing on the rocks far below. Tucked into the walls of the fortress are two whitewashed buildings. One houses the reception area, a small bar, and the cozy dining room with its lovely wood ceiling. The other building contains the small bedrooms. Each exudes a rustic, appealing simplicity with brick-red tile floors, regional-style dark-wood furniture, and homespun-looking bedspreads. Only one of the bedrooms (# 4) has a clear view of the ocean—the others look onto the seaside terrace or into the interior courtyard, which is graced by a tiny white chapel. The dramatic setting is ideal for those seeking tranquility, but is still readily accessible for touring the Algarve. *Directions:* Take N268 to Sagres. Just before the town, take the road to the right marked to Cabo São Vicente.

CASA DE CHÁ DA FORTALEZA DO BELICHE
8650-385 Sagres, Portugal
Tel: 282.62.41.24, Fax: 282.62.42.25
4 rooms, Double: €66–€89
Open: Feb to Nov
Credit cards: all major
Region: Algarve
www.karenbrown.com/portugal/fortaleza.html

Pousada de Sagres–Infante has a prime location overlooking the merging waters of the Mediterranean and the Atlantic. Named after Prince Henry the Navigator, the pousada is a long, two-story, whitewashed building with a red-tiled roof punctuated with elaborate chimneys. A large statue of Henry the Navigator marks the front of the hotel. Once inside you realize how well-thought-out the site is—the pousada faces onto a large grassy terrace (with a swimming pool) that stretches out to the very edge of the bluff. Most of the public rooms and all the bedrooms face this same direction, capturing the splendid view of the sea. Inside, the pousada has an appropriate nautical theme. There is a spacious tiled lounge with a large fireplace and cozy furniture, tastefully decorated in greens, browns, and blues. In addition to good food, the dining room has a fireplace, an arched ceiling, and colorful tiles that climb halfway up the walls. The good-sized bedrooms are not opulent, but they are newly refurbished in regional-style furniture and are very pleasant. Some of the bedrooms have balconies (at no extra cost). The Pousada de Sagres–Infante provides serenity and comfort in a relatively untamed, western edge of the famous Algarve coast, while still offering easy access to the long beaches, hidden coves, and fishing villages. *Directions:* Take N268 toward Sagres. Just before the town, take the road to the left, then follow the signs to the pousada.

❄ ⚓ ▣ ▦ 👫 🍴 ⚲ 🎿

POUSADA DE SAGRES–INFANTE
8650-385 Sagres, Portugal
Tel: 282.62.42.22, Fax: 282.62.42.25
39 rooms, Double: €135–€198
Open: all year
Credit cards: all major
Region: Algarve
www.karenbrown.com/portugal/pousadasagres.html

The Pousada de Santa Clara-a-Velha is tucked high up in the hills north of the Algarve in a region of untouched natural beauty. As you approach the pousada, you can see it from afar—a low, white structure hugging the top of a hill. There has been a pousada in this spot for many years, but it provided only a few simple guestrooms until a recent renovation. It is now gorgeous and accommodates the many guests who flock here in the summer (and weekends the entire year) to relax in this beautiful, pristine setting and enjoy the pool, country walks, or fishing and boating. Below the hotel is the featured attraction, a beautiful lake created by the dam. There is no development around it to disturb the eye—only gently rolling, tree-covered hills rise from its shores. The hotel is very cleverly designed to take advantage of its 360-degree view—all of the spacious bedrooms have a balcony and look out either to the lake or the equally splendid low, wooded mountains on the opposite side. Wrapping almost totally around the hotel is a wide balcony off which are located the dining room, bar, and lounge—all with walls of glass. Both the interior and exterior are as fresh and attractive as can be, with pastel colors, appealing fabrics, and lovely traditional furnishings in light wood. *Directions:* Located above the lake, near Santa Clara-a-Velha. From town, follow pousada arrows south to the hotel.

❄ ☕ 💳 🚻 🏃 🍴 ≈ ⛴ ♿

POUSADA DE SANTA CLARA-A-VELHA
7665-879 Santa Clara-a-Velha, Portugal
Tel: 283.88.22.50, Fax: 283.88.24.02
19 rooms, Double: €126–€172
Open: all year
Credit cards: all major
Region: Planícies
www.karenbrown.com/portugal/pousadasantaclara.html

The Pousada Quinta da Ortiga is located only a few kilometers from the town center, yet tucked in a farming estate of 4 hectares (10 acres), one feels secluded in the country. The approach to this charming white manor is by a long country lane and from first sight the quinta has a cozy appeal. A row of tall pine trees accents the garden of box hedges laid out in an intricate design. To the right is a tiny chapel, lovely in its utter simplicity, with blue-and-yellow tiles adorning white walls and a blue-and-gold altar with a statue of Mary and infant Jesus. The quinta has a rustic simplicity and yet is bright and cheerful, with the walls in the living room and the dining room opened up with large windows to let in plenty of sunshine and to capture a pretty view of the tall trees in the garden. The living room looks like one in a private home, with comfortable chairs and sofas informally grouped around the fireplace. The dining room is also extremely welcoming, with pretty fabrics, country-style wooden chairs, and large brass chandeliers. Bedrooms in the main house are not large, yet they are attractively decorated and as tidy as can be. Cottages scattered about the property house guestrooms with living rooms—perfect for families. There is horseback riding available as well as a pool shaded by a gorgeous old eucalyptus tree. *Directions:* Coming on the IP8 from Sines, directional pousada signs begin about 4 km from town.

POUSADA DE SANTIAGO DO CACÉM–
QUINTA DA ORTIGA
7540 Santiago do Cacém, Portugal
Tel: 269.82.28.71, Fax: 269.82.20.73
13 rooms, Double: €118–€133
Open: all year
Credit cards: all major
Region: Costa de Lisboa
www.karenbrown.com/portugal/pousadaortiga.html

The Pousada de São Brás de Alportel, in the hills 3 kilometers above the village of São Brás, is one of Portugal's earliest pousadas. Built in 1943 with only six guestrooms, it typified the small wayside inns that paved the way for the more elegant pousadas of today. Resembling a whitewashed manor house with red terra-cotta roof, it retains the flavor of a roadside inn, offering travelers a peaceful spot, removed from the heavily traveled coastal route, but still readily accessible to its activities. The hotel is surrounded by pine and eucalyptus and its bedrooms all have balconies and enjoy views overlooking São Brás, Faro, and the Atlantic in the distance. The pousada was closed for several years for a total renovation. The new look is fresh and pretty. No effort is made to create an antique ambiance, but rather a happy color scheme of crisp white and bright yellow is displayed throughout, beginning with the whitewashed exterior accented by yellow shutters. Inside, the mood is one of comfortable informality and good taste. The semicircular restaurant is locally popular, and has lovely views over the garden terrace and the countryside. On a terrace below the pousada is an excellent large swimming pool, a nice respite after a day of sightseeing. This is an excellent base for visiting the market town of Loulé, the white town of Montes Novos, and the ruins of Milreu. *Directions:* Located 2 km north of São Brás de Alportel, on the N2.

❄ ⚓ ☕ 💳 🛗 🚶 🍴 ≈ 🎿 ♿

POUSADA DE SÃO BRÁS DE ALPORTEL–SÃO BRÁS
8150-054 São Brás de Alportel, Portugal
Tel: 289.84.23.05, Fax: 289.84.17.26
33 rooms, Double: €126–€169
Open: all year
Credit cards: all major
Region: Algarve
www.karenbrown.com/portugal/pousadasaobras.html

Serpa is not quite as idyllic as some of the other old towns with Moorish influence that seem to crown every commanding hilltop in the Alentejo, but it is definitely picturesque. Set in the countryside just a few kilometers outside Serpa, the Pousada de Serpa-São Gens is a contemporary rather than a historical building. As you drive up the low incline to the pousada, your first sight is of a white structure without much personality: the exterior is trimmed in a shiny green tile continuing into the reception area, which has a rather dreary, dated look. But don't give up-from here on, everything perks up considerably and the ambiance greatly improves. The lounge is quite pretty, with white-colored walls and sofas and chairs upholstered in shades of peach and green. Numerous potted plants and a collection of colorful plates on the walls give a homelike look. Beyond the lounge is a sunroom with rattan furniture and large doors opening onto a spacious deck, which captures an immense vista stretching all the way to Spain. Ensconced on a lower terrace is a splendid, king-sized swimming pool, which also has a lovely view. The bedrooms have balconies and are well designed to overlook the gently rolling countryside, which is studded with centuries-old olive trees and twisted oaks. *Directions:* From Serpa take the road marked to São Bras. The pousada is well signposted just a few kilometers from town.

❄ ☕ 💳 🚶 🍴 ≈

POUSADA DE SERPA–SÃO GENS
7830 Serpa, Portugal
Tel: 284.54.47.24, Fax: 284.54.43.37
18 rooms, Double: €126–€172
Open: all year
Credit cards: all major
Region: Planícies
www.karenbrown.com/portugal/pousadaserpa.html

This impressive pousada is installed in the São Filipe Castle, which was built in the 16th century to defend against a possible attack from the British armada. Today, perched high on a hilltop towering above Setúbal, it has a commanding view of the bay. Wind your way up to the impressive castle and leave your car outside the walls. From here, well-worn stone steps take you past a tiny blue-and-white-tiled chapel to the broad terrace where you find the reception area. Further flights of stone steps (no elevator) lead to the whitewashed bedrooms with high ceilings and walls thick enough to accommodate window seats. Large baths, red-tile floors, traditional carved-wood furniture and earthtone, floral-print spreads and drapes combine to create extremely comfortable surroundings with a somewhat rustic flavor. Unfortunately, not all of the rooms have a view of the city and the bay—which is enchanting—so be sure to request one. Some of the rooms are small, former monastic cells, so also inquire about the size of the room. On the main level is a tiled lounge with well-worn, cozy furniture, a television, and a small bar. The restaurant is appealing, overlooking the sun-washed terrace and the sea, and specializes in superior regional cuisine. Note: A maze of narrow tunnels spider-web beneath the castle. Ask to see them as one was a secret escape route to the sea in case the castle was conquered. *Directions:* The castle is on the hilltop.

❄ ⊺ ☕ 🪙 🚶 🍴

POUSADA DE SETÚBAL–SÃO FILIPE
2900-300 Setúbal, Portugal
Tel: 265.52.38.44, Fax: 265.53.25.38
16 rooms, Double: €159–€216
Open: all year
Credit cards: all major
Region: Costa de Lisboa
www.karenbrown.com/portugal/pousadasetubal.html

Sintra, a colorful town nestled in the hills near Lisbon, is without a doubt one of the most charming places in Portugal. We highlight several superb places to stay in the surrounding countryside, but for those who prefer to be right in town, the Casa Miradouro makes an excellent choice. In fact, you would not even need a car because you can take a taxi from the train station and the heart of town is only a ten-minute walk away. The home dates back to the end of the 19th century. It was in sad disrepair when your gracious Swiss host, Frederico Kneubühl, purchased and totally renovated it. Even the exterior has returned to its original glory, gaily painted (as it was originally) in horizontal zebra stripes of pink and creamy yellow—a popular motif in its heyday. The gardens, too, have been meticulously restored and there is a pretty terrace at the front of the house. Inside, guests are made to feel at home and relax in the comfort of the attractively decorated lounges. There are six guestrooms individually decorated with pretty color-coordinating fabrics and attractive furnishings including a few antiques, and each has a brand-new bathroom. Although the Miradouro is in town, there are lovely views of the countryside. *Directions:* The villa is reached by taking Rua Sotto Mayor, a street that slopes down the hill from near the center of town. Casa Miradouro is on a corner, on your left.

CASA MIRADOURO
Host: Frederico Kneubühl
Rua Sotto Mayor, 55
2710 Sintra, Portugal
Tel: 219.23.59.00, Fax: 219.24.18.36
6 rooms, Double: €92–€122
Closed: Jan 12 to Feb 23
Credit cards: all major
Region: Costa de Lisboa
www.karenbrown.com/portugal/casamiradouro.html

The pale-melon façade of Lawrence's Hotel, established in 1764 and the oldest hotel on the Iberian Peninsula, seems to have taken shape following the contours of the road as it weaves up from the center of Sintra. A stone entryway welcomes you then you step down from the reception area to a cozy and intimate, pine-paneled bar with a theme of golf. Across from the bar is an inviting sitting area but don't miss the steps up to a library, gorgeous in paneled wood, with its fireplace and comfortable seating. Descend one level to a charming restaurant whose windows frame a scene of a forested hillside that drops dramatically away from the hotel. Below the restaurant is a lovely sheltered terrace, which enjoys the tranquility of the setting and views across the rooftops of Sintra. Surprisingly, the hotel has just eleven bedrooms and five suites, all exceptionally handsome in their decor, with rich fabrics, warm colors and tiles, exposed woods, and gorgeous furnishings. I loved the Lord Byron, a back garden suite whose handsome red decor contrasts beautifully with the backdrop of leafy greenery, and the Eça de Queiros Suite with its rich earth colors of sand, brown and rusts. Although not a suite, my favorite room was the Jane Lawrence, a pretty back corner room whose soft-yellow fabrics drape a four-poster bed and are restful against a backdrop of greenery. *Directions:* Up from the main square of Sintra, following the road to Monserrate.

LAWRENCE'S HOTEL
Host: Bos family
Rua Consigliere Pedroso, 38–40
2710-550 Sintra, Portugal
Tel: 219.10.55.00, Fax: 219.10.55.05
11 rooms, 5 suites, Double: €236–€395
Open: all year
Credit cards: all major
Region: Costa do Lisboa
www.karenbrown.com/portugal/lawrences.html

A splendid example of late-18th-century architecture, the Hotel Palácio de Seteais (Palace of Seven Sighs) is so-called due to a legendary love story involving a Portuguese nobleman and a Moorish princess. The exceptionally glamorous pastel-yellow and white palace is set amidst sculpted gardens and surrounded by expansive panoramas of the lush, emerald-green countryside. From the front lawn you can see the ornate Palácio de Pena on a hill above town. The grand-scale public rooms are nothing short of spectacular, decorated in pastel colors, with high, molded ceilings, hand-painted walls, wood or marble floors covered with Oriental rugs, and abundant antiques topped by fresh-cut flowers. Each of the mostly twin-bedded, spacious bedrooms is unique, furnished mainly with richly upholstered period pieces and decorated in muted earth tones. Bucolic views from tall windows complete the picture. The first-floor bedrooms have the added attraction of extra-high ceilings, augmenting their already generous proportions. One of my favorite rooms in the old wing was #14, a large corner room with serene views of the valley and down to the pool. There is a charming bar downstairs, an appealing awning-covered outdoor terrace, and an exceptional dining room. A pool is tucked in the beautiful gardens. *Directions:* Located 1.5 km from Sintra on the road to Monserrate.

HOTEL PALÁCIO DE SETEAIS
Manager: Paulo Geirinhas
Rua Barbosa do Bocage, 8
2710 Sintra, Portugal
Tel: 219.23.32.00, Fax: 219.23.42.77
30 rooms, Double: €250–€273
Open: all year
Credit cards: all major
Region: Costa de Lisboa
www.karenbrown.com/portugal/seteais.html

Quinta das Sequoias is truly a jewel. This charming farm was obviously home to a family of means and the estate is still quite sizeable, almost 40 acres surrounding the manor house with its white façade, red-tiled roof, and cheerful green shutters. Inside, the home reeks of comfort and the hand of someone who loves her property. Candida González treats her guests as she would friends—her home is your home for the lucky few who snare a room. There is a cheerful living room (warmed by an open fire in winter) with French windows opening onto the garden. The breakfast room, which was once the kitchen, is picture-perfect, with an enormous open fireplace and a large table where guests gather family-style for breakfast. Breakfast is the only meal officially served, but for guests enjoying a lengthy stay, a light supper can be provided with advance notice. The individually decorated bedrooms are as pretty as can be, with fine antiques used throughout and lovely color-coordinated spreads and curtains. The setting is fairy-tale perfect—the manor looks across a wooded oasis to the stunning Pena Palace crowning the top of the opposite hill and out back over the valley to the blue waters of the Atlantic. There is a beautiful swimming pool in the garden. *Directions:* From Sintra take the Monserrate road. Approximately 1 km after passing the Seteais Palace Hotel, turn left at a road marked Quinta das Sequoias and weave about 2km up the hill.

QUINTA DAS SEQUOIAS
Host: Candida González
Road to Monserrate
2710 Sintra, Portugal
Tel: 219.24.38.21, Fax: 219.10.60.65
6 rooms, Double: €135–€145
Closed: Dec 24 & 25
Credit cards: all major
Region: Costa de Lisboa
www.karenbrown.com/portugal/quintadassequoias.html

The Pousada de Sousel-São Miguel is one of the Pousada affiliation's newer buildings. Its architecture is interesting and the furnishings are very appealing, and it was built to take full advantage of its spectacular setting. A small road meanders through the countryside and then winds up a hill on top of which the pousada reigns supreme. What is so glorious about this utterly tranquil setting is that from the hotel (especially from its rooftop terrace) you have a 360-degree panorama of great beauty-in all directions there is a sea of olive trees whose mellow-green leaves and black trunks stand out like an abstract work of art against the clay-red soil. Slightly above the pousada is a very old church and, next to that, a centuries-old bullring. The surrounding area is excellent for hunting, attracting many sportsmen during the winter, so the pousada has a sporting theme-in the lobby a huge wild boar is displayed in glass and on the walls are trophies of deer, while the bedrooms are named for birds and wild game. The decor, however, is more like that of a sophisticated English gentlemen's club, extremely attractive with its predominant use of rich dark green accented by beige and red. The bedrooms are all large and each has a deck or balcony capturing the idyllic sweeping view of fields of olive trees. *Directions:* Go into Sousel and follow signs to the pousada, which is located several kilometers from town via a small country road.

❄ ☕ 💳 🏃 🍴 ≈

POUSADA DE SOUSEL–SÃO MIGUEL
7470-999 Sousel, Portugal
Tel: 268.55.00.50, Fax: 268.55.11.55
32 rooms, Double: €126–€156
Open: all year
Credit cards: all major
Region: Planícies
www.karenbrown.com/portugal/pousadasousel.html

The Paço de São Cipriano is a beautiful estate outside Guimarães. Although the home is near the city, it is totally secluded by its own farmlands, with no intrusion of civilization in sight. Over the years the house, one part of stone, another painted a deep mustard yellow, has been added onto many times, so each portion has its own personality, which creates a certain charm. In front of the house is a lovely formal garden of clipped hedges and sculpted trees, while behind the house, sequestered by a high hedge of centuries-old camellias, you find a swimming pool. There are seven guestrooms, each individually decorated and furnished with antiques. The old stone tower houses the most outstanding bedroom, a very large room painted a pretty color of green. This room has a canopy bed and is especially bright and cheerful with windows looking out in two directions. My favorite room in the house is the one used for breakfast, a charming room that was once the old kitchen. Breakfast is served on a gorgeous antique round table and in the corner is a cozy little niche with an open fireplace and an oven where bread used to be baked. *Directions:* From Guimarães take N105 toward Santo Tirso. After 2.5 km, make a sharp turn to the left in Covas and follow signs to Taboadelo. The house is on the right after 3km.

PAÇO DE SÃO CIPRIANO
Host: Don João Almeida Santiago de Sottomayor
Taboadelo, 4800 Guimarães, Portugal
Tel & fax: 253.56.53.37
7 rooms, Double: €100
Minimum nights required: 2
Open: all year
Credit cards: AX
Region: Costa Verde
www.karenbrown.com/portugal/cipriano.html

Casa do Sol Nascente gives new meaning to the word "rural"—it is truly off the beaten path, but this is exactly what attracted the Arbuckles here. After traveling throughout the world, Ian wanted utter tranquility and wife Chizu (whom he met while living in Japan) seems also to love the rural life. Intending part of the house to be an apartment for Ian's family, they built it larger than they needed but his father died unexpectedly so, with more bedrooms than they could use, Ian and Chizu decided to open their home as a bed and breakfast. It is a perfect outlet for their talents. Both are extremely gracious hosts who have the knack of making guests feel right at home, quickly leaving behind the tensions of daily life. The home is built in the traditional style of white stucco and red-tiled roof, but because the house is new, there are windows everywhere, filling the rooms with sunlight. Chizu is an excellent housekeeper as well as an artist whose paintings decorate the walls. For those on a budget, two small but attractive bedrooms on the first floor share a bathroom. Upstairs are two very spacious, nicely decorated bedrooms, each with its own large private bathroom. *Directions:* Taipa is not on any map we could find, so don't worry about it. It is off the N230 about midway between Aveiro and Águeda. In Eirol there is a sign for Taipa and Requeixo—turn south here for 1.4 km and then follow signs to Casa do Sol Nascente.

CASA DO SOL NASCENTE
Hosts: Chizu & Ian Arbuckle
Taipa, 3800 Aveiro, Portugal
Tel: 234.93.35.97, Fax: 234.93.35.98
4 rooms, Double: €45–€78
Meals on request
Open: all year
Region: Costa da Prata
www.karenbrown.com/portugal/casadosolnascente.html

A well-traveled friend said we must not miss Quinta do Caracol, her favorite hideaway in the Algarve, and this tiny inn is indeed a jewel, within walking distance of the quaint town of Tavira but, inside its gates, insulated from the bustling crowds. This ever-so-charming fantasy of white cottages laced with pink and yellow bougainvillea has been in the Viegas family for many generations. However, until João Viegas first began to take guests, Quinta do Caracol was a farm, producing olives and almonds. As word spread about the magic of this tiny hotel, more of the original buildings were renovated into suites, most with a sitting room, bedroom, and kitchenette. The decor throughout is charming: nothing fancy, just sweet and simple with provincial-print fabrics, antique furniture, colorful tiles, and white embroidered curtains at the windows (handmade by João Viegas's mother). There are also many beautiful watercolors on the walls, most of which were painted by Susel Viegas, a talented artist. As you walk through the meticulously kept gardens and see the lovingly decorated rooms, it is obvious that the owners have a real flair for making this small inn a very special place to stay. They also have a gift for making each guest feel very welcome—it is no wonder so many come back year after year. *Directions:* Take Avenida Miguel from the center of Tavira. After going over the railroad tracks, turn sharp left—the quinta is on your left.

QUINTA DO CARACOL
Host: João Viegas
8800-405 Tavira, Portugal
Tel: 281.32.24.75, Fax: 281.32.31.75
7 rooms, Double: €112
Minimum nights required: 3
Open: all year
Credit cards: all major
Region: Algarve
www.karenbrown.com/portugal/caracol.html

Although the address reads "Torrão" the hotel is actually about 12 kilometers away, in a beautifully secluded setting overlooking the lake of Vale do Gaio. Your first sight is of the back of the pousada—a boxy white building with not much architectural interest, but this impression is totally misleading. Inside the entrance gate flanked by two giant palm trees, a whole new image emerges. Here you see a small, attractive, red-brick structure with an extremely appealing wisteria-covered terrace looking out to the lake where boats bob in the water. The lake is formed by a dam, and the hotel was originally built to house the engineers who built it, later being converted by the government into a simple little inn with only a few rooms. The pousada began to show its age so was closed, totally renovated, enlarged, and redecorated, then reopened, revealing an excellent job. From the moment you enter, you will be impressed by the fresh, pretty look. Polished wood floors, lovely pastel colors, light woods, and pretty print fabrics give the feeling of being in a home. This is a small pousada and the public rooms are intimate in size but the bedrooms are spacious and appealingly decorated with light-wood furniture. All the guestrooms have a view of the lake, but those on the top floor have the bonus of balconies. *Directions:* From Torrão follow signs west toward Alcácer do Sal. After about 8 km there is a sign to the left to the pousada.

❄ ⚓ ☕ 💳 👫 🍴 ≋

POUSADA DO TORRÃO–VALE DO GAIO
7595-034 Torrão, Portugal
Tel: 265.66.96.10, Fax: 265.66.95.45
14 rooms, Double: €115–€121
Open: all year
Credit cards: all major
Region: Planícies
www.karenbrown.com/portugal/pousadatorrao.html

Unable to find a charming hotel in the colorful fishing village of Nazaré, we were delighted to discover a stately quinta just 5 kilometers away. From the moment you drive through the gates and see the impressive large courtyard, you know this was no ordinary farm. It was in fact once attached to the nearby important medieval monastery of Santa Maria in Alcobaça and was purchased by an ancestor of the present owner in the early part of the 19th century. There is a marvelous homelike atmosphere throughout, with family antiques in all the rooms—nothing is contrived or decorator-perfect, but the mood is one of appealing authenticity. Guests can make themselves at home in the parlor and fix themselves a drink from the honor bar. The eight bedrooms, all of which are individually decorated, are in the main house, which is painted a pretty, soft yellow with white trim highlighted by appealing blue doors. One of my favorite rooms is number 2, which is larger than some of the others and has exquisite antique headboards on the twin beds. There are also seven apartments with kitchenettes independent from the main house, each with a private terrace with pretty views of the rolling farmland. This is not a fancy hotel, but ideal for those who want to sample life on a once-grand estate. *Directions:* From Nazaré take the road toward Alcobaça. After 5 km, turn right and go to the center of Valado dos Frades, then follow the blue signs to the quinta.

☕ 💳 🚶 P 🏊 🚶

QUINTA DO CAMPO
Host: João Pedro Collares Perreira
Valado dos Frades, 2450 Nazaré, Portugal
Tel: 262.57.71.35, Fax: 262.57.75.55
8 rooms, Double: €90–€155, 7 apartments
Open: all year
Credit cards: MC, VS
Region: Costa da Prata
www.karenbrown.com/portugal/quintadocampo.html

Valença do Minho, a charming walled medieval hill town whose castle dates back to the 13th century, stretches across a hilltop overlooking the River Minho, which divides Portugal from Spain. There is just one gate that leads through the thick walls of the fortress and into the quaint town where tiny, whitewashed houses huddle over narrow cobblestone streets. The Pousada de Valença do Minho-São Teotónio (named after Portugal's first saint) huddles next to the thick stone ramparts and has a remarkable view across the river. The public rooms of the pousada are modern. The bright, airy lounge and bar are mostly furnished with tan leather chairs and sofas. The outdoor terrace features a fountain and overlooks cool, green lawn and old stone walls leading down to the riverbank. The same dramatic panorama is shared by the dining room with its floor-to-ceiling windows, which in the evening capture a view of the romantically illuminated castle perched across the river. Every bedroom also has a view, but not all have terraces. The guestrooms are comfortable (those with twin beds slightly larger), and all have large, tiled baths, parquet floors, and handcrafted, regional wood furniture. *Directions:* Enter through the narrow gate into the old town, then continue following the one-way arrows through the town, then through a second gate. The pousada is well marked to the left of the road at the end of the second part of the village.

❄ ☕ 💳 🚶 🍴

POUSADA DE VALENÇA DO MINHO–
SÃO TEOTÓNIO
4930-619 Valença do Minho, Portugal
Tel: 251.80.02.60, Fax: 251.82.43.97
18 rooms, Double: €115
Open: all year
Credit cards: all major
Region: Costa Verde
www.karenbrown.com/portugal/pousadavalenca.html

The Casa do Ameal is located in the residential outskirts within walking distance of the large port town of Viana do Castelo. Tucked off a narrow side street, this large and elegant white-stucco home with tiled roof is set behind its own gates and wall and is buffered from the city by a beautiful courtyard entrance with fountain and garden. When you enter, be sure to notice the hanging family coats of arms that drape the back wall. Guestrooms are found around the side of the house and enjoy individual entries off a cobbled walkway. A few rooms are located in what was once the servants' wing. The rooms range from an apartment with a small kitchen, lovely little living room with fireplace, a double-bedded room and a twin-bedded room sharing a bathroom, to a small room with a loft sitting area and kitchenette, to a cozy, simple, small double room—all set up against thick old stone walls. Next door an ivy-covered two-story building houses additional guestrooms and a large, open, second-floor breakfast room. Enclosed by a garden hedge, a large pool is set in the lawn, surrounded by garden. *Directions:* From the south, take the IC1 and its bridge across the river to Viana. After crossing the bridge, follow signs to Viana (ignore the turn to Meadela/Ponte de Lima). After 2 km turn right, following signs to Transito Local and after 200 meters, at a set of traffic lights, turn right—the entrance is on the left 50 meters up the street.

CASA DO AMEAL
Host: D. Maria Elisa Faria de Araújo
Rua do Ameal, 119, Meadela
4900 Viana do Castelo, Portugal
Tel: 258.82.24.03, Fax: none
2 rooms, Double: €75, 6 apartments (up to €120)
Minimum nights required: 2
Open: all year, Credit cards: AX, VS
Region: Costa Verde
www.karenbrown.com/portugal/ameal.html

The Pousada de Viana do Castelo is a luxurious, turn-of-the-century inn that shares a splendid hilltop (forested with pine and eucalyptus) with a dramatic pilgrimage church of the same name. They both also share a spectacular view of the small port town of Viana do Castelo, which hugs the banks of the River Lima. The large, pale-stone pousada is a majestic white building, which although not old, is traditional in style and beautifully constructed. The interior decor is outstanding—elegant yet welcoming and of such style that it rivals the finest hotels. This pousada is not old and stuffy, but fresh and airy, with grand-scale public rooms featuring splendid light-wood parquet floors, beautiful pastel-upholstered furniture, huge crystal chandeliers, and large windows to capture views of the town and estuary far below. The theme of taste and refined style is continued in the spacious bedrooms. Be sure to request one of the many rooms that overlook the church and river. The dining room and a wide verandah stretching the length of the pousada also enjoy the extensive panorama. In the garden there is a beautiful oval swimming pool encircled by trees. The Pousada de Viana do Castelo is more like a deluxe hotel than a typical pousada, but you will love it. *Directions:* You cannot miss this one. It is perched on top of the hill, visible from everywhere in town. Just follow signs to Santa Luzia—the pousada is just beyond the church.

POUSADA DE VIANA DO CASTELO–
MONTE DE SANTA LUZIA
4901-909 Viana do Castelo, Portugal
Tel: 258.82.88.89, Fax: 258.82.88.92
48 rooms, Double: €135–€236
Open: all year
Credit cards: all major
Region: Costa Verde
www.karenbrown.com/portugal/vianadocastelo.html

The secluded Vidago Palace Hotel, nestling in its own forest, is revealed at the end of a tree-lined drive. It is an impressive and beautiful salmon-colored, four-story building that indeed once was the residential palace of the Portuguese kings. Climb the palace steps and enter into a world fit for royalty, with gorgeous tiled floors, ornate ceilings, gilded columns, and a stunningly beautiful double stairway sweeping up from the entry. Off the entry is a small bar and beyond that a spectacular restaurant, painted in soft colors of salmon and soft green, with towering windows draped in yards of fabric, tables elegantly set with linens and crystal, and a ceiling that soars up to a second-story balcony-surround. Upstairs, guestrooms are decorated in traditional colors and, apart from a few two-room suites, differ essentially only in whether they are set with one or two beds. (Be sure to step off the first-floor landing to look down on the restaurant from the balcony-surround.) Off the back courtyard is a large pool with terrace bar where on weekends one can enjoy a lunch buffet and barbecue poolside. Proximity to the thermal waters, tennis, golf, table tennis, billiards-this hotel offers it all! The hotel is also popular as a conference center. *Directions:* Vidago is located 12 km southeast of Chaves along the N2. Travel through Vidago following signs to the Palace Hotel.

VIDAGO PALACE HOTEL
Director: Hein Demyttenaere
Parque de Vidago
5425-307 Vidago, Portugal
Tel: 276.99.09.00, Fax: 276.90.73.59
83 rooms, Double: €73–€180
Open: all year
Credit cards: all major
Region: Montanhas
www.karenbrown.com/portugal/vidagopalace.html

The enchanting Quinta das Torres, located on the outskirts of Vila Nogueira de Azeitão (home of Lancers wine), is surrounded by 34 acres of wooded park and farmland. Sculpted gardens and a large stone pond, complete with gazebo and swan, add to the idyllic scene. A private manor house for centuries, Quinta das Torres was built in 1570 as a palace for the Count of Aveiro. The family of the proprietors has called this home for over a hundred years, offering guests accommodation since 1931. Two of the brothers in the family now manage the inn. The ivy-covered, low stone manor surrounds a central patio with fountain. The main house contains splendid, if not perfectly preserved, public rooms, an extremely charming, intimate restaurant with windows overlooking the reflecting pool, and some of the guestrooms—the other guestrooms are across the patio. All of the accommodations, which vary in size and decoration, are furnished with antiques. An old-world ambiance prevails—electric blankets and modern plumbing being among the few concessions to progress. Our favorite rooms are #6, which has twin canopy beds and two comfy blue chairs in a cozy niche by a fireplace and #2, which has twin beds, pretty rose-floral fabrics, windows on three sides, and a rooftop terrace. *Directions:* From Lisbon go south on A2. Take the Seisimbra/Sétubal exit and stay on the N10, direction Sétubal. 15 km after leaving the A2, the Quinta will be on your right.

QUINTA DAS TORRES
Hosts: António & João Ferrão de Sousa
Estrada Nacional no. 10
Vila Nogueira de Azeitão, 2925-601 Setúbal, Portugal
Tel: 212.18.00.01, Fax: 212.19.06.07
12 rooms, Double: €100–€167
Open: all year
Credit cards: all major
Region: Costa de Lisboa
www.karenbrown.com/portugal/quintadastorres.html

The Pousada de Vila Nova de Cerveira-D. Diniz, named after the 14th-century king who fortified the town against Spanish aggression, is located in the cute town of Vila Nova de Cerveira, which hugs the banks of the River Minho as it makes its way to the Atlantic. The pousada is installed in the heart of the village. With the exception of the reception, which is housed in an old mansion, the inn is entirely built within the ancient ramparts. In fact, the pousada's public rooms and guestrooms are incorporated into the original dwellings that, until 1975, were inhabited by townsfolk. Once you've settled in, don't fail to visit the tiny, 13th-century chapel with its ornate painted ceiling and wood-slat floors. Just behind an old pillory is a pretty white-plaster and stone-framed building (previously the prison) containing the bar, lounge, and sitting rooms, with wood floors and cozy leather furniture. The spacious bedrooms are located in a cluster of remodeled village houses, and feature pale-wood, carved beds with woven wheat-colored spreads and windows with pretty white embroidered curtains. The restaurant is within still another building and its wall of windows allows beautiful views of the river. From the dining room, doors lead out to a large terrace, enclosed by the ramparts of the town. *Directions:* When you enter town, park in the square. The entrance to the pousada, located just across from the church, is a bit discreet.

❄ ☕ 💳 ⚐ 🍴

POUSADA DE VILA NOVA DE CERVEIRA–D. DINIZ
4920-296 Vila Nova de Cerveira, Portugal
Tel: 251.70.81.20, Fax: 251.70.81.29
28 rooms, Double: €117–€145
Open: all year
Credit cards: all major
Region: Costa Verde
www.karenbrown.com/portugal/pousadavilanova.html

In the mid-17th century King João IV, formerly the Duke of Bragança, built a tiny, picture-perfect stone castle in the remote fishing village of Vila Nova de Milfontes, overlooking the placid River Mira. For centuries it hosted royalty and nobility from all over Portugal and Europe. The unmarked, ivy-covered castle (complete with dry moat and drawbridge) sits on its own rocky outcrop that drops down to the river. As long as you've made reservations (an absolute must), don't be put off by the "Private Property" sign on the iron gates-just ring the bell on the massive wood door. When you stay at the Castelo de Milfontes, it is like being a privileged guest in a private home. Your hostess, Ema do Camara Machado, is a member of the family that has owned the property for many generations. Fine heirlooms furnish the living room, small bar, and dining room. Dinner is included with the your lodging, and the family shares it with guests at a large, handsome antique table. Narrow stone steps lead up to stone hallways, off which are smallish bedrooms. When we last visited, the castle was in the midst of a total renovation, so by the time you visit, the accommodations should be even nicer. An added bonus is a romantic arcaded, ivy-draped terrace at the back overlooking the river. The guest book is full of laudatory comments. *Directions:* Located in the center of town, on a tiny rocky outcrop overlooking the river.

☕ 👥 P

CASTELO DE MILFONTES
Host: Ema do Camara Machado
7645 Vila Nova de Milfontes, Portugal
Tel: 283.99.82.31, Fax: 283.99.71.22
7 rooms, Double: €144–€155*
*Includes breakfast & dinner
Closed: 15 days in Jan
Region: Planícies
www.karenbrown.com/portugal/milfontes.html

Vila Viçosa, home in the 16th century to the powerful Dukes of Bragança, is a small town brimming with palaces, museums, castles, and an impressive long, tree-lined plaza that stretches for blocks. Since this was a town of political importance, it is not surprising to find nearby a farm estate that hints of these bygone days of grandeur—the impressive Casa de Peixinhos, which dates back to 1595. Built on a knoll, the striking manor has a crisp-white façade enhanced by doors and windows trimmed with yellow. Three slender, whimsical turrets accent the front of the home, giving it a miniature-castle look. What makes this such a special place to stay, however, is not the dramatic façade, but the interior—the decor and ambiance are outstanding. The living room looks rather like an English country manor with comfortable brown leather chairs and sofas grouped around a large fireplace, hung with the family coat of arms. Fine-quality antiques abound. Beyond the living room is a splendid large dining room with oil paintings on the walls and a handsome brass chandelier over a beautiful table. There are eight guestrooms, one of these a pretty suite with a separate sitting room. Each of the beautifully decorated rooms has a huge bathroom and looks out to a fragrant grove of orange trees. *Directions:* Head east through town on the Avenida Duques de Bragança. After passing the Praça da República, turn right and then left, following signs to the inn.

■ ✎ ☎ P 🖼 ♿

CASA DE PEIXINHOS
Host: Passanha family
7160 Vila Viçosa, Portugal
Tel: 268.98.04.72, Fax: 268.88.13.48
8 rooms, Double: €98–€165
Dinner available upon special request
Open: all year
Region: Planícies
www.karenbrown.com/portugal/peixinhos.html

The Pousada de Vila Viçosa–D. João IV is a stunning hotel that not only is built within a fabulous 16th-century convent, but also has a romantic setting next to an exquisite palace and across from an appealing church. At first glance the large square reception lounge might seem a bit sterile with its white walls and white marble floors. However, on second glance you realize that part of the floor is glass and if you look down, below you—spread out like a museum—are the ruins of a very old building that date back far before the Convent of Chagas de Cristo was built. As you proceed through the pousada you will notice that marble from nearby quarries is used extensively. The decorator-perfect public rooms display a sophisticated elegance, fine-quality fabrics, beautiful furniture, and accents of antiques. Although much renovation has taken place, the architects have cleverly incorporated some of the original artwork—look carefully and you will see some of the original frescoes peeking through the new plaster. There is an exquisite cloister with the characteristic fountain and garden at the core of the hotel and many of the bedrooms are on corridors that wrap around this. All of the bedrooms are very large and, like the public rooms, furnished with great taste. As might be expected in a new pousada, there is also a large swimming pool. *Directions:* The pousada is well signposted once you arrive in Vila Viçosa.

❄ ☕ 💳 ⛲ 🏋 🚶 🍽 ≈

POUSADA DE VILA VIÇOSA–D. JOÃO IV
7160 Vila Viçosa, Portugal
Tel: 268.98.07.42, Fax: 268.98.07.47
36 rooms, Double: €159–€279
Open: all year
Credit cards: all major
Region: Planícies
www.karenbrown.com/portugal/pousadavilavicosa.html

The Casa de Vilarinho de San Romão is a wonderful old farmstead dating from 1462, set in its own vineyard acreage. Restoration work, which involves taking it apart stone by stone and then putting it back together, is a remarkable effort but Christine continues with the never-ending task. Inside, the decor is light and airy, with new, light-pine floors and whitewashed walls. The entry is spacious and dramatic under a traditional Douro ceiling and displays a wonderful old royal carriage. Guests have the use of a sitting area off the entry and a large library opening onto the front courtyard. Three guestrooms are found down each of two wings of the building. I liked the three in the wing with its hallway overlooking the central courtyard, whose windows open onto valley views. These have stone loveseats set in the deep window openings both in the bedrooms and bathrooms. I especially loved the cozy Cornucopia room, which enjoys the best view in the house. Given advance notice, Christine offers dinner at a table set under the original Douro ceiling with an oval carving of wheat. The pool is set on a grassy terrace of lawn looking out to vineyards. *Directions:* Leave Pinhão in the direction of Sabrosa and travel about 12 km to the town of Vilarinho de S. Romão. In town watch on the right for the arched gateway under the big trees, just to the left of the church next to the ruins of its own chapel.

CASA DE VILARINHO DE S. ROMÃO
Host: Christine van Zeller
Vilarinho de S. Romão, 5060-630 Pinhão, Portugal
Tel & fax: 259.93.07.54
6 rooms, Double: €75
Dinner available upon special request
Closed: Dec 23 to 27
Region: Montanhas
www.karenbrown.com/portugal/casadevilarinho.html

Key Map

Valença

Bragança

Braga

1

Vila Real

Porto

Lamego

Aveiro

Viseu

Figueira da Foz

Coimbra

2

Batalha

Óbidos

Lisbon

3

Estremoz

Évora

Azores (not to scale)

Sines

Beja

4

Sagres

Faro

Map 1

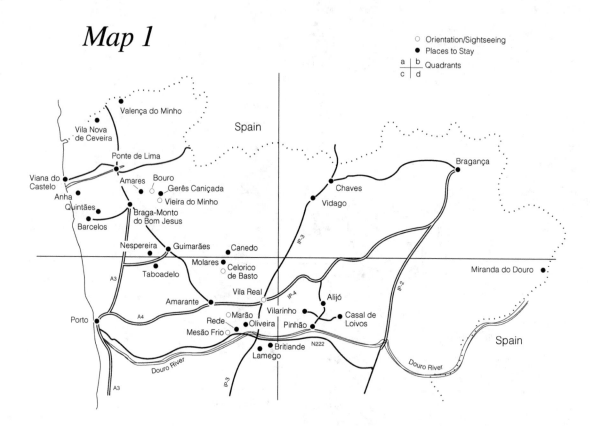

○ Orientation/Sightseeing
● Places to Stay

a	b
c	d	Quadrants

Valença do Minho

Vila Nova
de Ceveira

Ponte de Lima

Spain

Bragança

Viana do
Castelo

Amares · Bouro
○ Gerês Caniçada
○ Vieira do Minho

Chaves

Vidago

Anha

Quintães

Braga-Monto
do Bom Jesus

Barcelos

Nespereira · Guimarães

Canedo

IP-3

Molares

Taboadelo

○ Celorico
de Basto

Miranda do Douro

A3

Vila Real

Amarante

Vilarinho

IP-4

Alijó

Porto

A4

○ Marão

Rede · Oliveira

Mesão Frio ○

Pinhão

Casal de
Loivos

IP-2

· Britiande

N222

Spain

Lamego

Douro River

IP-3

A3

Douro River

260

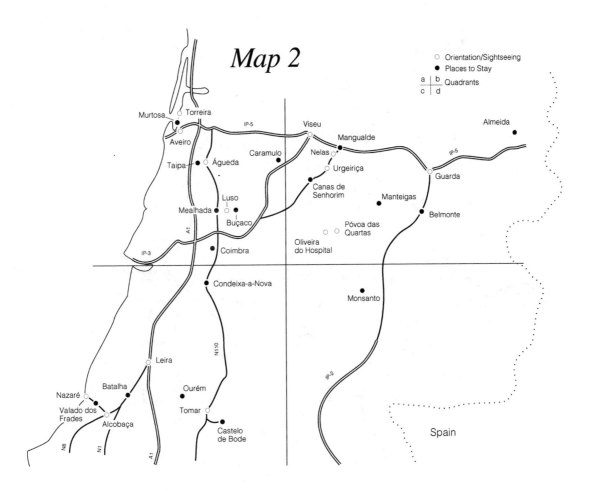

Map 2

○ Orientation/Sightseeing
● Places to Stay

a	b
c	d

Quadrants

Murtosa ○ Torreira
Aveiro ●
Taipa ○ ● Águeda
Caramulo ●
Viseu ○
Mangualde ●
Nelas ○
Urgeiriça ○
Canas de Senhorim ●
Manteigas ●
Guarda ●
Almeida ●
IP-5
IP-5

Mealhada ○ ●
Luso ○
Buçaco ●
Póvoa das Quartas ○ ○
Oliveira do Hospital
Belmonte ●

Coimbra ●
IP-3
A1

Condeixa-a-Nova ●

Monsanto ●

N110

Leira ○
IP-2

Nazaré ○
Batalha ●
Valado dos Frades ○
Alcobaça ○
Ourém ●
Tomar ○
Castelo de Bode ●

N8
N1
A1

Spain

Map 3

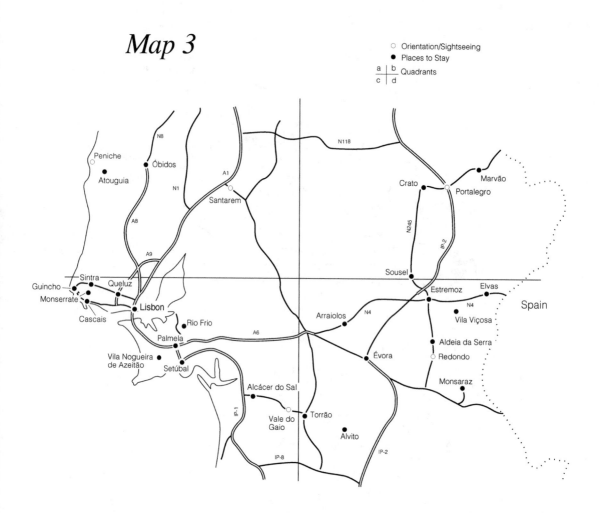

○ Orientation/Sightseeing
● Places to Stay

a	b
c	d

Quadrants

Peniche
Atouguia
Óbidos
N8
A1
N1
Santarem
A8
A9
Sintra
Guincho
Queluz
Monserrate
Lisbon
Cascais
Rio Frio
Palmela
Vila Nogueira
de Azeitão
Setúbal
Alcácer do Sal
Vale do Gaio
Torrão
Alvito
IP-1
IP-8
A6
Arraiolos
N4
Évora
IP-2

N118
Crato
Marvão
Portalegre
N245
IP-2
Sousel
Estremoz
Elvas
Spain
Vila Viçosa
Aldeia da Serra
Redondo
Monsaraz

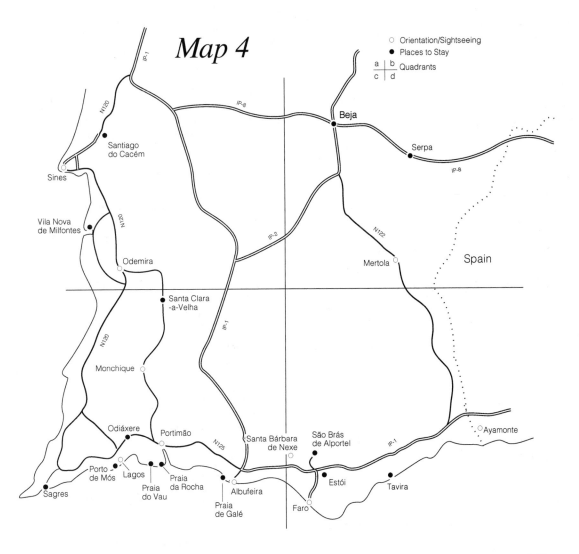

Map 4

○ Orientation/Sightseeing
● Places to Stay

| a | b |
| c | d |

Quadrants

Beja

Serpa

Santiago
do Cacém

Sines

Vila Nova
de Milfontes

Odemira

Mertola

Spain

Santa Clara
-a-Velha

Monchique

Odiáxere

Portimão

Santa Bárbara
de Nexe

São Brás
de Alportel

Ayamonte

Porto
de Mós

Lagos

Praia
do Vau

Praia
da Rocha

Albufeira

Estói

Tavira

Sagres

Praia
de Galé

Faro

Index

S

CYNTHIA SAUVAGE was born in Denver and graduated from the University of Colorado where she earned a degree in Spanish and French. Cynthia has traveled throughout the world and has lived in Mexico, Spain, and France. Cynthia traveled frequently to Portugal and became well acquainted with its culture, history, and customs. Cynthia now lives in Denver, Colorado, with her husband, David, and their two sons, Evan and Michael.

KAREN BROWN'S personalized travel series has grown to 17 titles. Karen, her husband, Rick, and their children, Alexandra and Richard, live in Moss Beach. They settled here in 1991 when they opened Seal Cove Inn. Karen is frequently traveling but when she is home, in her role as innkeeper, enjoys welcoming Karen Brown readers.

CLARE BROWN was a travel consultant for many years, specializing in planning itineraries to Europe using charming small hotels in the countryside. The focus of her job remains unchanged, but now her expertise is available to a larger audience—the readers of her daughter Karen's country inn guides. When Clare and her husband, Bill, are not traveling, they divide their time between Hillsborough, California and Vail, Colorado.

JUNE EVELEIGH BROWN'S love of travel was inspired by the *National Geographic* magazines that she read as a girl. June hails from Sheffield, England and lived in Zambia and Canada before moving to northern California where she lives in San Mateo with her husband, Tony, their daughter Clare, their two German Shepherds, and a Siamese cat.

JANN POLLARD, the artist responsible for the beautiful painting on the cover of this guide, is well known for her outstanding impressionistic-style watercolors, winning many awards. Jann travels frequently to Europe where she loves to paint historical buildings. Jann's original paintings are represented through The Gallery, Burlingame, CA, 650-347-9392 or www.thegalleryart.net. Fine-art giclée prints are also available at www.karenbrown.com.

BARBARA TAPP, the talented artist who produces all of the hotel sketches and delightful illustrations in this guide, was raised in Australia where she studied in Sydney at the School of Interior Design. Although Barbara continues with freelance projects, she devotes much of her time to illustrating the Karen Brown guides. Barbara lives in Kensington, California, with her husband, Richard, their two sons, Jonothan and Alexander, and daughter, Georgia.

Enhance your Guides—Visit us Online

www.karenbrown.com

- Hotel specials
- Color photos of hotels and B&Bs
- 20% online discount for book purchases
- Discount airfare, both business and coach class
- Direct links to individual property websites and e-mails
- Up-to-the-minute phone, fax, and e-mail information
- Rental cars, travel planning, trip insurance, itineraries, maps, and more

Become a Member of the Karen Brown Club

- Additional specials and offers from our travel partners
- Exclusive access to "new discoveries" from our current research
- An additional 20% savings on purchases from our online store

A complete listing of member benefits can be found on our website

Don't delay, join online today!

www.karenbrown.com

auto æ europe.

Karen Brown's Preferred Provider of

Car Rental Services
&
Discount Air Travel

Regularly scheduled flights on major carriers to Europe
Including discounts on both coach & business class

For special offers and discounts on car rentals and
An additional 5% off published air fares in 2003
Be sure to identify yourself as a Karen Brown Traveler and
Use your Karen Brown ID number 99006187

Make reservations online via our website, *www.karenbrown.com*
Just click
"Auto Rentals" or "Discount Airfares" on our home page

or call
800-223-5555

Marketing Ahead

POUSADA AND HOTEL RESERVATIONS

Reservations for all of the pousadas and many of the hotels featured in this guide can be made with Marketing Ahead.

Identify yourself as a Karen Brown reader using the code number KBG2003MA to get a 5% discount
(individuals only, please—this offer is not available through your travel agent)

Marketing Ahead
433 Fifth Avenue
6th Floor
New York, NY 10016
tel: (212) 686-9213 or (800) 223-1356
fax: (212) 686-0271
e-mail: mahrep@aol.com
www.marketingahead.com

or

click across from our website, *www.karenbrown.com*

Icons Key

This year we have introduced the icons listed below in the guidebooks and on our website (*www.karenbrown.com*). These allow us to provide additional information about our recommended properties. When using our website to supplement the guides, placing the cursor over an icon will in many cases give you further details.

❄	Air conditioning in rooms	🍴	Restaurant
	Breakfast included in room rate		Swimming pool
	Children welcome		Tennis
	Cooking classes offered		Television
CREDIT	Credit cards accepted		Wedding facilities
☎	Direct-dial telephone in room		Wheelchair friendly
	Dogs by special request		Golf course nearby
	Elevator		Hiking trails nearby
	Exercise room		Horseback riding nearby
	Mini-refrigerator in room		Skiing nearby
	Non-smoking rooms		Water sports nearby
P	Parking available		Wineries nearby